The Sharing Economy

The Sharing Economy

The End of Employment and the Rise of
Crowd-Based Capitalism

Arun Sundararajan

The MIT Press
Cambridge, Massachusetts
London, England

This book was set in Sabon LT Std by Toppan Best-set Premedia Limited. Printed and bound in the United States of America.

Library of Congress Cataloging-in-Publication Data

Names: Sundararajan, Arun, author.
Title: The sharing economy : the end of employment and the rise of crowd-based
  capitalism / Arun Sundararajan.
Description: Cambridge, MA : The MIT Press, 2016. | Includes bibliographical
  references and index.
Identifiers: LCCN 2015039935 | ISBN 9780262034579 (hardcover : alk. paper)
Subjects: LCSH: Economic geography. | Space in economics. | Capitalism—Social aspects. |
  Business networks.
Classification: LCC HF1025 .S86 2016 | DDC 330—dc23 LC record available at
  http://lccn.loc.gov/2015039935

10   9   8   7   6   5   4

For my parents, who taught me how to write; my sister Anu, who showed me, through her prose and poetry, how it's done well; and my dearest little girl Maya, who inspires me every day to imagine and create a better future.

Contents

Author's Note and Acknowledgments

This is my first book, so I am tempted to reach far back into the past to acknowledge all of the people who have shaped the thinking it contains. To ensure that this note does not rival a book chapter in its length, I am forced to focus on a select few. If I have inadvertently failed to include you, and you know me, then you know that I'm both forgetful and grateful. Thank you. (And visit http://oz.stern.nyu.edu/thanksforsharing where I will continue to update this note.)

I see the changes we label "the sharing economy" as the current phase of an ongoing evolution of the economy and society that is shaped in part by digital technologies. This is the topic of my program of research and scholarship at NYU. When I began investigating this evolution many years ago, two colleagues—Vasant Dhar and Roy Radner—were especially important intellectual influences and mentors. As I have continued to study the economics and sociology of digital technologies over the past decade, I have benefitted immensely from conversations with a number of current and former colleagues at NYU, including Ulrich Baer, David Backus, Yannis Bakos, Luis Cabral, Rohit Deo, Cynthia Franklin, Scott Galloway, Anindya Ghose, Peter Henry, John Horton, Joanne Hvala, Panos Ipeirotis, Srikanth Jagabathula, Sarah Labowitz, Natalia Levina, Hila Lifshitz-Assaf, Geeta Menon, Elizabeth Morrison, Beth Murray, Rika Nazem, Jessica Neville, Mandy Osborne, Patrick Perry, Michael Posner, Foster Provost, Paul Romer, Clay Shirky, Kristen Sosulski, Raghu Sundaram, Prasanna Tambe, Jamie Tobias, Alexander Tuzhilin, Mike Uretsky, Timothy Van Zandt, Niobe Way, Lawrence White, Norman White, Luke Williams, and Eitan Zemel. I am also eternally grateful to Sharon Kim and Shirley Lau, who inject some semblance of organization and structure into my professional life, and without whom I would not have managed to create the time to write this book.

I have had hundreds of conversations with executives, activists, policy makers, and thinkers connected to the sharing economy. I recount many of these in the book, and am particularly happy that Jennifer Billock, Brian Chesky, Antonin Leonard, Adam Ludwin, Frédéric Mazella, Benjamin Tincq, and John Zimmer took the time to sit down and speak to me specifically in connection with its writing. Numerous other fascinating conversations have helped me fit together the pieces of the complex puzzle that is the sharing economy. Some that were quite influential early on were with Odile Beniflah, Lauren Capelin, Shelby Clark, Sunil Paul, Jessica Scorpio, Erica Swallow, Molly Turner, and Hal Varian. Some of the others that were especially notable and/or frequent were with Bhavish Aggarwal, Alisha Ali, Douglas Atkin, Michel Avital, Emily Badger, Mara Balestrini, Yochai Benkler, Rachel Botsman, danah boyd, Nathan Blecharczyk, Jennifer Bradley, Erik Brynjolfsson, Valentina Carbone, Emily Castor, David Chiu, Marc-David Chokrun, Sonal Choksi, Peter Coles, Chip Conley, Ariane Conrad, Arnab Das, Cristian Fleming (and his team at the Public Society), Richard Florida, Natalie Foster, Justin Fox, Liz Gannes, Lisa Gansky, Marina Gorbis, Neal Gorenflo, Alison Griswold, Vijay Gurbaxani, Tanner Hackett, Aassia Haroon Haq, Scott Heiferman, Jeremy Heimans, Sara Horowitz, Sam Hodges, Milicent Johnson, Noah Karesh, Stephane Kasriel, Sarah Kessler, David Kirkpatrick, Marjo Koivisto, Karim Lakhani, Kevin Laws, Michael Luca, Benita Matofska, Andrew McAfee, Ryan McKillen, Lesa Mitchell, Amy Nelson, Jeff Nickerson, Melissa O'Young, Janelle Orsi, Jeremy Osborn, Jeremiah Owyang (to whom I owe a special debt of gratitude for his remarkably selfless sharing of ideas and data), Wrede Petersmeyer, Ai-Jen Poo, Andrew Rasiej, Simone Ross, Anita Roth, Chelsea Rustrum, Carolyn Said, Marcela Sapone, Marie Schneegans, Trebor Scholz, Swati Sharma, Clay Shirky, Dane Stangler, Alex Stephany, James Surowiecki, Jason Tanz, Marie Ternes, Henry Timms, Viv Wang, Cheng Wei, Adam Werbach, Jamie Wong, Caroline Woolard, and numerous members of the OuiShare collective (including Flore Berlingen, Julie Braka, Albert Cañigueral, Simone Cicero, Javier Creus, Arthur De Grave, Elena Denaro, Diana Fillipova, Marguerite Grandjean, Asmaa Guedira, Ana Manzanedo, Bernie Mitchell, Edwin Mootoosamy, Ruhi Shamim, Maeva Tordo and especially Francesca Pick).

I have also benefitted from numerous focused discussions about specific topic areas. These include conversations with: Neha Gondal about the sociology of the sharing economy; Ravi Bapna, Verena Butt d'Espous, Juan Cartagena, Chris Dellarocas, Alok Gupta, and Sarah Rice about trust; Paul Daugherty, Peter Evans, Geoffrey Parker, Anand Shah, Marshall Van Alstyne, and Bruce Weinelt about platforms; Brad Burnham, Kanyi Maqubela, Simon Rothman, Craig Shapiro, and Albert Wenger about venture capital; Janelle Orsi, Nathan Schreiber, and Trebor Scholz about cooperatives; Umang Dua, Oisin Hanrahan, Micah Kaufmann, and Juho Makkonen about marketplace models; Gene Homicki about alternative rental models; Primavera De Filipi and Matan Field about the blockchain and decentralized peer-to-peer technologies; Ashwini Chhabra, Molly Cohen, Althea Erickson, David Estrada, Nick Grossman, David Hantman, Alex Howard, Meera Joshi, Veronica Juarez, Chris Lehane, Mike Masserman, Padden Murphy, Joseph Okpaku, Brooks Rainwater, April Rinne, Sofia Ranchordas, Michael Simas, Jessica Singleton, Adam Thierer, and Bradley Tusk about regulation; Elena Grewal, Kevin Novak, and Chris Pouliot about the use of data science in the sharing economy; Nellie Abernathy, Cynthia Estlund, Steve King, Wilma Liebman, Marysol McGee, Brian Miller, Michelle Miller, Caitlin Pearce, Libby Reder, Julie Samuels, Kristin Sharp, Dan Teran, Felicia Wong, and Marco Zappacosta about the future of work. I am also thankful to Congressman Darrell Issa, Congressman Eric Swalwell, and Senator Mark Warner for their leadership and for many conversations about critical sharing economy policy issues.

My current and former students and collaborators have provided me with invaluable assistance and inspiration as I have explored the varied facets of this new model of organizing economic activity. My scientific research about the sharing economy would not have been possible without Hilary Jane Devine, Apostolos Fillipas, Samuel Fraiberger, Carlos Herrera-Yague, Marios Kokkodis, Marella Martin, Mareike Mohlmann, Lauren Morris and Lauren Rhue. I am also grateful for financial support for some of this research from the Ewing Marion Kauffman Foundation and Google Research. The results of a wide variety of independent study projects undertaken by my NYU undergraduates and MBA students have helped mold my early-stage research and thinking: the ones that stand out were by Humaira Faiz, Sydnee Grushack, Andrew Ng, and Jara Small (on inclusive growth in the sharing economy); Jonah Blumstein, Valeriya Greene and Eric Jacobson (on Airbnb and city regulations); Andrew Covell, Varun Jain, and June Khin (on the organization of sharing economy platforms); Phil Hayes (on surge pricing); Dmitrios Theocharis and Siri Zhan (on the on-demand workforce); Ann Dang, Louise Lai, and Daniella Tapia (on the global variation in regulation); Lauren Tai (on regulating autonomous vehicles); Karl Gourgue, Manasa Grandhi, and Joyce Fei (on decentralized models of research); Arra Malek, Ansh Patel, and Haley Zhou (on apparel rental models); Laura Kettell and Karina Alkhasyan (on peer-to-peer finance); and Keerthi Moudgal (on peer-to-peer retailing).

Although I have been captivated by the sharing economy for many years now, the emergence of this book was catalyzed by a series of email messages that my editor at the MIT Press, Emily Taber, sent me in April 2015. She was simply amazing in the months that followed as I rapidly wrote the first two drafts of the book. If you ever write a first book, I hope you are fortunate enough to have an editor like Emily. Through this process, I have also been privileged to benefit from the sage advice of the legendary literary agent Raphael Sagalyn and publicity guru Rimjhim Dey. I am grateful to numerous others at the MIT Press, including Marcy Ross (for her infinite patience as I constantly shifted revision deadlines), Jane Macdonald, and Colleen Lanick. Mary Bagg was an amazing copy-editor, and Kate Eichhorn helped me develop the flow of the book early in its evolution. I am also thankful to my wonderful friend Rakhi Varma for agreeing to undertake the hazardous mission of reading and giving me feedback on my first draft of this book, and to four anonymous book referees for their comments.

As I scripted and refined this book over the summer and fall of 2015, my (now twelve-year old) daughter Maya frequently had to deal with the inconvenience of a distracted father with an unusually busy work sched-ule, a situation she accepted with a quiet understanding well beyond her years. As the pages of content emerged, she shared in the excitement of creating something new, and marveled at a project whose scale could be quantified in the tens of thousands of words. She motivates me to imag-ine, and aspire to fashion, a better future. I hope the ideas in this book, in some small way, will help us find this future for her generation. (Meanwhile, she is pleased that I am finally done writing.)

Introduction

The stuff that matters in life is no longer stuff. It's other people. It's relationships. It's experience.
—Brian Chesky, *Today*, March 29, 2013

I live in Manhattan. I don't own a car, which isn't unusual. Less than one in four Manhattan households own a car. But sometimes, I need a car. And it's hard to find an affordable rental car in Manhattan. You often have to travel a few miles, to Queens or New Jersey, to rent one that costs less than a hundred dollars a day.

Meanwhile, the streets around my apartment are filled with hundreds and hundreds of parked cars. Beat-up old Corollas and snazzy new BMWs. (Although I haven't seen a Tesla in my neighborhood as yet. That's the car I really want to drive.) Back when my daughter was in second grade, I'd sometimes be running late getting her to school. On many a cold winter morning, while frantically trying to hail a taxi, I'd think, wouldn't it be nice if I could just borrow one of these parked cars instantly, drive her to school, and return it to where I found it, perhaps with a $10 bill and a note on the dashboard that said "Thank you!"

There's a company that lets you do this now using a mobile phone— borrow someone else's parked car for an hour at a time, instantly, for about $10 an hour. It's called Getaround. (I came across Getaround quite by accident in 2011, and not while trying to boost a vehicle during an early morning school run. I'll get to this in a few pages.) I thought about Getaround and my vision of Manhattan-wide seamless peer-to-peer car borrowing when, in December 2012, I read Mary Meeker's supplement to her annual *Internet Trends Report*.[1]

Meeker, a pioneering technology analyst during the "dotcom" era of the late 1990s, has been issuing this influential annual report since 1995. Her supplement emphasized how we are now reimagining everything from interfaces to lending in a way that foreshadowed the ascent of an "asset-light" generation. In settings that ranged from commercial real estate and corporate labor to personal banking, travel, entertainment, and transportation, Meeker illustrated a range of digitally enabled business models and consumer experiences that were catalyzing the descent of our industrial-era structures. A series of juxtaposed contrasting images in her PowerPoint slides pictured the stark differences between the so-called asset-heavy versus asset-light generations: an elderly vinyl enthusiast amid boxes and boxes of records versus screenshots from the streaming music services Spotify, Pandora, and iTunes; a high-rise Ramada Inn versus a tree house for rent on the peer-to-peer accommodation platform Airbnb; full-time workers seated ear-to-ear in endless rows versus an Internet-based freelancer marketplace.

As straightforward as an illustrated children's book, the message from Meeker's slides was clear—stuff owned for one's personal use, brick-and-mortar institutions, hard currency, and on-site, salaried, permanent jobs were on their way out, and shared access, virtual exchange, digital money, and flexible on-demand labor were in.

At the time I leafed through Meeker's slides, I knew that her prediction of an "asset-light" generation was merely one slice of a broader economic and social change that was already well under way—a radical shift toward new ways of organizing economic activity that will become increasingly dominant in this century. The assortment of behaviors (and organizations) that many of us optimistically call the "sharing economy" are early instances of a future in which peer-to-peer exchange becomes increasingly prevalent, and the "crowd" replaces the corporation at the center of capitalism.

A radical shift is underway. This kind of statement has become all too commonplace over the last two decades. Business executives seem resigned to the eventuality of persistent change, and especially change caused by digital technologies. Radical disruption, a concatenation of words that seems to suggest something quite avoidable in most situations, is a harbinger of wealth creation actively pursued by Silicon Valley investors. We have been nurtured by a steady diet of TED talks to expect bold claims about digital technologies being a catalyst for revolution, a panacea for the world's big problems. I would therefore not be surprised if some readers met my assertion of impending transformation with weary skepticism.

So let's step back and start to understand what the sharing economy is by considering a small sample of these "new" behaviors. Many of us (some 70 million as of 2016[2]) have stayed in someone's spare bedroom or rented someone's entire home through the Airbnb platform as a way of getting accommodation in a city or town we are visiting for a few days. Many others have swapped their homes through LoveHome-Swap, Debbie Waskow's membership platform that I discovered in February 2012 when Mashable's Erica Swallow (a technology entrepreneur and one of my favorite former NYU students) discussed her excellent early article on the sharing economy with my undergraduate class.[3] You can transport yourself across short distances using apps like Lyft and Uber, platforms that connect drivers who have cars and are willing to give rides to people who need them. If a chauffeured car or taxi on-demand doesn't suit your mobility needs, you can get space in a bus using the Didi Kuaidi app in China, or hail an auto-rickshaw using the Ola platform in India. You can get access to someone else's car for a few hours or a few days through the peer-to-peer rental platforms Getaround and Turo (formerly RelayRides) in the United States, Drivy in France and Germany, SnappCar in the Netherlands, EasyCar Club in the UK, and Yourdrive in New Zealand. You can get a meal with others at someone's dining table through social dining platforms, like EatWith in Barcelona, Feastly in New York, or VizEat in Paris, that allow people who enjoy cooking to have others visit their home and join a lunch or dinner. With as little as £100 in liquid assets, you can make an interest-bearing loan of £20 or more to a small business that you like through the peer-to-peer lending platform Funding Circle.[4] You can offer up your services as a home cleaner, handyman, plumber, electrician, or painter (or hire a freelance worker who has these or other skills) through the labor marketplaces Handy, TaskRabbit, and Thumbtack.

Getting set up to receive these services from your peers is often as easy as installing an app and proving your identity by sharing data from a valid Facebook account. Becoming a provider—a supplier who is a source of these shared services—is quite simple as well. In his informative and entertaining February 2015 *Time* magazine cover story, "Tales from the Sharing Economy," the journalist Joel Stein described his journey through different roles as a provider in the sharing economy. "Besides a rental-car company, I became a taxi driver, restaurateur and barterer," as he put it, further noting that he would have also become a kennel and a hotel if it weren't for the objections of "my lovely wife Cassandra."[5]

If these activities—borrowing someone's home, getting a ride, borrowing a car, sharing a meal, lending money, getting help with your home improvement—don't seem especially new to you, it's because they aren't. Perhaps, then, what is new is the fact that this isn't "gift economy" exchange, but mediated by money. Stein's use of commercial labels for the sharing he engaged in underscores the point that while all of these examples do involve sharing, in a sense—of space, of a car, of food, of money, of time—none of these services are offered for free. You get paid by the person you provide to. You pay the provider who shares with you.

So let's now consider whether peer-to-peer *commercial* exchange is new. How long has the world's economy been dominated by large corporations? How has the way we organize economic activity developed through human history? The Industrial Revolution, which sparked the emergence of mass production, mass distribution, and the modern corporation, began a little over 200 years ago.[6] In his retelling of the story of modern American capitalism, *The Visible Hand*, the economic historian Alfred Chandler paints a vivid picture of the US economy of that period:

In 1790 general merchants still ruled the economy. In this economy, the family remained the basic business unit. The most pervasive of these units was the family farm. ...The small amount of manufacturing carried on outside the home was the work of artisans in small shops. ... As Sam Bass Warner wrote of Philadelphia on the eve of the American Revolution: "The core element of the town economy was the one-man shop. Most Philadelphians labored alone, some with a helper or two."[7]

A quick glance at the evolution of economic activity suggests that prior to the Industrial Revolution, a significant percentage of economic exchange was peer-to-peer, embedded in community, and intertwined in different ways with social relations.[8] The trust needed to make economic exchange possible came primarily from social ties of different kinds.[9] It is easy to accept that hosting visitors from out of town, sharing food with visitors, giving someone a ride, or borrowing money from a peer are hardly new human activities. But engaging in some form of small-scale commercial entrepreneurship, or in trade or craft ("making") as an independent provider isn't radically new either. In fact, at the turn of the 20th century, almost half of the compensated US workforce was self-employed.[10] By 1960, this number shrank to less than 15%. (See figure 0.1.) It is also very likely that the self-employed constituted more than half of the compensated workforce at some point prior to 1900.

One reason for this significant shift in workforce composition over the first few decades of the 20th century was the economy-wide move away from farming (which, at the time, was largely practiced by independent farmers) and toward other forms of making a living. But even outside of agriculture, over the same period, the percentage of the US workforce

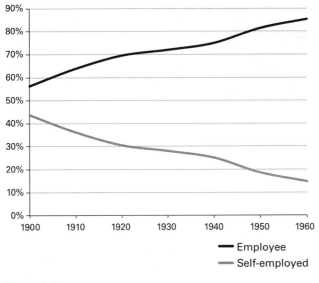

Figure 0.1
Paid US workforce, 1900–1960.

that was self-employed (and unincorporated) fell from almost 30% in 1900 to about 10% in 1960, and it remained at about the same level for the ensuing 50 years, during which time the US economy was dominated by large corporations.[11]

My point is therefore not merely that the industrial era is a blink in the eye of human history, but rather, that the forms of exchange, of commerce, and of employment associated with the sharing economy are not new. Today's digital technologies seem to be taking us back to familiar sharing behaviors, self-employment, and forms of community-based exchange that existed in the past. This "not entirely new" aspect, of both the nature of the activities and the form of work, is important because an improved form of something familiar will gain widespread adoption more rapidly and have greater economic impact than the invention of entirely new consumption experiences or models of employment.

A natural question at this point might be whether there's anything new about the sharing economy at all. If all of these seemingly "new" activities were widely prevalent in the past, then why is there so much excitement? Well, first, these new ways of doing familiar things are being powered by technologies that extend your economic "community" far beyond family or friends who live in your neighborhood, to a digitally vetted subset of the population at large: allowing us to engage in what the

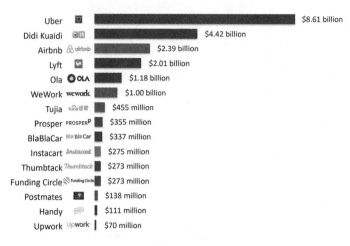

Figure 0.2
Some sharing economy platforms and the venture capital they have raised as of December 2015.

sociologist Juliet Schor calls "stranger sharing."[12] Second, the capitalist engine of technology-powered markets has dramatically scaled these "sharing" and entrepreneurial behaviors, taking them orders of magnitude beyond their recent prevalence in modern economies, shifting the source of what we value commercially away from traditional corporations and toward a crowd of entrepreneurs we find through a digital marketplace. It is for these reasons that I sometimes refer to the subject of this book as *crowd-based capitalism.*

Between 2010 and 2015, new companies that are shaping this new form of capitalism have raised a staggering amount of money from investors. Figure 0.2 summarizes the equity venture capital invested in some of the most active platforms, most of which are what we now call "unicorns," valued at over $1 billion. But the implications of the transition they are enabling go well beyond this venture capital activity. Crowd-based capitalism could radically transform what it means to have a job. Our regulatory landscape will be reshaped. Our social safety net, often funded by corporate employment, will be challenged. The way we finance, produce, distribute, and consume goods, services, and urban infrastructures will evolve. New ways of organizing economic activity will redefine whom we trust, why we trust them, what shapes access to opportunity, and how close we feel to each other.

I have been fascinated by these new developments for a few years now. But when I started to notice the proliferation of digital peer-to-peer markets in 2011, I was puzzled. I have been doing research on and teaching about the impacts of digital technologies on business and society since the late 1990s. The first large Internet-enabled peer-to-peer market, eBay, was founded in 1995, went public in 1998, and it remains visibly successful as I write this book in 2015. Why did it take until 2007 for Airbnb and the others to emerge? What was missing until recently?

Airbnb—Design Your World Right

I first met Brian Chesky, the CEO of Airbnb, as a dinner guest in the summer of 2013, at a loft in Manhattan's Hell's Kitchen, where I mingled with a group of Airbnb hosts, NYC entrepreneurs, and sharing advocates. Chesky, a designer who trained at the Rhode Island School of Design (RISD), sees his foray into entrepreneurship with Airbnb as being part of the fifth chapter of his life. "I really loved hockey growing up," he recounted when we spoke in the spring of 2015. "I went to Canada, then went to a youth sports academy for hockey. And then I realized I wasn't going to be a professional hockey player." Next, while at Niskayuna High School, a teacher recognized Chesky's artistic abilities—"growing up, I really looked up to Norman Rockwell"—and encouraged him to pursue his art, which culminated in his work being exhibited at the US Capitol when he was 16. The artistic path led to his education at RISD, which Chesky sees as the next chapter, and then to his training in industrial design.

Chesky's vision for Airbnb was modest when he began. "The motivation for starting Airbnb was to be able to pay our rent in October 2007. I remember I had a rent check that was $1,150. Our landlord had raised our rent. This international design convention was coming to San Francisco one weekend. All the hotels were sold out. And so we had this idea: what if we turned our house into a bed and breakfast for the design conference. Joe (Gebbia, also an Airbnb co-founder, as well as Chesky's college friend and apartment-mate at the time) had three airbeds. We pulled them out of the closet. We called it the 'AirBed and Breakfast.'"

"That its mission was kind of pure, to solve a problem and to help people—I think that maybe therein lies a little bit of the beauty in it," Chesky continued. Of course, by the time I met Chesky in 2013, he and his co-founders Gebbia and Nathan Blecharczyk had taken Airbnb from the tiny AirBed and Breakfast to a global platform with hundreds of thousands of "hosts"—people who rent their spare bedrooms, apartments, houses, tree-houses, beach homes, boats, and more to millions of paying guests—and over $100 million in venture capital funding. And as of 2016, their exponential growth continues. As Blecharczyk noted during a panel discussion at the 2016 World Economic Forum meeting in Davos, "To date, 70 million guests have now stayed in a stranger's home, and 40 million last year alone, so last year was more than the previous 7 years combined."

Part of the promise I have always sensed in Airbnb's business model is the huge economic efficiency it seems to represent. People have accommodation space they aren't always using. Other people sometimes need space for a short period of time. If an Internet-based platform can connect the people with space with the people who need it, won't the economic gains have to arrive at some point? Rather than making billions of dollars of capital investment into constructing dedicated units for short-term accommodation—hotels—why not tap into the millions of sometimes-empty apartments and spare rooms around the world?

The Airbnb way could thus be a compelling microcosm for why the economic fundamentals of crowd-based capitalism are simply superior to those of the industrial era. The interest Airbnb and its sharing economy brethren attract from government regulators reflects, in part, this disconnect between the new and the old. Could it be that the regulations developed to keep guests safe in an era of full-time hoteliers with dedicated buildings may simply not fit the world of Airbnb where the boundaries between one's personal space and what's available for rent by a guest are rapidly blurring? Might the genesis of a different regulatory approach already be taking place across peer-to-peer platforms?

But there's more to why I find Airbnb interesting as a company. The company has rapidly created a sophisticated organization, its public relations and marketing is among the savviest of all the sharing economy startups I have encountered, it conducts government relations with nuance, and perhaps most compellingly (and often in contrast with Uber), its community of providers genuinely seems to love the platform and what it represents. In November 2014, I wrote an article for *Harvard Business Review* contrasting the "platform culture" of these two giants of the sharing economy, conjecturing that part of the difference, perhaps, has to do with Chesky's background in design.

Chesky agreed. "One of the guiding principles of my life is to live in a world of my own design," he told me. "And that can be your life, a company, the world you want to live in. And so I think we have rethought a lot of things, starting with our core business and going to our culture. Our culture is designed. I don't believe in inevitability or destiny. I believe that whether you design a culture or not, it will be designed for you, so you better design it because you might not otherwise like where you end up."

It's an inspiring philosophy. Design your world right. If you don't, it will be designed for you, and you might not like what you end up with. But it makes me wonder. Might the same hold true for our future regulatory structures?

Lyft—Hospitality in Transportation

A few blocks down the street from Airbnb's shiny new corporate headquarters at 888 Brannan in San Francisco's SoMa district is a small building at 568 Brannan, the site of Lyft's original offices. In it's simplest form, Lyft is a chauffeured car, on demand. You open the app, you tell it where you are, it shows you cars nearby, you request a car, and you get picked up in a few minutes. In a more sophisticated use case, you turn on your Lyft app when you drive to work, put in your destination, and others who might want to travel a similar route can pay you a little for a seat in your car. Carpooling on demand, but flexibly, on your own schedule.

Over the years, my Lyft drivers have included stand-up comedians, software engineers, deejays, schoolteachers, a retired CIO, a digital marketing executive between jobs, and numerous college students. Taking a Lyft is a completely different customer experience from hailing a cab. You sit in the front seat and have a conversation with a peer. It is like getting a ride with a new acquaintance.

I visited Lyft at 568 Brannan in fall 2012 at the invitation of Emily Castor, an early employee who is currently their self-described "resident transportation wonk," and who was kind enough back then to accelerate my approval as a Lyft passenger so that I could use their service to get to the meeting. The car that came to pick me up was instantly recognizable, adorned with Lyft's giant pink mustache. (Noticing the branded corporate swag I was carrying from a different company at the end of our meeting, Emily grabbed one of these pink mustaches from an office cabinet and tossed it to me before I left. It is still in my office, and has attracted many a puzzled look from my students over the years.)

My first Lyft driver was an artist who was driving her car to earn some extra money while she pursued her art. There was no formal fare in 2012, since Lyft was not yet legally allowed to offer "taxi" service, but instead, the app suggested a "donation" to my driver in exchange for her being nice enough to come to where I was, pick me up, and give me a ride. A high point of the visit was the opportunity I got to try on a Lyft employee's Halloween costume. He had dressed up as a Lyft car, using a skillfully constructed cardboard contraption.

Three years later, Lyft had raised over a billion dollars in venture capital (including $100 million from the legendary investor Carl Icahn) and was in 60 cities around the United States. Although often in the news because of the bruising battles it has waged with Uber for market share, Lyft projects a decidedly kinder and gentler feel than their larger competitor, even as they have graduated from the giant pink mustaches to a more subtle branding strategy. Their co-founder and president John Zimmer, with whom I have had many fascinating conversations over the years, has famously said that he doesn't see Lyft as competing with Uber, but rather, as competing with "people driving alone."[13]

"For me, personally, it was my interest in hospitality," Zimmer told me, when I asked him about his motivation for starting Lyft. "There are two main pieces in hospitality success: providing an amazing, delightful experience, and having high occupancy. Both of these aspects were missing from transportation." He broke the occupancy dimension down further for me. "Vehicle utilization is about 4%, occupancy in those cars is about 20%. So you basically have about a 1% utilization rate on something that accounts for about 13% of global GDP. I saw that as a big opportunity."

Zimmer has a point. There's immense excess capacity in cars around the world. Americans alone spend about a *trillion* dollars *each year* buying new and used cars. Around the world, governments spend billions of dollars building elaborate public transit systems, often imposing crippling costs of both money and inconvenience on their city economies. Could apps like Lyft promise a different approach to building urban transportation infrastructure, foreshadowing a new kind of crowd-based public-private partnership, one that uses digital technology to tap into decentralized excess capacity rather than creating new monolithic centralized systems?

The Rise of the On-Demand Workforce

One of the things that set Lyft and Uber apart from Airbnb is that the weekly time commitment of their "providers"—the folks who are sharing their time and assets to provide a service through the platform—is markedly higher. Although David Estrada, Lyft's (then) head of government relations, told me in 2014 that two-thirds of Lyft's drivers drive less than

15 hours a week, that's still a number approaching what might be considered a "part-time occupation" of sorts. The same is true for the providers of assorted forms of labor and services on the TaskRabbit and Handy marketplaces, and of the shoppers, contractors and part-time employees alike, who buy the groceries and bring them to you when you order them through the Instacart app. And many of these providers put in much longer hours—often 40 to 50 a week—through these different platforms.

A growing number of people worry if this is an early glimpse into a future of work with less reliable benefits and more uncertainty about where your next paycheck is coming from. Of course, it is not immediately clear that this future is inferior. Perhaps the flexibility and fluidity of contracting through digital platforms rather than working a day-job can be empowering. Indeed, as Zimmer pointed out to me, "We have a lot of single parents who are doing this because they really can't work a nine to five job when they have to pick their kids up from school, from appointments, and they always want to be available for the activities their kids have."

Granted, working on demand for multiple platforms can be appealing, maybe even empowering, but there's also something empowering about getting a fixed periodic paycheck. It helps plan a future, something that is challenging when one's income fluctuates based on the vagaries of supply and demand on a set of apps. Besides, as other platforms specialize service labor more and more, there's a growing specter of enhanced future social inequality. The winner of *TechCrunch*'s widely observed Disrupt entrepreneurs challenge in 2014 was a platform for personal home assistants founded by two Harvard Business School MBAs, Marcela Sapone and Jessica Beck, called Hello Alfred, a name evocative of the eponymous butler whose dedicated service assists his employer's secret life as Batman. (Of course, unlike the original Alfred, as noted by journalist Sarah Kessler in her delightful 2014 article about the challenges of making one's apartment butler-worthy, this modern-day platform based version is "a butler that doesn't have to live in your home."[14])

And Alfred is just the tip of the on-demand personal service iceberg. In a May 2015 *Wall Street Journal* article titled "There's an Uber for Everything," Geoffrey Fowler describes a subset of the dizzying array of new and narrow personal services, starting with his favorite, Luxe:

A marvel of the logistics only possible in a smartphone world, Luxe uses GPS to offer a personal parking valet. It's magical. When you first get in your car, you open the Luxe app to tell it where you're going. Then Luxe tracks your phone as you make your way, so that one of its valets meets you at your destination just in the nick of time. Last Friday, my Luxe valet Kevin—dressed in a blue uniform and fully vetted, trained and insured—greeted me at my office in San Francisco's Financial District around 8:45 a.m. I handed him my keys and he whisked away my car.

At 6 p.m., I pulled up the Luxe app again and requested my car be returned in a different part of town. No problem. In under 10 minutes, a valet named Ross was there with my car, along with his foldable scooter, and a ukulele, in my trunk. The scooter is for getting up and down the hills of San Francisco, he says, and the ukulele fills time between jobs.[15]

Besides Luxe, other popular on-demand services include having someone pick up anything for you and bring it to you in an hour (Postmates), come over to your house to pack and ship stuff for you (Shyp), pick up your dirty laundry, wash it, and bring it back to where you live (Washio), walk your dog (Wag), bring you a gourmet meal (Munchery), and deliver your drinks (Minibar, Drizly).

Are we heading toward an economy in which the on-demand many serve the privileged few? And if the efficiencies of crowd-based capitalism lead to an economy that relies increasingly on peer-to-peer platforms to organize economic activity, how do we supply its on-demand providers with a social safety net—health insurance, worker's insurance, paid vacations, maternity leave? Do we need a government-provided basic income? Or is there some clever new public-private partnership model that can make benefits portable and stabilize people's incomes over time?

BlaBlaCar—Global Infrastructure Built on Trust

Interestingly, Lyft's original business plan wasn't about transforming urban and suburban transportation. Rather, it was started by Zimmer and CEO Logan Green as Zimride, a city-to-city ridesharing system, and "pivoted," as the Silicon Valley folks say when shifting to a new business model, after the original idea didn't gain traction fast enough in the United States. Meanwhile, the idea of using an app to hitch a ride to another city in a stranger's car is hugely popular in Europe and other parts of the world. The company that dominates that market—by connecting drivers who have empty seats in their cars with passengers who want to buy them, and moving, as of 2015, more people every day than the US national rail system Amtrak—is France-based BlaBlaCar.

Much like Zimmer, BlaBlaCar's co-founder Frédéric Mazzella, who boasts degrees in computer science and business from Stanford and INSEAD, and who worked as a researcher for NASA for three years, was motivated to start BlaBlaCar by the immense inefficiencies he observed. "The initial motivation was the waste, the unbearable waste that empty cars on the road represent," said Mazzella during a conversation at his

Paris headquarters in 2015. "I think everyone needs to reach a point where, one day, you open your eyes, and you're like 'Oh my God! All the cars are empty!'" Mazzella continued to explain, "I love to optimize things. And there is this tremendous reservoir for optimization here in cars."

Companies that try to do what BlaBlaCar does—use a website or mobile app to match empty seats with willing passengers—have emerged in numerous countries. Between 2014 and 2015, Mazzella's company expanded by acquiring five of these companies in five different countries—including key competitor carpooling.com—leveraging capital infusions totaling over $300 million, the highest ever level of venture capital financing for a French startup. The company seems extremely well run—like a streamlined Silicon Valley software company, but with a decidedly French socialist sensibility. Even its whimsical name came out of careful market research (and allegedly has no connection, despite the striking similarity, to Le Bla-Bla, a restaurant two minutes from their headquarters). "We had 250 names," Mazzella told me. "We narrowed that list to a shortlist of 30. I send this list to friends of mine, and a month or two after, we asked them, 'Okay, do you remember the list of names I sent you?' And more than half of them would name BlaBlaCar."

Mazzella loves to discuss trust. He believes it is absolutely central to his company's business, and is passionate about its importance. (BlaBlaCar's corporate headquarters has a life-sized cardboard cutout of "Trust-Man," a cape-wearing superhero with a "T" emblazoned on his jumpsuit.) His conception of trust is based on what he calls the D.R.E.A.M.S. framework (Declared, Rated, Engaged, Activity-Based, Moderated, Social), and the company is constantly working on deepening its understanding of trusted exchange.[16]

This focus on trust is understandable, of course. Sure, people have been sending each other packages using the peer-to-peer marketplace eBay for a couple of decades now, so society has developed systems to build trust digitally when transacting with a semi-anonymous peer over the Internet. But how does one move from generating the level of trust needed to receive a UPS box from a stranger, and get to the level where people are willing to get into a stranger's car and say, "Drive me to another city"?

The Melding of Commerce and Community

I connect easily with Mazzella's obsession, because my own interest in trust is what led me to discover the sharing economy. In 2011, I was collaborating on a research project with my colleagues Ravi Bapna and Alok Gupta of the University of Minnesota, and Sarah Rice from the

University of Texas. We were using a Facebook app running economic experiments to measure how much Facebook friends trusted each other, and how closely these levels of economic trust were connected to their social interaction on the platform.

We thought this was a really cool question and approach. But when we presented our findings at academic conferences, people would ask, "Can you give us some examples of how these results might be useful?" So we hunted for businesses on the web that seemed like they were using Facebook friendships as the basis for trusted exchange. And we came across a little startup—Getaround. Saliently, connecting using Facebook (ubiquitous today, but not back in 2011) was a form of identity and trust provision that Getaround required.

I connected with Getaround's co-founder Jessica Scorpio in August 2011, and while we weren't able to find a way to collaborate on research about trust at the time (Getaround was at a really early stage), I kept track of the company's progress. Their CEO Sam Zaid and policy czar Padden Murphy began enabling some of my research a couple of years later. They've been a fabulous resource, a company that epitomizes a no-strings-attached support of science—providing me with data critical to developing my models of economic impact. (They've also collaborated with Susan Shaheen of the University of California to help improve our understanding of the environmental benefits of car sharing.)

Getaround is growing rapidly, fuelled in part by over $40 million in venture financing, and a bet that its "Instant" model—where you can get a car as soon as you book it without owner approval—is what will really shift behavior from buying to sharing. Its peer-to-peer rental model is a central part of the sharing-economy narrative, the perfect confluence of two ideas: *access without ownership* and *networks replace hierarchies*.

But there haven't yet been any large-scale, digital, peer-to-peer rental marketplaces for assets other than automobiles. Snapgoods was an early effort at creating a peer-to-peer rental marketplace for everything from power saws to Roombas, but it couldn't find a profitable business model. Marketplaces that enable the rental of expensive equipment owned by people who aren't very wealthy might represent a new pocket of opportunity. For example, KitSplit, funded in 2014 by NYU students Lisbeth Kaufman and Katrina Budelis, is a peer-to-peer rental marketplace for independent filmmakers to get cameras, lenses, Oculus Rift headsets, and other professional equipment from each other. But as of late 2015, other success stories that have scaled are hard to find, and peer-to-peer rental activity is often conducted through bulletin-board-esque services like Alan Berger's NeighborGoods.

Many others have successfully facilitated household asset rental using a different, more traditional form of organizing short-term borrowing: the library. Gene Homicki, who founded and ran the West Seattle Tool Library until 2012, now runs a software company called myTurn that makes it easy for any neighborhood to set up an asset library. According to Homicki, community often emerges naturally at these lending sites. "One of the things we've seen," he told the online magazine Shareable in 2014, "is tool libraries that start makerspaces. The other thing we've seen is co-working spaces and makerspaces that are adding lending libraries. It's a natural evolution in both directions."[17]

A seemingly unrelated opportunity for peer-to-peer rental seems to be in high-end apparel and accessories. Following the runaway success of Rent the Runway, a business that lets you rent expensive outfits for a few days at about a tenth of retail price (as of 2015), there's a growing number of early-stage peer-to-peer apparel rental marketplaces. These include StyleLend and Rent My Wardrobe in the United States, RentezVous in Europe, and Designer-24 in Dubai.

I had an interesting meeting early in 2015 with Lona Duncan, a former fashion model and serial entrepreneur, and co-founder and CEO of StyleLend, during which she highlighted the immense potential of peer-to-peer for apparel and accessories. "Access over ownership is more natural than purchasing. Women want to have greater flexibility over what they wear," said Duncan, as we shared a pot of Buddha's Blend at Greenwich Village's David's Tea. "And besides, the prospect of revenue from renting out might induce more impulse buying." Fiona Disegni, the founder of RentezVous, further highlighted the value of this business model to smaller, niche designers in a 2014 conversation we had, noting that the peer-to-peer rental activity increases visibility for fashion lines with new potential buyers, builds community between users who share similar tastes, gives the designer a conduit to feedback and a form of market research, and creates a more seamless path to eventual purchase. (Interestingly enough, this is a list of benefits to a brand that sounds a lot like what I used to tell my students were some of the commercial sources of value from social media back in 2007.)

But the key challenge, said Duncan, is in the logistics. Items have to be transported from owner to renter, dry-cleaned after use, and returned reliably, activities done quite efficiently at scale by business-to-consumer rental companies like Rent the Runway, but an ongoing challenge for smaller peer-to-peer marketplaces. As a consequence, as of mid-2015, both StyleLend and RentezVous operate largely by organizing events akin to clothes-swaps, where customers meet face-to-face in preorganized physical spaces to transfer or exchange clothing. The melding of commerce and community that both Disegni and Duncan have described to me actually doesn't seem too far removed from the co-evolution of meeting and exchange in the tool libraries described by Homicki.

And yet, a central question remains. While there's clearly tremendous potential efficiency from "access over ownership," are peer-to-peer rental markets viable at scale for anything other than really expensive assets like homes and cars? Is their long-run value tied to this connection between community and commerce? And if they do take off, how will that impact the economy? Will they induce growth because there's a lot more exchange going on? Will Duncan's vision of "impulse buying, then renting out" materialize? Or will the economy slow because people stop buying things?

La Ruche Qui Dit Oui—Redefining Perfection

Back in Paris, there's another face-to-face, peer-to-peer model that's been gaining popularity in a different vertical—grocery shopping. In spring 2014, accompanied by a wonderful NYU Stern MBA student team (Humaira Faiz, Sydnee Grushack, Andrew Ng, and Jara Small), I met Marc-David Choukrun, the co-founder and CEO of La Ruche Qui Dit Oui, which translates roughly to "the beehive that says yes," and is also known in English-language countries by the easier-to-remember name The Food Assembly. The model Choukrun and his buoyant team in Paris are pioneering is a remarkable blend of the virtual and the physical, a new digitally enabled way of scaling the familiar real-world farmer's market.

Here's how Choukrun explained the business to me. A volunteer in a neighborhood decides to set up a local "ruche." The platform provides the ruche with software that allows local farmers to post availability and prices of produce in advance. (The software also provides tools to promote the marketplace.) Customers place orders for the produce that they want. A couple of times a week, the farmers and the customers meet during a specific time window at a physical space provided by the local volunteer, and the produce is picked up. The volunteer gets a small commission (about 8%), the platform gets an additional 8%, and the rest goes to the farmer.

La Ruche Qui Dit Oui has grown from an idea in 2010 to over 700 ruches as of mid-2015, when they received an €8 million investment led by the New York venture capital firm Union Square Ventures (USV). This was USV's first investment in a French firm. "We went to a ruche on a Saturday morning, we had coffee, watched people come by. To me, that was the moment when I realized that they were doing something different, unique—something that nobody in the U.S. has done, at least successfully," Fred Wilson told *TechCrunch* in a 2015 phone interview.[18] The merriment in a ruche, the happy faces and social buzz, contrasts quite starkly with the quintessential image of a lone American pushing a grocery cart through fluorescent-lit aisles.

There's another potentially broader shift that La Ruche Qui Dit Oui embodies. As anyone who has shopped at a farmer's market knows, the fact that the produce doesn't have the perfection of hue and appearance one has come to expect from big box grocery chains takes some getting used to. But according to Choukrun, there's more to the adjustment than just product appearance. And maybe this isn't a bad thing. "Consumers need to change their expectations in terms of service," he told me during a summer 2014 panel at the La French Touch conference in New York. "We're used to big brands that are streamlining very consistent experiences. In our system, it's not possible to propose a streamlined system. It's going to be very different from one community to another. People need to also accept some kind of imperfection because it's very difficult to propose perfect service when you put very small farmers in direct contact with consumers. They need to accept that sometimes a product will be missing, that sometimes a farmer can be delayed on the road. But we see a real shift in what people expect. People start to understand."

I often think back to what Choukrun said when I see the perfectly folded towels and "everything in place" appearance of my hotel rooms, or when I sense my growing impatience if a room service order runs a minute over the promised delivery time. Have we, as a society, overinvested during the industrial era in aspects of product and service quality that, upon reflection, aren't especially important? Will our return to peer-to-peer cause a natural shift back to focusing on the dimensions of quality that really matter?

How to Read This Book

Over the last few pages, I've raised a number of questions. I wrote this book to start answering these questions. I hope to provide you, the reader, with a deeper understanding of the ongoing transition toward crowd-based capitalism, and why the implications of these shifts could be profound over your lifetime.

I've organized the ideas in two broad sets: *cause* and *effect*. (Yes, I'm an academic nerd.) Of course, the best way to read this book is from start to finish. However, if you are looking for a different arc, the following notes might help.

In chapters 1 through 4, I deal with "cause," looking both back at the past and into the future. The discussion about whether the sharing economy is a market economy or a gift economy, in chapter 1, provides an important foundation for what's in the second half of the book. The evolution of thinking about the sharing economy, also in chapter 1, should be of particular interest to my fellow academics.

I wrote chapter 2 primarily for people who are genuinely curious about why we have seen the sharing economy emerge suddenly over the last few years. However, those of you who want a framework for thinking about future changes that digital technologies might cause would also benefit from reading it. It's not overly technical, but it also isn't a prerequisite for what follows. Similarly, in chapter 4, I provide an overview of emerging "blockchain" technologies that may alter crowd-based capitalism over the coming decade. (As I will explain later, they move the crowd from being the source of supply to being the "intermediary" that actually runs and, implicitly, collectively owns the market itself.) There's a parallel between the "blockchain" discussion of 2015 and the idealistic discussions of 1995, at the dawn of the commercial Internet, especially around the topic of permissionless innovation. Blockchain technologies may well power a new generation of peer-to-peer markets and digital disruption. But again, reading this chapter isn't a prerequisite for the second half of the book.

In chapter 3, I delve deeper into the nature of the new "institutions" that are being created by different sharing economy platforms. This discussion draws on years of research into how digital technologies have changed the boundaries between organizations and markets. It will be useful if you are looking for frameworks to organize different sharing economy businesses, or if you are interested more generally in what determines how economic activity is organized.

In chapters 5 through 8, I deal with "effect": economic, regulatory, and workforce impacts. I've tried to write chapter 5 on economic impacts and chapter 6 on regulatory issues as readable by themselves, although you're likely to get more out of each if you read the first few chapters as well. If you are solely interested in workforce issues, then I recommend reading chapters 3, 7, and 8.

* * *

James Surowecki framed the opportunity for crowd-based capitalism nicely in his 2013 *New Yorker* article "Uber Alles." After noting that Uber raised a quarter-billion dollars in venture capital (an amount which had seemed so high at the time), he concluded:

The flood of new money into all these new businesses feels like a mini-bubble in the making. But beneath all the hype is a sensible idea: there are a lot of slack resources in the economy. Assets sit idle—the average car is driven just an hour a day—and workers have time and skills that go unused. If you can connect the people who have the assets to people who are willing to pay to rent them, you reduce waste and end up with a more efficient system.[19]

Internet-enabled marketplaces are one kind of "community" through which the connection Surowecki refers to can be made. But, of course, there are other kinds. In keeping the scope and arguments of the book focused, I have left out a wide variety of sharing activities that are also gaining popularity: among them, food cooperatives, car-sharing cooperatives, time banks, bike-sharing initiatives, co-housing, and co-working. I don't mean to suggest through this omission that these activities aren't important or desirable. However, they don't fall as naturally under my umbrella of crowd-based capitalism.

But let's return now to the examples I have discussed in this chapter. These are a small subset of so many interesting executives, thinkers, and organizations, both corporate and otherwise, all of which I've encountered in what we call the sharing economy. You'll encounter many more of them in the pages that follow. Together, they weave a fascinating tapestry of innovation, one that provides an early glimpse of what capitalist societies might evolve into over the coming decades.

But they also raise a lot of questions—about trust, about new digital foundations like the blockchain, about economic impacts, about what it means to have a job, about the social safety net, and about what shape regulation should take. Together we'll also explore answers to each of these questions and many more as the book progresses.

Starting with the question perhaps most salient on your mind—how exactly do we define "sharing economy," anyway? To answer that one, I'll begin by taking you back again to Paris, to OuiShare Fest.

I

Cause

1

The Sharing Economy, Market Economies, and Gift Economies

In the present century the opposition between negative and positive reciprocity has taken the form of a debate between "capitalist" and "communist," "individualist" and "socialist"; but the conflict is much older than that, because it is an essential polarity between the part and the whole, the one and the many. Every age must find its balance between the two, and in every age the domination of either one will bring with it the call for its opposite.
—Lewis Hyde, *The Gift*, 49

It is May 2015, and I'm contemplating the future of capitalism at OuiShare Fest, a gathering in Paris with a decidedly non-capitalist vibe.[1] Over a thousand sharing-economy enthusiasts have gathered in and around the main venue, a giant red tent called Cabaret Sauvage, for a celebration that feels part TED, part Burning Man, and part Woodstock. I'm sitting outdoors enjoying the springtime sun with two of the founders of OuiShare and eating my conference-provided lunch, a bowl of organic lentils and beets. Behind me, preparations are afoot for the Love Fest, an all-night party that brings the three-day event to a close. Volunteers take turns on a pedal-powered generator connected to large acoustic speakers, producing short bursts of piped-in music that compete with the enthusiastic live singing of a band nearby. Across the courtyard from me, a mother nurses her infant child. Meanwhile, participants discuss, in a variety of languages, a fascinating array of topics. New investments by the New York venture capital firm Union Square Ventures. Pia Mancini's Democracy OS, a YCombinator-backed collaborative decision-making platform.[2] A notion of "new power" championed by the 92nd Street Y CEO Henry Timms and Purpose co-founder Jeremy Heimans.[3] And the environmentally conscious conference toilets that use recycled wood chips rather than water or chemicals.

Co-founded in 2011 by Antonin Léonard, Benjamin Tincq, Edwin Mootoosamy, and Flore Berlingen, OuiShare in 2015 is an increasingly influential arbiter in the vibrant marketplace of ideas about crowd-based capitalism. Léonard, youthfully charismatic and politically ambitious, sees OuiShare playing a role that extends beyond facilitating thought and dialog in the future. "We see ourselves as a creator of meaningful projects, trying to change our society into a better one, one with more social justice," he tells me.

The origins of OuiShare can be traced to consocollaborative.com, a blog started by Léonard in 2010. A year later, a group of "sharing" advocates started meeting every month in Paris for potluck dinners. Those conversations evolved into what is now a global entity with a consulting arm, a burgeoning project incubator, and a maker network. OuiShare's presence extends to more than 20 countries, primarily in Europe but including those as diverse as Chile, Lebanon, Morocco, and Canada, with each OuiShare community's presence overseen by a democratically nominated "connector."

OuiShare tries to embody the phenomenon of the dialog it facilitates, making a genuine attempt to create a collaborative organization with a cooperative decision-making process that values consensus over speed.[4] As OuiShare Fest co-chair Francesca Pick explains in a 2015 blog post, "That's why rather than calling it a think tank, a non-profit or anything else, I like to think of OuiShare as an incubator of people: a shared platform for experimentation that gives Connectors and members access to a commons of knowledge, tools and an international network of people they can learn and draw inspiration from."[5]

I'm chatting with Léonard and Tincq about the tension I sense at the Fest between the profit-motivated and purpose-driven sides of the sharing economy, between people who see the sharing economy as a market economy and those who envision it more as a "gift economy."

"I think the confusion comes from all the hope people had in those platforms, to really change the world. And because there was so much hope, the ones that were once so hopeful are now so disappointed, in a way," says Léonard. "But maybe the problem is not so much how much money was invested, but why did we have this hope?"

This "hope" that Léonard refers to is explained well in a 2015 interview by Neal Gorenflo, a former Wall Street equities analyst who started the Shareable project in 2009 to aid "democratizing how we produce, consume, govern, and solve social problems." Gorenflo points out how the Industrial Revolution could have spread abundance, but that over time, society's focus shifted to private accumulation instead of widespread prosperity and freedom. He posits that the sharing economy can serve to redress this imbalance, and in the process help to address some of the other big world challenges like environmental degradation.[6]

Tincq, understated and measured, a deep thinker who has told me that he co-founded OuiShare to get away from a corporate job he was "super-bored at," nods in agreement with Léonard. In his opinion, to bring one's sharing economy idea to market, there are few alternatives to venture capital. "Right now," Tincq says, "there is no other practical alternative for somebody who has an idea for a project to raise this first amount of money to build a platform, especially to build a community, grow to critical mass, because you need a lot of resources to do that. Right now, we all think, 'Okay, we should try to find a way for value and governance to be shared more democratically and more equally,' and that's a good objective. But to do that, you need to find a way to bridge the early-stage gap. How do you do that? Right now, it seems like only venture capital can do this."

The previous morning, Jeremiah Owyang, the founder of the brand council Crowd Companies and an active writer about the space, spoke about the massive infusions of venture capital that sharing economy platforms have raised, already far exceeding all the money social media companies, Facebook included, had garnered before they went public.[7] Owyang, a champion of calling the phenomenon the "collaborative economy," sees a close structural connection between the phases of evolution of the sharing economy and the corresponding phases the social media industry went through a few years earlier. In many ways, he's right. But to me, the connection is deeper than even Owyang might concede. Without social media, the sharing economy probably wouldn't exist in its current form. In some ways, as I explore at length in the next chapter, it laid the digital tracks upon which the platforms now rest.

A number of corporate executives no doubt started to pay attention to the sharing economy because of the venture capital and other pre-IPO financing raised by Uber (over $8 billion as of late 2015), China's Didi Kuaidi (over $4 billion), and Airbnb (close to $3 billion). These executives are present in growing numbers at events like OuiShare Fest (something my friend Charly Strum had pointed out to me earlier in the day with a sardonic remark about there being "more high heels than Birkenstocks this year"). Active investors range from New York's Union Square Ventures and Silicon Valley's Andreessen Horowitz to the hedge funds Black Rock and Tiger Global Management, the investment banking firm Goldman Sachs, the business magnate Carl Icahn, General Motors, and the Indian media company Bennett and Coleman. Of particular interest is the Collaborative Fund, founded by Craig Shapiro in 2011, which invests almost exclusively in the sharing economy.

The infusion of venture capital and the emergence of platforms with large corporate investors lead many to believe that any ideals associated with a pre-2010 sharing economy cannot be sustained. As Arthur De Grave, the editor of OuiShare's magazine stated in a 2014 post: "Simply put, under a modern capitalist mindset, shareholders are not peers (from Latin *par*, "equal"), but overlords. And if your business model is based on your ability to sustain a community, it is not absurd to expect a contradiction between your duty to serve your investors a high return on investment and the egalitarian spirit of P2P (peer-to-peer) services. In the end, you will have to choose one or the other."[8] The inherent tension in making this choice is perhaps what leads to the disappointment Léonard refers to. It is also reminiscent of the sentiment expressed by the public intellectual Diana Fillipova in her 2014 essay, "The Mock Trial of the Collaborative Economy," in which she noted: "Of course, as with technology, the problem is not the collaborative economy itself but, at least partly, the way we have been thinking about it and the unlimited hopes we were putting into it."[9]

This discussion within OuiShare as well as at their Fest, mirrors both the evolving use of the term "sharing economy" and the nature of the exchange it is used to describe. Looking at the sharing economy as I write this book in 2015, I see commercial activity resembling that of a fairly standard market economy. Yet I also see exchange that might best be described as part of a "gift economy" that serves not only an economic purpose but also has other social and cultural function. Most exchange, however, seems like an interesting meld of market and gift.

As I will argue later in this chapter, it is quite natural that the sharing economy spans the continuum between market economies and gift economies. But to get there, I first need to better bound the scope of what is meant by the "sharing economy," and discuss the evolution of recent thinking about it.

What Is the Sharing Economy?

In the introduction, I provided a number of examples that fall under the umbrella of what I call the "sharing economy" or "crowd-based capitalism," terms I use more precisely (and interchangeably) to describe an economic system with the following five characteristics:

1. Largely market-based: the sharing economy creates markets that enable the exchange of goods and the emergence of new services, resulting in potentially higher levels of economic activity.

2. High-impact capital: the sharing economy opens new opportunities for everything, from assets and skills to time and money, to be used at levels closer to their full capacity.

3. Crowd-based "networks" rather than centralized institutions or "hierarchies": the supply of capital and labor comes from decentralized crowds of individuals rather than corporate or state aggregates; future exchange may be mediated by distributed crowd-based marketplaces rather than by centralized third parties.

4. Blurring lines between the personal and the professional: the supply of labor and services often commercializes and scales peer-to-peer activities like giving someone a ride or lending someone money, activities which used to be considered "personal."

5. Blurring lines between fully employed and casual labor, between independent and dependent employment, between work and leisure: many traditionally full-time jobs are supplanted by contract work that features a continuum of levels of time commitment, granularity, economic dependence, and entrepreneurship.

I am unaware of any consensus on a definition of the sharing economy. So I am quite sure that some readers may object to my definition, and perhaps feel that it is biased toward the capitalist side of the phenomenon, and further, that it misuses the term "sharing" in describing what is often commercial exchange. As my colleague Paul Romer lamented in a June 2015 blog post, we may be losing a good verb.[10] (I agree. Much like we lost a good adjective when "social" media platforms emerged, and a good noun when Facebook converted "friend" into a verb.)

Although I find "crowd-based capitalism" most precisely descriptive of the subject matter I cover, I continue to use "sharing economy" as I write this book because it maximizes the number of people who seem to get what I'm talking about. It is interesting, nevertheless, to consider the range of labels associated with these new economic systems. Beyond Owyang's "collaborative economy"—favored over "sharing economy" by the authors Rachel Botsman and Robin Chase, and, somewhat ironically, by OuiShare—writers and thinkers since 2010 have experimented with the use of the terms "gig economy," "peer economy," "renting economy," and "on-demand economy" (the latter deemed most accurate by the venture capitalist Chris Dixon[11]). A study by *Fortune* magazine of term usage in the *New York Times,* the *Wall Street Journal,* and the *Washington Post* revealed that "sharing economy" was used five times as frequently as "on-demand economy" and "gig economy" in the first six months of 2015, but that the latter two terms were gaining popularity.[12]

Before I delve into the intellectual precursors to today's sharing economy, I'd like to consider the definitions implicit in two influential books that have appeared concurrent with the mainstream emergence of the sharing economy—Rachel Botsman and Roo Rogers's *What's Mine Is Yours: The Rise of Collaborative Consumption* (2010) and Lisa Gansky's *The Mesh* (2010)—and look as well at the ideas in Alex Stephany's more recent book, *The Business of Sharing* (2015).

Botsman and Rogers attempt in their book to lay out what they consider a broad shift in consumption from the 20th century to the 21st. The authors maintain that the 20th century was defined by "hyper consumption," whereas the 21st century stands to become the century of "collaborative consumption." Access in hyper consumption is defined by credit, whereas access in collaborative consumption is driven by reputation; choice in hyper consumption is defined by advertising, whereas choice in collaborative consumption is driven by community. Hyper consumption is defined by ownership, collaborative consumption by shared access. As they observe: "The Collaboration at the heart of Collaborative Consumption may be local and face-to-face, or it may use the Internet to connect, combine, form groups, and find something or someone to create 'many-to-many' peer-to-peer interactions. Simply put, people are sharing again with their community—be it an office, a neighborhood, an apartment building, a school, or a Facebook network."[13]

Botsman and Rogers define collaborative consumption, their preferred term, in accordance with a set of principles that include critical mass, idling capacity (the untapped value of unused or underused assets), belief in the commons, and trust in strangers. Botsman has since expanded on these ideas in numerous talks around the world, and in some definitional articles in 2014 and 2015 that I return to in chapter 3.

Gansky's thoughtful 2010 book focuses not on "collaborative consumption" but yet another concept—"the Mesh." Gansky, a good friend of mine as well as a serial entrepreneur who sold her company oFoto to Kodak prior to the dotcom bubble of 2000, is now a respected Silicon Valley angel investor who consults widely. She has an uncanny ability to see just a little further into the future of digitally enabled change than most others I know.

As many people know, mesh is a fabric, of sorts, but with lots of holes. Hammocks are made of mesh but so are football jerseys and onion bags. Not quite a fabric, nor simply a tangle of strings, mesh is difficult to categorize, has many uses, and unlike most fabrics is largely transparent. Gansky's "Mesh" is also somewhat difficult to categorize, but she emphasizes that at its heart the term applies to "a type of network that allows any node to link in any direction with any other node in the system."[14] In other words, it is rhizomatic rather than linear.

More specifically, Gansky maintains that the Mesh has five central features. First, the Mesh is defined by shareability—products or services can be easily shared within a community and that community can take any form (local or global). Second, the Mesh relies on advanced digital networks (data, about what is being shared, and by whom, can be tracked in real time). Third, the Mesh is about immediacy (goods can be shared whenever and wherever). Fourth, in the Mesh, advertising is replaced with promotions driven by social media platforms (user reviews that appear on the platforms in question or other sites, such as Facebook and Twitter). Finally the Mesh economy is global in scale and potential.

Gansky's perspective on the sharing economy focuses heavily on the enabling power of digital technologies. As she explains, "Using sophisticated information systems, the Mesh also deploys physical assets more efficiently. That boosts the bottom line, with the added advantage of lowering pressure on natural resources." In other words, people's spare time as well as their space capacity in assets and space are, in effect, being rendered detectable because of digital networks, and by virtue of this new transparency, increasingly shareable. On this basis Gansky optimistically describes "the Mesh" as the "next big opportunity—for creating new businesses and for renewing old ones."[15]

The ideas and predictions of Botsman and Gansky formed an integral part of my own original conception of crowd-based capitalism in 2011. My thinking has been influenced significantly by reading their books and engaging in many conversations with each of them. I also spoke frequently to Alex Stephany as he was writing his 2015 book, which benefits significantly from him being not just a thinker, but an active entrepreneur in the business he writes about: he is the founder of JustPark, a peer-to-peer marketplace that matches people who have empty parking spaces with those looking for a place to park. (One might imagine this as having being described at some point as the "Airbnb of parking spaces.")

Early in his book, Stephany, with a nod to the influence of the "geeky school" that sent him to the dictionary for answers to his questions,

provides a short definition of the sharing economy: "The sharing economy is the value in taking underutilized assets and making them accessible online to a community, leading to a reduced need for ownership of
those assets."[16]

He then explains each of the five limbs of his definition: (1) value (the
exchange creates economic value, either through the use of money or
through barter); (2) underutilized assets (akin to Botsman's idling capacity); (3) online accessibility (the enabling power of the Internet); (4) community (the facilitation of more fluid exchange through community trust,
social interaction, or shared value), and (5) reduced need for ownership
(goods become services).

Stephany, in his definition, does not focus exclusively on peer exchange,
but rather encompasses companies like Zipcar and Rent the Runway that
rent directly to consumers instead of only facilitating individual-based
supply. He is explicit, however, in his interest in the "business" of sharing,
and, realizing the inherent potential contradiction, explains his use of the
term "sharing economy":

Why am I using the term "sharing economy" time and time again in this book?
In part, I do so because this term has come to dominate discourse on the subject.
The genie is out of the bottle. It would be near-impossible to dislodge the term
without the risk of fracturing a growing movement of people who largely have
no problem with the term, and who are building something that—for the most
part, as we will see—is a social and economic good.[17]

How Key Early Thinking on the Sharing Economy Evolved

What I defined as the sharing economy (or as crowd-based capitalism)
emerged at scale around 2010. Different conceptions of a "sharing economy," however, predate the point at which the conditions were finally in
place for it to expand beyond niche markets. It is useful to step back here
and consider the perspectives of several earlier thinkers on the sharing
economy, exploring in the process some of the sharing economy's historical precedents, and its connection to even earlier thought on the gift economies that human societies have relied on for centuries.

In 2004, the NYU professor Yochai Benkler (now at Harvard) published "'Sharing Nicely': On Shareable Goods and the Emergence of
Sharing as a Modality of Economic Production." Motivated in part by the
rapid growth of Wikipedia since 2001, Benkler observed the ascendance
of social sharing and exchange, and predicted that sharing would soon
be at "the very core of the most advanced economies—in information,

culture, education, computation, and communications sectors."[18] He argued that the change has much to do with the growing availability of free software, distributed computing, and population-scale digital networks. According to Benkler, the most notable shift is the extent to which "these technologies have allowed various provisioning problems to be structured in forms amenable to decentralized production based on social relations, rather than through markets or hierarchies."[19]

Notice that Benkler does not argue that we have shifted to some kind of unique moment of humanistic sharing. Rather, he suggests we are experiencing a new model that combines older economic models marginalized under capitalism. And this new model is enabled by the emergence of digital technologies:

The capital cost of effective economic action in the industrial economy shunted sharing to its peripheries—to households in the advanced economies, and to the global economic peripheries that have been the subject of the anthropology of gift or common property regime literatures. The emerging restructuring of capital investment in digital networks—in particular the phenomenon of user-capitalized computation and communications capabilities—is at least partly reversing that effect.[20]

Much of Benkler's core argument rests on the observation that some material resources, like cars, are, as he puts it, "lumpy" and of "medium granularity." "Lumpy" for Benkler refers to any good that you must purchase "as is," whether or not you will use all its features. For example, to carry out your work, you may not need all the CPU power the manufacturer has pre-installed on your computer, and yet you likely have no choice but to purchase a machine more powerful than you need. "Granularity," on the other hand, refers to use—the extent to which an object is or is not being used at capacity. Cars, for example, are usually not driven 24 hours a day (sometimes only once in a day or a few times a week) and therefore not used at capacity. For this reason, most cars can be described as possessing "medium granularity."

These lumpy and mid-grain material goods represent under-used physical-capital resources. The innovation, Benkler suggests, is not whether and how these idle resources emerged, but rather the uptake of once-neglected resources. Why now? The shift, he reminds us, is not necessarily because society has suddenly decided to embrace sharing for ethical reasons but because digital platforms—the availability of free software, distributed computing, and wireless networks—enables these resources to be shared and used at capacity more easily. He does, further, see the sharing activities among peers as resembling market-based interaction, but with a key difference, the ascendance of social cues as an economic coordination mechanism:

The claim, then, is that phenomena I describe here and elsewhere—sharing of material shareable goods and peer production of software, information, and cultural goods more generally—resemble an ideal market in their social characteristics, but with social cues and motivations replacing prices as a means to generate information and motivate action.[21]

He also suggests that the economic shift we are witnessing raises several new policy issues. Moving forward, he suggests, somewhat presciently, we will need to "adjust our expectations, assumptions, and, ultimately, policy prescriptions to accommodate the emerging importance of social relations in general, and sharing in particular, as a modality of economic production."[22]

Benkler's measured approach to describing the sharing economy contrasts with the more ecclesiastical pronouncements of the scholar Michel Bauwens. While consistent with Benkler's notion of commons-based peer production, Bauwens's vision and writing aptly captures not only the strength of resistance from the "purpose-driven" community to the "profit-driven" sectors of the sharing economy that we discussed earlier in this chapter, but also the fervor with which some thinkers and users have embraced the sharing economy. The introduction of Bauwens's 2005 essay "The Political Economy of Peer Production," for instance, has a decidedly manifesto-like feel:

Not since Marx identified the manufacturing plants of Manchester as the blueprint for the new capitalist society has there been a deeper transformation of the fundamentals of our social life. As political, economic, and social systems transform themselves into distributed networks, a new human dynamic is emerging: peer to peer (P2P). As P2P gives rise to the emergence of a third mode of production, a third mode of governance, and a third mode of property, it is poised to overhaul our political economy in unprecedented ways.[23]

A central takeaway from Bauwens's article is his clearly articulated definition of peer-to-peer projects. First, he maintains that they are processes happening over distributed networks. These networks are places where individuals have a certain degree of agency. So unlike, let's say, the US airport system (a decentralized system where planes still must go through pre-determined and centrally allocated hubs), the Internet, powered by the TCP/IP protocol, is a truly decentralized system, since transmission paths are determined in a distributed way, and there are robust ways to work around predetermined routes if network resources fail. In Bauwens's words, "P2P is based on distributed power and distributed access to resources." Second, Bauwens maintains that P2P projects are defined by their "equipotentiality" or "anti-credentialism." Said simply, anyone, rather than a permissioned few, can participate in these networks. The guiding philosophy again is perhaps TCP/IP, a "permissionless" protocol that allows any device to transmit over a network, irrespective of the nature of content they are transferring.

Finally, Bauwens contends that P2P projects are defined by their "holoptism," contrasting the idea with "panoptism." Under panoptism, total knowledge is reserved for a single person or elite group, and participants only know what they must know to carry out their work. Holoptism represents a reverse order—knowledge is distributed among all users. In other words, it aims to reduce the information asymmetry and redefine the power balance that has typically characterized relationships between users and providers, between workers and owners. This in turn means that in P2P projects, communication is distributed rather than hierarchal.

Bauwens's vision is more in line with what we see emerging in the decentralized blockchain-based peer-to-peer systems we will discuss in chapter 4. Today's crowd-based capitalism, however, has a closer connection to the "hybrid" Lawrence Lessig characterizes in his 2008 book *Remix: Making Art and Commerce Thrive in the Hybrid Economy.*

In *Remix* Lessig uses a stark definition of a sharing economy in the context of culture, distinguishing it definitively from what he calls a "commercial economy." He writes: "There exists not just the commercial economy, which meters access on the simple metric of price, but also a sharing economy, where access to culture is regulated not by price but by a complex set of social relations."[24] Later in the same chapter, Lessig qualifies his point: "Of all the ways in which the exchange within a sharing economy can be defined—or put differently, of all the possible terms of the exchange within a sharing economy—the one way in which it cannot be defined is in terms of money."[25]

Lessig himself then draws a parallel between his thinking and Benkler's. "As Yochai Benkler puts it, in commercial economies 'prices are the primary source of information about, and incentive for, resource allocation'"; in sharing economies "non-price-based social relations play these roles."[26] However, he argues, this "is not because people are against money (obviously)" but rather because "people live within overlapping spheres of social understanding. What is obviously appropriate in some spheres is obviously inappropriate in others."[27]

In other words, Lessig contends that there is more circulating in sharing economies than services and goods. To put it simply, "good feelings" are what circulate in Lessig's version of a sharing economy. So, as Lessig asserts, "not only is money not helpful, in many cases, adding money into the mix is downright destructive."[28]

Lessig further contends that not all sharing economies are built alike. On the one hand there are "thin sharing economies" or "those economies where the motivation is primarily me-regarding" or meant to serve the individual (and not necessarily on a monetary level, for example, as with joining a local softball league). On the other hand, there are "thick sharing economies" or "economies where the motivations are at least ambiguous between me and thee motivation"[29] or meant to serve communities (for example, volunteering at a local soup kitchen).

This diversity in sharing economies leads to the central argument Lessig makes in his 2008 book. He contends that we are now seeing the rise of a "third way"—a hybrid economy, which he characterizes as follows:

Commercial economies build value with money at their core. Sharing economies build value, ignoring money. Both are critical to life both online and offline. Both will flourish more as Internet technology develops. But between these two economies, there is an increasingly important third economy: one that builds upon both the sharing and commercial economies, one that adds value to each. This third type—the hybrid—will dominate the architecture for commerce on the Web. It will also radically change the way sharing economies function. The hybrid is either a commercial entity that aims to leverage value from a sharing economy, or it is a sharing economy that builds a commercial entity to better support its sharing aims. Either way, the hybrid links two simpler, or purer, economies, and produces something from the link. That link is sustained, however, *only if the distinction between the two economies is preserved.*[30]

To summarize: there appears to be a general consensus that any kind of sharing economy will likely yield a greater range of available options for its participants and possibly a greater attention to long-term goals like sustainability, as well as an increased reliance on social rather than economic cues to facilitate the organizing of economic activity. However, I believe we are witnessing new "hybrids" (to use Lessig's term) in which, *rather than being preserved, the distinction between the two economies— commercial and sharing—will get increasingly blurred.* Some hybrids that may take the form of commerce leading sharing, like Airbnb, or a form where commerce is leveraged but sharing is the real objective (for example, the time banking platform TimeRepublik where time rather than money is exchanged[31]).

Is the Sharing Economy a Gift Economy?

Beyond the public relations efforts of platforms like Uber and Airbnb, there may be deeper reasons why the term "sharing economy" is so popular: It captures some of the thinking and the idealism of the early proponents of economy-wide sharing approaches. It hints at the shift away from faceless, impersonal 20th-century capitalism and toward exchange that is somehow more connected, more embedded in community, more reflective of a shared purpose.

In this section I dwell at some length on one central point—the social versus the commercial as a facilitator of exchange. Yes, it is a unifying theme among prior thinkers. But its manifestation is quite different across these different authors. For Botsman and Stephany, and to some extent, Gansky, the role of social cues is contained largely in the creation of trust, reputation, or "digital community" that facilitates economic exchange. For Lessig, the social versus the nonsocial drivers are precisely what draws the line between sharing economies and commercial economies. For Benkler, the social cues are a replacement for economic cues (prices or managerial oversight) in the creation of a third way, commons-based peer production.

In many ways, in their thinking about the integration of social aspects into economic exchange and activity, both Benkler and Lessig point frequently to the "gift economies" that have existed for centuries. This is a critical connection. There are numerous parallels between the behaviors I see emerging in the modern sharing economy and what we have observed in these gift economies of the past. Simply put, I believe that some of the shifts we will see in capitalist exchange over the coming years will reflect a reintegration of gift economies into a system that has become inefficiently impersonal and commercial.

Perhaps the earliest work on gift exchange was the 1924 essay by Marcel Mauss, "Essau sur le don," in which he characterizes gift economies as having three obligations: to give, to accept, and to reciprocate.[32] My own understanding of gift economies, however, has relied extensively on Lewis Hyde's remarkable 1983 book, *The Gift: Creativity and the Artist in the Modern World.*

Hyde's book is too richly layered to reduce to a useful, succinct definition of a gift economy. And yet he draws on a different (and interesting) contrast with a market economy: "Works of art exist simultaneously in two 'economies,' a market economy and a gift economy. Only one of these is essential, however: a work of art can survive without the market, but where there is no gift, there is no art."[33]

A first critical link—between gifts and the creation of community—is made early in his book: "To begin with, unlike the sale of a commodity, the giving of a gift tends to establish a relationship between the parties involved. Furthermore, when gifts circulate within a group, their commerce leaves a series of *interconnected relationships* in its wake, and a kind of *decentralized cohesiveness emerges*."[34]

Hyde contrasts this creation of a complex of relationships with a purely commercial exchange. (The following passage is one of many crucial to Lessig's shaping of *Remix*.)

It is the cardinal difference between gift and commodity exchange that a gift establishes a feeling-bond between two people, while the sale of a commodity leaves no necessary connection. I go into a hardware store, pay the man for a hacksaw blade and walk out. I may never see him again. The disconnectedness is, in fact, a virtue of the commodity mode. We don't want to be bothered. If the clerk always wants to chat about the family, I'll shop elsewhere. I just want a hacksaw blade.[35]

The picture of a gift economy that Hyde presents is thus tied very closely to the creation of community. In fact, one theme of the book involves the nature of a gift: that its property value or consumption value is largely irrelevant, and that the *true purpose* of any exchange or transfer of objects is of increasing social cohesion.

A clear understanding of this dimension of gift economies is what prompts Benkler to explicitly distinguish them from his idea of peer production. He explains, "I hesitate to use the term 'gift exchange' because the highly developed gift literature ... has focused very heavily on the production and reproduction of social relations through the exchange and circulation of things. As will soon become clear, I am concerned with the production of things and actions/services valued materially, through nonmarket mechanisms of social sharing."[36]

A second important aspect of gift economies is that there is no expectation of bilateral reciprocity. A barter economy is not a gift economy. Using examples ranging from the ceremonial exchange of the Massim of the South Sea Islands (the Kula ring) to Scottish folk tales, Hyde explains how gift "circles" allow for the sustained flow of social value between people while avoiding the commercial nature and expectations induced by bilateral gift exchange.[37]

What does this flow of gift objects from person to person lead to? Hyde says that gift circles "give increase." Put differently, since the purpose of gift exchange is to facilitate the flow of "social value," a gift that is kept does not serve any purpose. One that is "paid forward" does. "Now that we have seen the figure of the circle we can understand what seems at first to be a paradox of gift exchange: when the gift is used, it is not used up," observes Hyde. "Quite the opposite, in fact: the gift that is not used will be lost, while the one that is passed along remains abundant." This observation contrasts gift economies with market economies, since, as Hyde further notes, "The distinction lies in what we might call the vector of the increase: in gift exchange it, the increase, stays in motion and follows the object, while in commodity exchange it stays behind as profit." Hyde also suggests that the ethos of gift economies leads to a culture that is better aligned with environmentally responsible or sustainable living: "the forest's abundance is in fact a consequence of man's treating its wealth as a gift."[38]

In a gift economy, debt may exist but without any clear sense of how much is owed. Again, as Benkler observes in "'Sharing Nicely'":

In many cultures, generosity is understood as imposing a debt of obligation, but neither the precise amount of value given nor the precise nature of the debt to be repaid or its date of repayment need necessarily be specified. Actions enter into a cloud of good will or membership, out of which each agent can understand himself as being entitled to a certain flow of dependencies or benefits in exchange for continued cooperative behavior. This flow may be an ongoing relationship between two people, sharing among members of a small group like a family or circle of friends, and more broadly, the general level of generosity among strangers that makes for a decent society.[39]

In other words, in a gift economy, while someone may owe something, it neither has a specific value nor is there, in some cases, an expectation that the debt will even be repaid to the giver. The radical reciprocity of gift economies also sometimes allows for the possibility of debts being repaid to anyone in the community—much like the "gift" of a user-generated review on a site like Amazon or a peer-to-peer marketplace like Airbnb.

Finally, the tension highlighted by Hyde from the parallel prevalence of gift economies and market economies seems oddly prescient of the "purpose versus profit discussion" at the start of this chapter. Again, quoting Hyde:

> In the present century the opposition between negative and positive reciprocity has taken the form of a debate between "capitalist" and "communist," "individualist" and "socialist"; but the conflict is much older than that, because it is an essential polarity between the part and the whole, the one and the many. Every age must find its balance between the two, and in every age the domination of either one will bring with it the call for its opposite. For where, on the one hand, there is no way to assert identity against the mass, and no opportunity for private gain, we lose the well-advertised benefits of a market society—its particular freedoms, its particular kind of innovation, its individual and material variety, and so on. But where, on the other hand, the market alone rules, and particularly where its benefits derive from the conversion of gift property to commodities, the fruits of gift exchange are lost. At that point commerce becomes correctly associated with the fragmentation of community and the suppression of liveliness, fertility, and social feeling.[40]

The Sharing Economy Spans the Market-to-Gift Spectrum

Hyde draws the examples in his book primarily from anthropological studies of small economies, he says, "not ... because gifts are a primitive or aboriginal form of property—they aren't—but because gift exchange tends to be an economy of small groups, of extended families, small villages, close-knit communities, brotherhoods and, of course, of tribes."[41]

Today's sharing economy is scaling behaviors and forms of exchange that used to be among such "close-knit communities" to a broader, loosely knit digital community of semi-anonymous peers. In asking whether we should expect the natural integration into the sharing economy of the "gift" motivations and practices that characterized the economies of these smaller communities, I have found that is useful to view the new economic activity as existing on a continuum between gift economies and market economies, with some cases at both ends of the spectrum, and many more in between. Let me illustrate this point with a few examples.

Accommodation: Couchsurfing, Airbnb, OneFineStay

Short-term accommodation platforms are among the most high-profile and high-use peer-to-peer platforms, transforming how people travel both domestically and abroad. On the gift economy end of the spectrum is Couchsurfing, a platform many people think of as the original sharing economy platform. You join Couchsurfing, get verified, and get an account. As a member, you are able to sleep on the couches of other members. You are also able to allow them to sleep on your couch, if they happen to be in your city and need a place to crash. No money exchanges hands, and there is no formal system tracking whether you are giving as much as you take. Indeed, someone may host people every week but never stay on another members' couch and vice versa.

In the past, you might have called up an old friend and asked to crash on his or her couch while visiting his or her city. Couchsurfing enables you to do the same thing but with one difference—your "old friend" may be a complete stranger. The platform, then, is designed to put you in touch with peers around the world and has the added benefit of ensuring that they are really who they say they are and not someone who might harm you. What separates this from the informal couchsurfing of previous eras is its reliance on networked technologies and the possibility of a trust built through the platform rather than through a history of personal contact.

I spoke at length to Jennifer Billock, the charismatic CEO of Couchsurfing, at OuiShare Fest in 2015. A veteran Web executive and a long-time yoga and meditation teacher, Billock doesn't view Couchsurfing as an accommodation platform; she views it as a social network. "If you ask people why they use Couchsurfing, they'll tell you they use it to meet people or to make new friends. They will generally secondarily say that they use it to find a place to stay," Billock notes. "The network is a means of social connection, whether you're a traveler or travel enthusiast, that range from 'I want to go on a bike ride,' or 'I'm traveling solo and I want to connect with somebody for a hike,' or whatever, to 'I'm putting myself in someone's home.' Those are the spectrum of use-cases for Couchsurfing."

In other words, hospitality and a desire to connect with other human beings are what drive Couchsurfing. There are members who have never actually stayed with any other member, but have hosted extensively. Similarly, there are members who have never hosted but are frequent guests. The act of hosting or being a guest induces no expectation of reciprocity, but is a conduit for the exchange of social value. Numerous members connect with Couchsurfing when they arrive in a new city with no interest in finding accommodation, but just to find community. As I write this book, it is the closest example to a pure gift economy that I have encountered in the modern sharing economy.

Couchsurfing, which is venture-backed, shares a board member with Airbnb: Joel Cutler, a travel industry veteran. In contrast with the social motivations of a Couchsurfing host, Airbnb hosts typically join the platform because they have space that they are hoping to rent out for a profit. Guests, likewise, are often on the platform because they are looking for accommodations that are larger, better located, less synthetic, or more affordable than hotels.

However, this is not to say that Airbnb is purely market driven. There is certainly a gift economy aspect to it as well. Even as money exchanges hands, a large number of hosts are, in a way, also giving the gift of their personal space to someone. There is an intimacy associated with an Airbnb stay. One sees family pictures, trinkets from travel to other countries, the choices made of linens and towels, spices in the kitchen. The space transitions from personal to something in between personal and public. As Hyde points out, "The way we treat a thing can change its nature."[42]

Furthermore, the gift aspect of Airbnb exchange changes our behaviors. Hosts often go out of their way to make guests feel at home by providing myriad extras (a glass of wine upon arrival, a tour of the neighborhood, or a free gym pass) and guests often go the extra mile, too (bringing gifts from their home country or treating a host to dinner). You'd leave the towels on the floor in a hotel without a second thought, but not at an Airbnb. Many guests have told me how they spend hours cleaning the host's apartment before they depart.

The reviews on the platform also operate, in part, as "gifts." Positive reviews for hosts help to support hosts by generating future business, and positive reviews for guests help travelers to secure future accommodations more easily. As we discussed, these are gifts in Hyde's sense of the word.

On the market economy end of the spectrum is OneFineStay, a UK-based platform that counts Hyatt Hotels among its investors, and that enables people to rent out luxury homes, luxury yachts, and vacation villas. When I spoke to its founder Evan Frank, in 2014 and in 2015, he didn't see Airbnb as his direct competitor. Rather, he sees OneFineStay as a challenger to a luxury hotel like the Ritz Carlton. If one delves a little deeper into the service, this distinction starts to make sense. The platform ensures that the well-heeled OneFineStay guests will enjoy all the amenities they might expect from a high-end hotel, including cleaning, fresh linens (on a daily basis if needed) and 24/7 guest services. In other words, while the space may be supplied by crowd, the hospitality is not provided by the homeowners but rather by the platform itself.

Funding: Kickstarter, Kiva, Funding Circle, AngelList

The peer-to-peer financing arena provides additional examples along the gift-market spectrum. The quintessential crowdfunding platform Kickstarter, for example, provides a way for people to fund a wide variety of projects, be it a new film or performance, the development of a new app, or a new product. A typical sequence of funding works like this. First, creative entrepreneurs launch their project with a funding goal. Second, people on the platform who feel strongly about the project contribute an amount they can afford. Often, the entrepreneur will offer rewards of different kinds for different levels of contribution. If the funding goal is reached, the creative entrepreneur receives their money. Between 2009 and 2015, close to nine million people pledged close to $2 billion for hundreds of thousands of projects on Kickstarter, and the word has entered the lexicon of popular culture. Every day, hundreds of people decide they are going to "Kickstart" their projects.

What's in it for the funders? Part of it is the pure joy of seeing a cool idea receive the funding it needs to get off the ground. Part of it has to do with getting early access to cool new things. However, even if the project is a commercial venture, investing in a Kickstarter gives you no ownership stake. I spoke to Kickstarter's founder and CEO Yancey Strickler about this in spring 2014, and at the time he asserted that he had no intention of taking the platform into the "capital for equity" realm. In fact, late in 2015, the company reaffirmed its position by becoming a benefit corporation, renewing its longstanding commitment to supporting the arts and culture, and articulating other values and commitments it intended to live by.[43]

If one looks at the composition of projects funded on Kickstarter, some of the "gift" motivations become clearer. A large percentage of Kickstarter projects are those that would have traditionally been funded by a foundation or a wealthy local business looking to support the arts, or through a charity walk, or by a group of friends. As Brian Meece, the founder and CEO of Kickstarter competitor RocketHub told me in 2013, crowdfunding is a social event, and a successful project is one that is curated in the same way you would a good party. In many ways, thus, the psychology of funding projects on Kickstarter is much more social than commercial. It is much more a gift economy than a market economy, with the norms associated with philanthropic giving.

The gift motivation is also central for funders on the microloan platform Kiva. Founded by Jessica Jackley and Matt Flannery in 2004, Kiva connects people who have money with people whose businesses need a loan. However, the funders are largely from wealthier countries, while the loan recipients are frequently in less wealthy countries. The requested loan amounts are also typically small (for a business)—a few hundred to a few thousand dollars—and the loans themselves are typically funded by pooling smaller contributions from multiple lenders.

Based on the numbers, a Kiva loan is an excellent investment. The repayment rates are extremely high. There are often well-developed on-the-ground verification entities, community groups, (and often commercial micro-lenders) who vet Kiva projects before they are listed. Furthermore, projects on Kiva compete for the same sources of funding. So there's clearly a market economy element to this. But lenders also give to feel connected to the lives of the recipients; this motivation is well reflected in the project descriptions that potential borrowers post, which are heavy on personal stories but light on financials. So Kiva's position in the sharing economy is somewhere on that continuum between the market economy and the gift economy.

Funding Circle, like Kiva, is a peer-to-peer lending platform offering loans that are funded by pooling small contributions from multiple lenders (often hundreds of lenders), to loan recipients (mostly small businesses). On the original UK-based Funding Circle platform, the funders—whether they have a few pounds or a few thousands pounds—select projects to back, and they receive interest on their loans, typically significantly higher than what one would earn from a savings account. Entrepreneurs who receive loans must pay them back in a set amount of time. But unlike Kiva there are few, if any, personal stories in the loan documents, which are instead laden with financial details. Although the platform eliminates traditional trusted third-party lenders (e.g., banks and mortgage brokers), it remains largely a market economy. Perhaps some lenders feel good about supporting their local businesses, but they view their contribution as an investment, not as a gift, and evaluate its performance through this lens.

Finally, on the opposite end of the spectrum are equity crowdfunding platforms like AngelList, which puts startups into contact with investors who make investments in early-stage companies. Funders get equity in exchange for their investments. AngelList and others like it almost always serve a pure market economy, bringing online the traditional activity of venture capital (VC) financing, structuring such financing using ideas from private equity, and perhaps expanding the set of people who can participate. One might occasionally see motivation to support a business in a specific area or a specific sector, but this is no different from what happens in traditional VC.

Service Platforms: Trade School, TimesFree, TaskRabbit, Handy

The final set of examples of peer-to-peer platforms I discuss focuses purely on service and, more notably, on leveraging participants' spare time along with their knowledge, skills, and talents. Platforms like the Brooklyn-based peer-learning initiative Trade School and barter market-place OurGoods, both communities for artists and other creative professionals started in Brooklyn by Caroline Woolard and Jen Abrams, are good example of platforms that are more gift economy than market economy. On Trade School, the platform's "teachers" share knowledge and skills in exchange for either others' knowledge and skills, or in exchange for material goods, but not for money.[44] For example, you might swap a tutoring lesson in math for help purchasing the best set of downhill skis in your price range. Someone else might offer personal training in exchange for French cooking classes. In short, on Trade School, knowledge and skills are reimagined as money-free trades.

Lessig's conception of a sharing economy, as we discussed earlier in the chapter, is well aligned with the motivations of Trade School and Our-Goods. In a 2014 conversation, Woolard explained to me how the value of what is created by an artist is not measured well by traditional money. Some art is priced very high, and most art cannot be exchanged for money at all. The pricing of art that emerges from the balancing of supply and demand therefore does not yield an appropriate allocation of money to artists, and as a consequence, alternative forms of exchange (ones not involving money), are necessary for their communities to get services as basic as childcare and education.

Similar to Trade School, the babysitting co-op app TimesFree, started by Francis Jervis, a PhD student at NYU, represents a gift economy with some market economy elements to it. Communities set up co-ops with a virtual currency: each participant is issued a set of "tokens"; one earns tokens by babysitting, and one spends tokens on getting sitters.

By contrast, labor markets like TaskRabbit and Handy have few, if any, gift economy dimensions. On TaskRabbit, prospective providers (called "taskers") are hired by clients at hourly rates chosen by the taskers, and can choose filters to ensure that they are only matched with jobs that meet their preferences, such as their minimum hourly rate or the times when they are available. TaskRabbit is thus a matching market for labor services. You might make friends with your tasker, but in the same way you'd make friends with your local grocery checkout clerk.

The Sharing Economy and Human Connectedness

There are numerous other sectors in which one sees platforms that span the market-to-gift continuum. Yerdle and Listia are platforms for exchanging owned assets (using virtual currencies), and represent an interesting middle ground between market and gift economies when considering substitutes for buying from a retailer—Rent the Runway and StyleLend being on the market extreme, and numerous clothing swaps on the gift extreme. Uber is very much a market economy, as is Getaround (although environmental concerns might lead one to use these as substitutes for auto ownership); BlaBlaCar and Lyft have some gift economy aspects to them, as does Bandwagon, a platform for sharing yellow cabs in New York, and Hitch, a carpooling network acquired by Lyft in 2015. Natalie Foster, the founder of the (then) sharing economy collective action platform Peers.org, quotes a Peers member named Justin, a ride-share driver in Los Angeles, who calls the ride-sharing experience a positive force in his life: "Often times because of how we run so close in our circles, we sometimes shut ourselves off from interactions with new people. Ride sharing has allowed me to interact with people whom I would never have met."[45]

The sharing economy is thus diverse not just in its industries, services and business models, but on the market-to-gift spectrum as well. It is neither the exclusive domain of altruistic givers nor full-steam-ahead capitalists.

Of course, this diversity may also explain the sharing economy's popularity and future potential. The sharing economy, although not politically neutral, is creating a new economic model—an interesting middle ground between capitalism and socialism—that also appears to lend itself to the fulfilling the desires and needs of people who identify with the extreme ends of both the economic and political spectrums. More importantly, it has developed as an economic model that appears to lend itself to fulfilling the desires and needs of people who identify with neither of those extremes.

In 2013, I joined a newly formed NYU collective, the Project for the Advancement of our Common Humanity (PACH), founded by the NYU professors Niobe Way, Carol Gilligan, and Pedro Nguera. PACH was formed to better understand "what lies at the root of our crisis of connection and what we can do to create a more just and humane world."[46] A number of the world's problems, ranging from violence to educational outcomes have been shown to stem from an insufficient level of human connectedness. I joined PACH to try and understand whether digital technologies were a part of the solution, or part of the problem.

My ongoing exposure to the sharing economy has made me wonder if we are reversing a now-familiar narrative about the isolating effects of digital technologies. MIT sociologist Sherry Turkle, the leading scholar on the topic, explains in her 2011 book *Alone Together* that "digital connections and the sociable robot may offer the illusion of companionship without the demands of friendship. Our networked life allows us to hide from each other, even as we are tethered to each other."[47]

However, this is a familiar narrative. In 1953, Robert Nisbet lamented that while he was not sure if it was the "presence of the machine and its iron discipline that creates, as so many argue in our day, the conditions of depersonalization and alienation in modern mass culture, the fact is plain that the contemporary sense of anxiety and insecurity is associated with not merely an unparalleled mechanical control of environment."[48] Nisbet further quotes the 19th-century classic, *Suicide*, in which Emile Durkheim worried that the forces of technological progress have "successively destroyed all the established social contexts; one after another they have been banished either by the slow usury of time or by violent revolution."

Could it be that we are at an inflection point in the social impact of digital technologies, from which a more connected society will emerge through Airbnb and Couchsurfing stays, Lyft carpools that take us away from driving alone to commuting together, VizEat social dining instead of TV dinners, and La Ruche Qui Dit Oui gatherings rather than solitary shopping carts? Or will we be increasing isolated as our Alfred butlers, Instacart shoppers, and Munchery deliveries fulfill our basic needs behind the closed doors of our high-rise apartments?

Scott Heifermann, the CEO of Meetup, a social platform whose headquarters are around the corner from my NYU office, constantly emphasizes to me that Meetup provides a purpose-driven rather than a social service, with millions of people coming together in small groups to learn or discuss a shared interest, and finding community as a by-product. Perhaps they are the 21st-century digital equivalent of a highly personalized

Rotary Club, reconstructing fragmented communities around shared interests.

Or maybe the blurring of lines between the commercial and the gift in tomorrow's sharing economy will organically weave greater levels of connectedness into our everyday economic activities—finding a place to stay, driving to work, getting a meal, buying groceries—and create new social contexts to replace the ones Durkheim lamented we lost through the Industrial Revolution.

Perhaps, over time, this will be the true gift of the sharing economy.

2

Laying the Tracks: Digital and Socioeconomic Foundations

There is now a new kind of relationship of trust for people to build on: trust in online profiles. This is not an incremental change to society—it's not a bit more, or a bit better of what went before—it's a disruptive change. Nothing will ever be the same. The building block of society, interpersonal trust, has been transformed from a scarce into an abundant resource. Our potential to collaborate and create value [is] also transformed.
—Frederic Mazzella, OuiShare magazine interview, January 14, 2013

The Internet has existed as space for commercial exchange for over two decades. Now well into the new millennium, it is easy to forget that in the mid to late 1990s, the Internet was both a scene of frenzied excitement and a site of deep apprehension, fear, and moral panic. After all, although some Internet enthusiasts like Howard Rheingold were staking out the "virtual frontier" of the Internet, others were warning people that the Internet was a potential minefield of illicit affairs, pornography, and (of course) fraudulent activities.

Over the past two decades, as both the utopian speculations and paranoid misconceptions about the Internet have receded, it has become an integral part of our everyday lives. However, although nearly as old as the commercial Internet itself, peer-to-peer exchange has only recently graduated from supplementing or extending existing forms of commerce to creating entirely new business models and consumer behaviors—models and behavior that were not fully conceivable in the early years of the Web.

Why did it take so long? Online consumer commerce was already part of the mainstream by the turn of the 21st century—Amazon.com, the world's largest online retailer in 2015, went public in 1997, and was generating over $3 billion in revenue by 2001. But the sharing economy as we know it today has emerged quite recently.

In this chapter, I explain how the emergence of today's sharing economy is largely due to the confluence of a set of digital enablers that have been a long time coming—critical among them now being mass-market smartphones, ubiquitous wireless broadband, and trust systems that include digitized real-world social networks. I discuss further how the potential of crowd-based capitalism is being expanded by an ongoing digitization of everyday physical objects, and by the coming of age of decentralized marketplace protocols like those underlying Bitcoin.

To better understand why it took so long and how the potential is expanding so rapidly, it is first helpful for us to consider some of the peer-to-peer precursors to today's sharing economy—eBay, Alibaba, Craigslist, Kozmo—that introduced a largely apprehensive group of consumers to some of the promise of peer-to-peer in the years following the birth of the commercial Internet, and, in some ways, were the conceptual ancestors of today's sharing economy platforms.

Precursors: eBay, Craigslist, Kozmo

Let's start with eBay, founded in September 1995. In its earliest iterations, eBay offered a commercial space for individuals to move their garage sales online and for isolated booksellers and thrift shop owners to expand their potential market by developing online shops that ran parallel to stores in physical locations. Today, eBay generates more than $80 billion in marketplace activities per year, more than the gross domestic product (GDP) of over 100 countries. (Despite its scope and size, however, eBay is still dwarfed by Alibaba's Taobao, China's dominant peer-to-peer retail marketplace, which mediates close to $300 billion in transactions annually, more than the GDPs of Finland, Ireland, or Portugal.)

While both eBay and Alibaba continue to represent important economic hubs on the web, neither exemplifies the sharing economy's most interesting economic activities. The transactions are quite different from those on Uber, Airbnb, Handy, or Getaround. In many ways, these differences explain why eBay and Alibaba came of age many years before the sharing economy did. First, they focus quite extensively on retail exchange. Buyers bid (or sometimes buy without bidding), and sellers put objects in boxes and ship them to buyers. By contrast, today's sharing economy is more about facilitating or providing services than exchanging objects. Money is generated from "renting out" rather than selling, and what can be borrowed ranges from a room or entire house (e.g., Airbnb) to a seat in someone's car (e.g., BlaBlaCar), to a few hours of someone's time (e.g., Postmates).

Second, with eBay, exchange is asynchronous and "low-stakes." A buyer purchases a product, a seller then ships the product, and the buyer finally receives the product. In this respect, while peer-to-peer, eBay still shares a great deal in common with older forms of long-distance retailing like mail order. While you might not receive the product you hoped to receive (e.g., the autographed baseball signed by Babe Ruth may be a mass-produced replica or the used jeans may not fit or be more faded than promised), the exchange is unlikely to result in serious harm. The risks aren't very high, and this is the sense in which I mean that the exchange is low-stakes. By contrast, the sharing economy often entails synchronous and high-stakes exchange. You are often collocated with the person who is providing your service, and there's a great deal more risk, for example, in sleeping in a stranger's spare bedroom than there is asking someone you don't know to send you a package. But correspondingly, because the sharing economy encompasses everyday physical-world services, it holds the potential to more profoundly impact people's everyday lives.

Finally, with eBay, proximity between the trading partners has little impact on the quality of the exchange. While proximity may reduce the cost of shipping, there are no other advantages to buyers and sellers being located close by. In the sharing economy, on the other hand, proximity is often a key factor. Indeed, as I discuss later in this chapter, peer-to-peer markets are especially robust in densely populated urban areas, and more advantageous there too, because they work more efficiently when their participants live in close proximity.

In many respects, eBay may be at best understood as a distant cousin of today's sharing economy. While it may have turned consumers into digital manifestations of Adam Smith's 18th-century "one-man shop," and helped build a first form of familiarity with the idea of trusting people on the other end of a digital interface, it was only a step or two away from catalog shopping. By contrast, Craigslist, which started as an e-mail service in 1995 and become a web-based service in 1996, is somewhat more in line with the contemporary sharing economy.

In a now-famous infographic from 2012, David Haber from SupplyDemanded.com mapped the different services of Craigslist to the specialized peer-to-peer marketplaces that were emerging to scale up exchange in each "industry vertical."[1] A subset of these marketplaces that were operational in December 2015, spanning a range of industries, is summarized in figure 2.1.

Figure 2.1
Sharing economy platforms across a few industries, 2015.

As anyone who has used it knows, Craigslist is a very general-purpose peer-to-peer marketplace, an "anything goes" digital bazaar of sorts. You can buy products like old and new electronics, furniture, and bicycles, but you can also get services, such as a man-with-a-van, a cleaner or home computer technician, or a piano tuner. If eBay is a distant cousin to the sharing economy, Craigslist may be a slightly closer cousin.

Of course, cousins don't always have much in common. On the one hand, as much as Craigslist is about buying and selling products, it is also about finding and delivering services. Furthermore, in the case of Craigslist, proximity matters. This is why Craigslist, while global in scope, has always been organized on a local basis.

On the other hand, Craigslist lacks many elements of today's sharing economy marketplaces. One element stands out most saliently—trust. You may be comfortable using Craigslist to hire someone to move a few boxes of books from your home to your office or to paint your kitchen, but as new peer-to-peer services appear, finding services on Craigslist seems increasingly perilous. After all, why hire a cleaner or repairperson on Craigslist when you can hire one who has been background-screened on TaskRabbit or Handy?[2]

True, the cleaner or repairperson you hire on TaskRabbit may end up having pretty much the same skills as one you could have found on Craigslist. You may be happy or unhappy with either person. But on Craigslist, there are no checks and balances. You could be letting anyone into your home. If you don't like the job these providers do, you can choose not to hire them again, but there's nowhere to launch a complaint if something is damaged or stolen.

Of course, this also means that there is less motivation for the cleaners and movers you find on Craigslist to do a great job. After all, while they may lose a potential repeat client, they won't lose future customers. In contrast, if you hire a cleaner or mover on TaskRabbit or Handy, you not only get someone who has been vetted by the platform but, more importantly, if that person does a bad job, you can give him or her a bad rating. Bad performance has consequences—it becomes part of the person's profile on the platform—and, as I discuss in chapter 8, spawns a new form of Darwinist evolution that is data driven. Similarly, if you're a provider through TaskRabbit or Handy, you never have to worry about doing a job and not getting paid, since the platform facilitates the transaction. This addresses an issue of huge concern for freelance workers. Sara Horowitz, the captivating founder of the Freelancers Union, notes that nearly 8 in 10 freelancers have faced client nonpayment at some point in their careers, or as she pointed out to US president Barack Obama at an October 2015 labor conference that we both attended and spoke at, "freelance isn't free."[3]

In this sense, while Craigslist expanded peer-to-peer forms of exchange and prepared us for today's sharing economy, it didn't do so in a way that engendered population-scale confidence about getting these services through digital platforms. In fact, over the past two decades, Craigslist has generated so many awkward and even dangerous encounters that there are now entire blogs and online forums dedicated solely to sharing disastrous Craigslist stories.

A final precursor to current sharing economy platforms is Kozmo—a less well known but nevertheless early relative of many of today's peer-to-peer delivery services. In many respects, Kozmo, established in the 1990s, was too far ahead of its time. It was the first "on-demand anything" service, offering to pick up and deliver a range of items to your home in one hour. The company raised $250 million in venture capital, employed over 1,000 delivery personnel, and in 2000, had partnerships with Starbucks to promote its service at their coffee shops and use these locations as drop-off points for rented items.

Today, your Kozmo delivery person would likely be an independent contractor or part-time employee with his or her own GPS-enabled smartphone. In 1999, however, Kozmo had to hire employees and equip them with its own hardware, sort of like what UPS drivers carry. An untenable cost structure, prices that started too low, and a plan that scaled too rapidly forced the company into bankruptcy in 2001.[4] (A similar competitor, UrbanFetch, went under in 2000.)

Postmates is now one of many peer-to-peer delivery services that is succeeding in the United States, has raised $80 million in venture capital in 2015, and operates a service almost identical to the one Kozmo conceived. All you need to be a Postmate is some spare time, a smartphone, and the Postmate app to keep track of clients, deliveries, and fees. As of 2015, payment is on a per-delivery basis, keeping overhead in line with demand.

Digital Determinants of the Sharing Economy

As the above examples illustrate, while the geneses of today's sharing economy date back at least two decades and some of these precursors, like eBay and Craigslist, continue to exist, the promise could not be fully realized until the economy had been sufficiently digitized.

What underlies this digitization of the economy we take for granted today, and how exactly is it related to the explosion of crowd-based capitalism? In 2007, my colleague Vasant Dhar and I published a research article for our academic peers in which we attempted to explain what fundamental forces had been shaping the evolution of the digital economy, what consequences these forces might have, and what this told us about the anticipated business and societal implications of information technologies.[5] At their core, we argued, what distinguished digital technologies from the other past revolutionary general-purpose technologies were three invariant factors that, over four decades, had defined the evolution of the technology and explained a wide variety of its consequences; these forces serve as foundations for thinking about what to expect from digital technologies in the future, and also explain some of the more visible digital determinants of the sharing economy.

Three Fundamental Forces

Let's begin with these three fundamental forces that distinguish digital technologies from the other economy-shaping "general purpose" technologies that preceded them. The first is the rendering of things as information and, in particular, representing that information digitally. A growing number of "things" of economic and social importance have "gone digital." For example, your money is information about wealth stored in a bank computer, a PayPal server, or the Bitcoin blockchain, and occasionally rendered into physical money—bank notes and coins. Music, voice, and video are today translated into digitally represented information about frequency, pitch, color, and their rates of change. A trading strategy today is a set of rules and algorithms that act on information. A commercial drug starts its life as information, and is then rendered into chemicals in a capsule. A growing array of physical products begin their lives as digitally represented designs, which are then converted by a manufacturing process into physical form—a chair, a telephone, a piece of jewelry, an airplane—for human consumption. Each of these kinds of information can be and is digitized today. Once digitized, this information is amenable to a variety of forms of manipulation and transport.

A second force is the sustained and exponential growth of hardware power, bandwidth, storage, and the accompanying miniaturization of digital devices. In the 1960s, Gordon Moore made a prediction that the number of transistors on a microchip would double roughly every two years. This now-fabled "Moore's law," which was often interpreted as a statement that the price-performance ratio of computers would halve every two years, is an empirical rendition of this second force. Although there was some evidence of a slowdown in Moore's law on the hardware front a few years ago, massive parallelization and the move of functionality and reliability to software—epitomized by the approach pioneered by Google, and adopted widely by companies including Facebook to build large-scale computing using mass-market hardware and software like Hadoop and Hive—continue to sustain the trend of exponential growth in raw digital power.

The final force is subtler but augments and adds power to the first two. It is the sustained increase in programmability, *in a modular way*, which enables increased complexity to be aggregated, codified, and eventually integrated into standardized software platforms. Put another way, digital "machines" are fundamentally different from all the other machines that preceded them because one can make these "machines" do entirely new things without rebuilding them physically, simply by sending them a new codified set of instructions. One can add new capabilities to existing digital devices merely with the addition of software. For example, what your smartphone can do is enhanced every time you download a new app, with no physical changes to the device itself. The increased programmability and modularity of hardware—computers, smartphones, and tablets—is already having powerful transformative effects on business and society. The addition and improvement of modular layers can enable capabilities and business models that would otherwise not exist.

There are a number of consequences we have already observed that flow directly from these three invariants: the separation of information from its physical artifacts as witnessed in the music, video entertainment, and publishing industries with the emergence of pure digital products delivered via iTunes, Netflix, and Amazon's Kindle; the creation of powerful shared digital platforms, ranging from Google Maps to Amazon; and the emergence of increasingly rich digital spaces like Facebook, Snapchat, and WeChat for human interaction of increasing complexity.[6]

I outline four additional consequences of these digital forces that I believe are fundamental to the emergence and sustained evolution of crowd-based capitalism. They are: (1) the consumerization of the digital; (2) the digitization of the physical; (3) the emergence of decentralized peer-to-peer, and (4) the digitization of trust.

The Consumerization of the Digital

In the late 1980s and early 1990s, the convergence of workplace personal computers, client-server technologies, and corporate Ethernet access resulted in a massive redesign of workflows within organizations, as the physical paper files of the 1980s were increasingly rendered into pure digital work documents. Today, consumers are the focus of digital industries, increasingly armed with their own digital devices, smartphones that are powerful general-purpose computers in their own right. Further, high-speed communications networks, both residential broadband and cellular Internet, are being built for them. It seems like we are now poised for phase 2 of this reengineering; except that this time, we will witness the *reengineering of everyday life.*

While digital technologies had their roots in the wartime information processing of the 1940s, it was not until the 1960s that their commercial sector came of age. Through the 1960s, 1970s, 1980s, and 1990s, information technology giants like IBM, Hewlett-Packard, Apple, and Microsoft emerged. With the exception of Apple, the primary customers for these companies were not individuals but private business and government agencies. Although the hardware and software created by these companies occasionally would be adapted for consumers, the so-called home computers produced by these companies were attempts to personalize products based on technologies designed for business and government clients, such as the wave of home computers in the 1990s adapted from PCs developed for businesses. Similarly, Microsoft's software was built for commercial use, and as an afterthought, a personal version would sometimes be created.

Then, quite suddenly, around the turn of the 21st century, this cycle reversed. The forces of exponential growth in digital power had progressed sufficiently to create cost-effective, mass-market, affordable digital consumer devices. Music had been digitized onto CDs for a few years by then. The separation of digitized songs from these physical artifacts and into MP3 files that people stored on their home computers occurred in the late 1990s. Coupled with sufficiently widespread Internet adoption among individuals, this made the market for a personal digital music device commercially viable.

Apple, long the exception in its consumer focus but almost tragically ahead of its time for two decades, was now uniquely poised to build products that were simultaneously usable and beautiful, and captured this market with the iPod. But the iPod was not just an immensely popular consumer product. As the first successful mass-market digital product developed primarily for consumers rather than for business or government users, it represented an inflection point, a pivot in the focus of digital development.

Over the following decade, many of the most important and innovative new digital products—smartphones, digital tablets, social media platforms like YouTube and Facebook, and applications like Google Maps—were developed for consumers and then adapted by business and government, not the other way around. And this trend continues today. Many of my colleagues and I refer to this as a "consumerization" of digital technologies. It is no longer assumed that hardware or software development must consider first the needs of businesses and governments. Indeed, the driving force in the IT industry today is in products developed with individual consumers' needs in mind.

As a consequence, today, concepts we once took for granted, like ownership, or purchase from large corporate brands, are no longer universal. Companies have started to rethink what they might deliver to this digitally enabled consumer base—imagine Uber without GPS-enabled smartphones; simply not possible at scale—and what workforce models might be now feasible when a smartphone-equipped crowd of independent contractors can seamlessly enter and exit digital labor markets.

The Digitization of the Physical

Alongside the consumerization of digital, we are now also witnessing a parallel yet equally important shift: the digitization of the physical. Two contemporary developments illustrate how the same three invariant forces, and thus the same economics, that led to the consumerization of digital may reshape our everyday physical objects: the Internet of Things and the emergence of additive manufacturing.

The Internet of Things   In the not-so-distant future, every "thing" will have the potential to be digitized and networked. In an iconic example (although perhaps not the most cost-effective), a milk carton nearing or getting close to its expiration date will communicate with your refrigerator, which will in turn communicate with your FreshDirect grocery list. Cartons of fresh milk will subsequently be delivered to your home, allowing you to focus your attention on more important things. This is the Internet of Things—a world where objects of all kinds from milk cartons to household appliances to items of clothing have a little bit of embedded digital intelligence, and are part of the network. The milk carton will not house a computer but simply some kind of transducer that can let the refrigerator, which is also networked, know that the milk's expiration date is imminent. The refrigerator will register this information and add milk to the grocery list at an online delivery service.[7]

In other words, in the near future, a growing number of quotidian objects will be able to talk to each other over a network. This is not, to be clear, the stuff of science fiction. After all, the Internet of Things does not promise to help us have intelligent conversations with our refrigerators or milk cartons (at least not anytime soon). Elevators imbued with a little intelligence are unlikely, as the humorist Douglas Adams posited, to get bored with their mundane jobs of traveling up and down and take to sulking in building basements. Yet the Internet of Things—though not yet delivering articulate appliances or portending device depression—will inevitably expand crowd-based capitalism.

As intelligence, even in the smallest increments, can be embedded more cheaply and readily in physical objects, the ability to track these objects will increase. In parallel, the ability to monitor their usage will also expand. As drone technology gets more advanced and accepted, the costs of transporting objects between peers will drop. Put differently, a physical object will know where it is, how much it is being used, and will be able to arrange automated, digitally enabled transport for itself to its renter without human intervention.[8] A physical object becomes, in a sense, like an intelligent iTunes movie file.

As a consequence, the "rentability" of objects also expands. On-demand services of all kinds become more viable, more efficient, and more ubiquitous with the Internet of Things.

3-D Printing and Additive Manufacturing   Until recently, if you wanted to get into the business of making and selling physical objects, you had to acquire the capabilities of manufacturing and find some way of distributing and selling objects (by connecting, for example, with a wholesaling or retailing network). We are now entering a world where you no longer need a factory or warehouse or distribution network to be engaged in the sale of physical objects. You no longer need a distribution network to get spare parts to machines in remote locations. All you need is a design.

The game-changing technology at work here is 3-D printing. Industrial era–manufacturing is typically "subtractive"; it starts with physical material—wood, metal, heated resin—and removes portions of it to create the components of the eventual product, using tools, machines, or a mold. Additive manufacturing is the opposite. It starts with a design, and uses a "printer" to additively construct the physical object.

How might this reshape the economy? Let's consider a digital analogue. (I enjoy having that pair of words next to each other.) Twenty years ago, most cities and towns had numerous music retailers with physical storefronts. Records and CDs, having been centrally manufactured and distributed to these stores, were sold from bins and shelves. If you wanted to succeed as a musician, you needed to be one of the few whose music made it into these stores. Similarly, to run a successful newspaper, you needed large-scale printing technology and a physical distribution infrastructure for the broadsheet newspapers. Have you been to a record store in the last year? How many people do you know who still get a physical newspaper delivered to them? Are you reading this book on a Kindle?

The digitization of music and publishing has radically altered the economics of their industries, shifting the basis for competitive advantage to the entity that controls the "interface"—Apple's iTunes, Amazon's Kindle, the YouTube platform. It has also made it possible for a far greater range of niche musicians, authors, bloggers, and YouTube stars to emerge.[9] As the University of Rochester professor Ravi Mantena forecasted in his 2004 doctoral dissertation at New York University, the coming of age of additive manufacturing could similarly radically alter the economics of many physical industries.

Imagine, for example, you are looking for a new phone case. Right now, most of us are constrained in our choices to the selection at the Apple Store, at BestBuy, on the street vendor's cart, or what's in Amazon's warehouse. With access to 3-D printing, you can now buy a design rather than a phone case. In other words, what once entailed the purchase of a physical object now simply entails the purchase of a design that can in turn be manufactured, in a sense, by the buyer, either on a 3-D printer at home or on one owned by a local print shop. If neither you nor your local print shop owns a 3-D printer, you can simply have your purchased design printed by a peer who owns a 3-D printer through a marketplace like 3DHubs, or browse the alternatives at Shapeways, an online retailer for 3-D printable designs.

As a consequence, the potential for commercial peer-to-peer interactions increases dramatically. Pure data is exchanged rather than physical objects. The need for wholesale distributors and traditional retailers diminishes. The economics of small-batch manufacturing by microentrepreneurs (who might then sell their additively manufactured craft through a marketplace like Etsy) improve dramatically.

Decentralized Peer-to-Peer and the Blockchain

In chapter 4, I discuss the emergence of a new form of decentralized peer-to-peer economic activity that may reduce the need for centralized intermediaries. To give you a sense of the potentially revolutionary impact of this kind of decentralization, I make an analogy illustrating the difference between Napster, the first really popular Internet-based peer-to-peer file-sharing network, and the "pure peer-to-peer" filesharing networks that followed.

Napster was created by Shawn Fanning, and released in June 1999, when he was a 19-year-old student at Northeastern University, in collaboration with his friend Sean Parker and his uncle John Fanning. Napster users, through the Internet, could find files (primarily MP3-encoded music files) that were stored on other Internet users' computers and then "download" one or more MP3 files directly from another user's computer. The service was instantly popular, peaking at 80 million users very rapidly.

In 2000, a year after its emergence and meteoric rise, Napster found itself the target of the heavy metal band Metallica's rage after band members discovered that a song they were about to release was already being traded by fans and even played on radio stations across the United States. Metallica launched a lawsuit against Napster and shortly thereafter, so did the rapper Dr. Dre. By July 2000, Artists Against Piracy had formed and taken out full-page advertisements in *USA Today*, the *New York Times*, the *Los Angeles Times*, and dozens of other national newspapers to express their concerns about the rising "theft" of music on the peer-to-peer platform Napster.

It's not entirely surprising, then, that within a year, Napster—at least the Napster that close to 80 million users had grown to rely on for music sharing—was effectively dead. Sued by the Recording Industry Association of America and facing an injunction, it shut down its network in July 2001.

Along with eDonkey, Napster can be thought of as the first generation of peer-to-peer. While the music industry may be responsible for the charges laid against Napster, its Achilles' heel was its technological design. It was a *centralized* index of music, along with a set of rules that allowed peers to directly transfer files to one another. This centralization of the index meant that it had a central point of failure. If the index was shut down, then even if two peers were willing to share music, there was no way they could find each other.

Napster's most popular immediate successor, Gnutella, solved this problem, in a sense, by breaking apart the index and distributing multiple copies of each piece to multiple peers on the network. The central database no longer existed. The index was distributed by design. In other words, the machines on the network informed the other machines on the network of what music was available. Faced with a Napster situation, it was impossible to shut down the network. There was no central point of failure. The "crowd"—manifested by a distributed and partially replicated index, and not a centralized server—matched a peer looking for a song with the peer who had the song.

Every subsequent successful peer-to-peer filesharing network uses some variant of this decentralized, replicated indexing approach. And in 2009, the emergence of the digital currency Bitcoin demonstrated a significant step forward in decentralized peer-to-peer technology by decentralizing and distributing not merely an index but an actual anonymized ledger of financial transactions, the *blockchain*. When combined with peer-to-peer filesharing technologies, cryptographic techniques, and a novel incentive system, Bitcoin showed how a blockchain-based system could be used as the basis for *trusted peer-to-peer transactions without a third-party intermediary*, instead using the crowd—a decentralized network of "verifiers"—to clear transactions.

The promise of blockchain-based systems like Bitcoin was encapsulated well in a January 2014 *New York Times* article by venture capitalist Marc Andreessen, a long-time Internet entrepreneur and investor who created the first web browser Mosaic in 1993:

Bitcoin gives us, for the first time, a way for one Internet user to transfer a unique piece of digital property to another Internet user, such that the transfer is guaranteed to be safe and secure, everyone knows that the transfer has taken place, and nobody can challenge the legitimacy of the transfer. The consequences of this breakthrough are hard to overstate.

What kinds of digital property might be transferred in this way? Think about digital signatures, digital contracts, digital keys (to physical locks, or to online lockers), digital ownership of physical assets such as cars and houses, digital stocks and bonds ... and digital money.[9]

The examples we have considered up to this point in the book constitute a "crowd" of new suppliers—of assets like Airbnb homes, of money, of their time or labor. The blockchain promises to take the role of the crowd from the *periphery* to the *center*. The peers become the market makers. I return to this topic at length in chapter 4.

The Digitization of Trust

The sharing economy has us trusting each other at levels that are quite surprising. Jason Tanz, the editor of *Wired* magazine, puzzled over this trend in his April 2014 cover story "How Airbnb and Lyft Finally Got Americans to Trust Each Other":

> But one consequence is already clear: Many of these companies have us engaging in behaviors that would have seemed unthinkably foolhardy as recently as five years ago. We are hopping into strangers' cars (Lyft, Sidecar, Uber), welcoming them into our spare rooms (Airbnb), dropping our dogs off at their houses (DogVacay, Rover), and eating food in their dining rooms (Feastly).[10]

Beyond the raw digital enablers we've discussed so far, the explosion of crowd-based capitalism over the last few years can be attributed to dramatic improvements in our ability to get people to trust others they don't know through the use of different systems generating reliable digital cues that together might be thought of as the "digital trust infrastructure."

But what exactly is trust? In many ways, the answer depends on the context. Trust in a romantic relationship might mean something different from trust in a commercial transaction. (I would certainly hope it does.) A particularly useful definition in the context of the sharing economy comes from a 1990 book by the sociologist James Coleman, who defined trust as *a willingness to commit to a collaborative effort before you know how the other person will behave.*[11]

Establishing trust seems like it would take time and depend on a multiplicity of dimensions. In a non-face-to-face (and sometimes face-to-face) setting, it first involves establishing authenticity. Is this person real, and are they who they say they are? Second, it involves assessing intentions. Does this person have good intentions? Do these folks really want to be guests on Airbnb or are they looking to rob me? Third, it involves assessing expertise or quality. Is this person a good plumber? Are these people truthfully representing how interesting their neighborhood is? Are they polite? Is that living room as airy as it looks? Does the car have as much legroom as the photo seems to indicate it does?

For some interactions, verifying that a person is good at what he or she does might be a primary consideration if, for example, you're hiring someone to paint your fence. For other high-stakes interactions, like getting a ride from a stranger, intentions may matter more than expertise; you're probably more interested that the person isn't a criminal, and might be forgiving if the person is not the best driver on the platform. For still other higher-stakes interactions, like hiring a babysitter for your children, you'd want to be satisfied with all three dimensions: some guarantee that the person is authentic and has good intentions, and that the person actually knows what he or she is doing.

If you interact repeatedly with someone, you start to learn about these aspects over time. But when you're trying to transact with a semi-anonymous peer, and for the first time, how do you verify identities, intentions, and capabilities? In many ways, the lower the stakes of the interaction, the easier it is to establish sufficient trust. This is why we saw the emergence of platforms like eBay at scale early in the evolution of the Internet, but it has taken an additional 15 years for platforms like BlaBlaCar to achieve population-scale success.

I think of trust in semi-anonymous Internet-based peer-to-peer settings as stemming from at least five cues: (1) from one's own prior interaction; (2) by learning from the experiences of others; (3) through brand certification; (4) by relying on digitized social capital; and (5) through validation from external institutions or entities, digital and otherwise, government and nongovernment. We've had digital access to some of the first three sources of trust for some time—arguably since eBay was established in 1995—but the other two have become digitally available at scale only recently.

Familiarity is a cumulative process, something that builds over time. Thus, trust increases with every positive experience. For instance, if you win a bid on eBay and the product shows up and it is exactly what you were looking for, you'll be more likely to return to the platform to purchase products in the future. Steve Tadelis from UC Berkeley and Chris Nosko from the University of Chicago have quantified these "reputation externalities" on eBay, externalities that are bound to exist on more recent sharing economy platforms as well.[12] In particular, if you have a good experience with a specific provider, you are especially likely to buy from him or her again. Of course, a positive experience on eBay may also prepare you to trust the new generation of platforms. Airbnb's early adopters probably had already had some positive experience with a pre-sharing economy platform.

Since the mid 1990s, we've also had the benefit of learning digitally from the experiences of others. Take, for example, the function of buyer and seller feedback on eBay. A seller who consistently fails to deliver products will get bad reviews. The same holds true for bidders who never actually complete their transactions. When the experiences of others get digitized and made publicly available through an online reputation system, our ability to trust people we don't know is enhanced because, in a sense, we can learn from the experiences of others who have interacted with them. Over the last 20 years, we have gained a fairly deep understanding of the potential and limitations of these feedback-based reputation systems.[13]

Then there's the trust built through brand recognition. As I discuss further in chapters 4 and 6, we are still at a phase of consumption in Western economies where we draw a lot of trust from placing faith in a brand name; eBay recognized this early on as it rolled out its "Power Sellers" feature as a way of signaling to potential buyers that some sellers had, in a sense, been vetted through the platform, and could therefore be trusted more. Additionally, the name recognition of eBay itself provided many users with a feeling of comfort.

It is important to recognize the huge role that brand and platform certifications continue to play in today's sharing economy. While there are other platforms that provide shared short-term accommodation (like Airbnb), or urban transportation (like Lyft and Uber), these platforms' brand recognition continues to be a powerful factor in shaping their growth.

In this respect, branding functions much like it does in traditional economies but with one exception. The fact that the brand is being built by a platform linked to hundreds of thousands (or even millions) of providers means that it is now much easier for smaller providers to attach themselves to a large brand. In a sense, it's a less formal version of what franchisees get when joining a franchise. They make money by leveraging an established brand and conforming to shared business practices, albeit for a small fee.

Prior interaction, feedback, and brand certification had their place in the world of eBay, but digitized social capital and digital conduits to validation by external institutions, which are critical sources of trust, are more recent developments.

Think of social capital as some kind of aggregation of the resources one might have access to on account of a network of relationships. These relationships may be of friendship, mutual acquaintance, or of recognition. Such ties give you access to a wide range of resources, now and potentially in the future. Collectively, these ties and their associated current and potential resources represent your social capital.[14] And your social capital is thus a signal of your trustworthiness, of your reliability when you commit to an interaction. Someone with a greater level of social capital is better known, has a greater presence in society, and, as a consequence, can be relied on to behave in a way consistent with what you'd expect. If you share friends with someone, you can rely on them more, perhaps because you feel they are "closer" to you, or because you know that the shared friendship is likely to deter bad behavior.

True, online social networking platforms like Facebook and LinkedIn have enhanced our ability to build new social capital digitally, but this is only a small part of their power in facilitating peer-to-peer exchange online. What's most important is that these platforms contain *digitized representations of our real-world, physical-world social capital.* Maybe we formed some of our Facebook friendships on the Facebook platform itself. Some friends are perhaps those attractive strangers you met at that conference or convention. But the more important ones are actual physical-world relationships: childhood friends, relatives, college classmates, and work colleagues. As Sean Moffitt and Mike Dover put it in *Wikibrands*, their engaging account of how brands are reshaped by social media, "collaborative technologies and social media that connect family, friends, colleagues and interest groups are not just a fad; they are the currency that runs the future marketplace."[15]

Making this network of real-world social capital digitally available provides a powerful cue of authenticity, of intent, and of reliability. This was not a source of trust that eBay's sellers had access to. But it is, as I discussed in the introductory chapter, a prerequisite for participating in a large number of today's sharing economy platforms. It helps raise the stakes of online exchange with semi-anonymous peers.

Finally, trust often comes from validation by external institutions not connected to the exchange. A government can certify that you are who you say you are by issuing you a government ID. An auto club can do the same, while also perhaps signaling your ability to drive well. Your possession of a mobile number tied to a monthly subscription plan is indicative of authenticity based on the screening process that issuing such accounts involves. A company that conducts a background check can verify that you don't have a prior criminal record.

Again, many of these services have been available for decades. But only recently have technologies emerged that allow you to digitize such external forms of validation and make them available as part of your online profile. You can hold your driver's license up in front of your webcam briefly, and in a matter of minutes, a service run by Jumio will validate your identity.[16] (Jumio can also verify the authenticity of your credit cards.) Airbnb uses this service as part of their "Verified ID" program. Once these real-world forms of validation can be digitized, they add further to the trust infrastructure, but again, by bringing online the cues previously only available in the real-world.

In the sharing economy of 2015, these trust infrastructures are, by and large, isolated islands. If you are a good eBay seller, you can't transfer that reputation to Airbnb: you have to rebuild it starting from scratch. A star rating of 4.9 on Uber doesn't help you get customers on Lyft.

But this may change over the coming years. For example, the Madrid-based startup Traity is building a general-purpose portable reputation

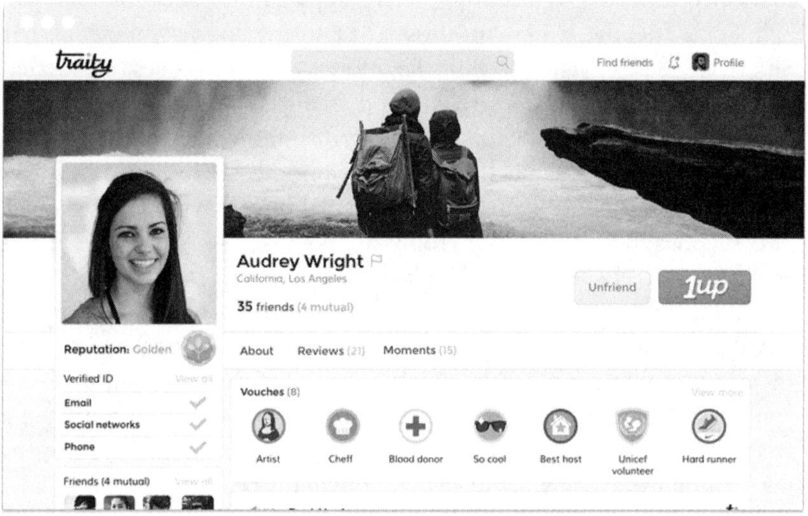

Figure 2.2
Example of a Traity profile.

platform it sees as powering a wide range of peer-to-peer exchange, both online and offline.[17] A small part of your Traity reputation is reflected by your user-generated feedback scores on platforms like Airbnb and eBay.[18] Traity also verifies your government ID and links to your digital social capital on Facebook or LinkedIn.

Your profile, however, goes well beyond your marketplace activities and ID. Traity collects and digitizes a wide variety of other cues, including your personality type, whether you are a blood donor, and what organizations you volunteer for. As I learned in 2015 from the platform's founders Juan Cartagena, José Ignacio Fernández, and Borja Martín over dinner at the Real Madrid stadium, this reflects a more holistic view of what drives trust online. Anything that might cause someone who doesn't know you to feel comfortable that you're going to do what you say you will—or, to return to Coleman's definition, that might make you willing to commit to a collaborative effort before you know how the other person will behave—could be credibly digitized, and added to your online Traity reputation.

Socioeconomic Drivers of the Sharing Economy

A final set of non-digital factors needs to be taken into account in order to understand why the sharing economy has only recently taken off and seen its greatest growth in urban areas. As I already discussed, the digital enablers were critical. But the predominance in urban areas is not a coincidence.

Following the Industrial Revolution, people around the world began moving to cities. The ensuing urbanization changed how we lived, how we obtained food, and eventually how we moved ourselves (and our commercial goods) from place to place. After a brief reversal in some Western economies in the second half of the 20th century, when there was a move away from cities and to the suburbs in countries like the United States, urbanization continues around the globe in the 21st century. In 2014, the United Nations reported that 54% of the world's population now lives in urban areas compared to 30% in 1950. It further projects that by 2050, 66% of the world's population will live in urban areas. It is worth noting, however, that in many parts of the world, we've already exceeded this projected number. In North America, 82% of people live in urban areas. Latin America and the Caribbean are not far behind at 80%. In Europe, 73% of people live in urban areas. It is precisely in these urban areas, and especially in the world's megacities (urban areas with 10 million residents or more), that the promise of crowd-based capitalism seems most salient.

Cities are sharing economies. When you live in a city, you share public parks. You share transportation using taxis, buses, and the subway. You share common areas in your apartment building. As a city resident you are naturally accustomed to a world of asset sharing rather than exclusive ownership. This makes you intrinsically better suited to adopt digitally mediated sharing behaviors.

Additionally, the larger the city and the more densely populated it is, the more viable is peer-to-peer exchange that requires geographic collocation. After all, if you live in a rural area, you likely don't want to drive 20 miles to rent camping equipment for an upcoming trip. Besides, you likely have a shed or garage and perhaps an entire barn where you can store your packs and tents and kayaks when you're not using them. If you live in a tiny apartment in a large city like London, you may still want to go camping, but it is less likely that you'll have any space to store your gear when you aren't camping. Rather than own, then, peer-to-peer renting becomes desirable because you don't have the space to store what you own. And a peer who does own is more likely to live nearby rather than far away.[19]

Finally, crowd-based capitalism, which often represents a move away from traditional forms of ownership, can also be attractive because it encourages behaviors that hold the potential to preempt or at least delay the onset of future environmental crisis. Renting, rather than owning, uses fewer products more efficiently among a wider group of people, which is in turn good for the environment—the ecological damage caused by manufacturing, packaging, and transporting new goods is reduced, and less stuff ends up in landfills.

In her 2015 book, *Peers Inc*, the author Robin Chase discusses many examples of how the sharing economy can solve what she sees as our impending ecological crisis. As she outlines in her introduction, she believes that the ideas embodied in the sharing economy are "the only way we are going to meet the speed, scale, and local adaptation requirements to address climate change in time to prevent the catastrophic change that we've set in motion."[20] The recent popularity of Uber's Uber-Pool and Lyft's LyftLine services, genuine ridesharing that pair travelers going in the same direction and assign them a shared vehicle in real time, is perhaps one of the most promising current developments in realizing this vision.

The digital and socioeconomic foundations I outline in this chapter have created a dizzying array of different platforms that are powering increasingly widespread crowd-based capitalism. What form is the ensuing reorganizing of economic activity taking? In the following two chapters, we will build on the foundations laid in this chapter to understand what kind of institutions today's platforms are, how they represent a new form of organizing economic activity that sits between the firm and the market, and how some of the digital changes we have discussed will shape and scale tomorrow's decentralized, peer-to-peer world.

3
Platforms: Under the Hood

As modern business enterprise acquired functions hitherto carried out by the market, it became the most powerful institution in the American economy and its managers the most influential group of economic decision makers. The rise of modern business enterprise in the United States, therefore, brought with it managerial capitalism.
—Alfred Chandler, *The Visible Hand* (1977)

In their 1987 article, "Electronic Markets and Electronic Hierarchies," MIT professors Tom Malone, Joanne Yates, and Robert Benjamin made a bold assertion: digital technologies will lead to an overall shift away from "hierarchies," the modern corporations that permeate mature economies, and toward "markets."[1] This was a startling prediction. At the time, electronic markets were largely unknown and very rudimentary, coordinated by bulletin board service providers that facilitated the exchange of software, or by Usenet groups, e-mail-like discussion forums resembling today's Google Groups, whose users sometimes facilitated the trading of items like live concert recordings.[2]

The emergence of Uber, Lyft, Airbnb, and Etsy might tempt one to conclude that Malone, Yates, and Benjamin had an especially astute view into the future. But are today's sharing economy platforms really "markets"? Or are they simply 20th-century organizations with a new employment model, and thus no more than old hierarchies in new digital bottles?

In this chapter I explain how sharing economy platforms may represent a new structure for organizing economic activity, one that is an interesting hybrid of a market and a hierarchy, and that could signal the evolution of 20th-century *managerial capitalism* into 21st-century *crowd-based capitalism*. To give this explanation some context, I'll need to provide a brief and selective overview of how economic activity is organized, so that we can contrast these two polar opposites, the market and the hierarchy, and understand the roles of each in the economy. I then look at how digital technologies—from the onset of their noticeable organizational impact through the emergence of early forms of crowd-based organizing like open innovation—have gradually reshaped and melded these alternatives for organizing economic activity.

To help situate sharing economy platforms (i.e., the new institutions of crowd-based capitalism) on the market-to-hierarchy spectrum, I chart more than 20 dimensions that can be useful for assessing the new hybrids and for highlighting how they are quite different from one another. I conclude the chapter with a quick overview of some other ways in which we might categorize these institutions, focusing primarily on frameworks developed by three thinkers whose ideas I have introduced in earlier chapters: Lisa Gansky, Rachel Botsman, and Jeremiah Owyang.

Markets and Hierarchies

Let's start by getting a better feel for what we mean by the terms "market" and "hierarchy." Capitalist economies have at least two ways of organizing economic activity. There are markets, in which individuals buy and sell from other individuals and invest their time and money into producing goods and services using their own equipment, sometimes perhaps financed by others who lend money. Markets are where Adam Smith's famed "invisible hand" determines the prices that balance supply and demand. And then there is the "visible" hand—the "hierarchies" that we typically think of as firms or organizations (or government entities). These entities contain within them a set of operating units that are managed by a hierarchy of salaried employees. Each operating unit has additional salaried employees who engage in various economic activities; there is coordination and exchange between the units that is facilitated by this hierarchy of executives, and the unit as a whole interacts with customers, as well as with suppliers, through the market.

To appreciate this distinction between markets and hierarchies, let's consider the example of buying fresh fruits and vegetables and, more generally, the farm crops (including meats, grains, and other goods) we call fresh produce. Some consumers favor a farmer's market. This is market-mediated exchange. The farmers who grow the produce bring it to the marketplace, and the consumers who want the produce come in, examine the selection, and buy what they want. Prices are often significantly higher than what you'd see in a grocery store.

In contrast, when you purchase your groceries from a store like Whole Foods in the United States, you are getting your produce from a hierarchy that has coordinated the delivery of fresh produce from hundreds of local farmers, perhaps using an operating unit dedicated to purchasing. The price you pay for that avocado or those organic chicken tenders is likely set by an operating unit dedicated to setting prices, often aided by sophisticated analytics. The layout of the store is determined in part by a different operating unit. The specific store you go to is perhaps its own little organizational unit making day-to-day decisions.[3]

It's hard to easily come up with other examples contrasting markets and hierarchies because in modern Western economies hierarchies are the dominant structures for organizing economic activity. The Nobel Prize–winning social scientist Herbert Simon summed up this dominance well in a 1991 essay about organizations and markets, when describing how a mythical visitor from Mars might be "astonished" by the references to our economy as being a "market economy":

Suppose that [our visitor] ... approaches the Earth from space, equipped with a telescope that reveals social structures. The firms reveal themselves, say, as solid green areas with faint interior contours marking out divisions and departments. Market transactions show as red lines connecting firms, forming a network in the spaces between them. Within firms (and perhaps even between them) the approaching visitor also sees pale blue lines, the lines of authority connecting bosses with various levels of workers. As our visitor looked more carefully at the scene beneath, it might see one of the green masses divide, as a firm divested itself of one of its divisions. Or it might see one green object gobble up another. At this distance, the departing golden parachutes would probably not be visible.

No matter whether our visitor approached the United States or the Soviet Union, urban China or the European Union, the greater part of the space below it would be within the green areas, for almost all of the inhabitants would be employees, hence inside the firm boundaries. Organizations would be the dominant feature of the landscape. A message sent back home, describing the scene, would speak of "large green areas interconnected by red lines." It would not likely speak of "a network of red lines connecting green spots."[4]

The transition of economies from market transactions governed by Adam Smith's "invisible hand" to the ones we observe today has been gradual. In *The Visible Hand*," a book I cite in the introduction and for the epigraph to this chapter, the economic historian Alfred Chandler traces this transition from the early 1800s through the late 20th century, documenting how although the United States in Adam Smith's time was largely a market economy, there began a steady transition to hierarchies of increasing complexity as a consequence of a series of technological changes spanning 200 years.[5] Chandler chronicles the creation of plantations, the emergence of textile mills, the use of armories, the revolutions in transportation and communication induced by the railroad and the telegraph in the mid-19th century, followed by the emergence first of mass distribution and then of mass production. He then records the emergence of the modern corporation through the integration of mass production and mass distribution, its spread—in a wide range of industries, from food and tobacco to oil, chemicals, and machinery—in the early 20th century, and leads up to the dominance of modern managerial hierarchies through the 20th century.

A key takeaway from Chandler's history is that technological progress seems to reinforce the move away from markets and toward increasingly sophisticated hierarchies. In this context, the prediction of Malone, Yates, and Benjamin (MYB for brevity in what follows)—that digital technologies will take us in the opposite direction—seems especially striking.[6]

How Digital Technologies Reorganize Economic Activity

Here is the gist of the MYB argument. The way economic activity is organized is based on the relative magnitude of production costs and the costs of coordinating different activities through the market. Let's call the latter "external coordination costs." When external coordination costs are low relative to production costs, this favors organizing economic activity through the market, where an individual will simply make products to sell to other individuals. If the opposite holds, it makes more sense to organize the activity within a firm or hierarchy.

More importantly, however, MYB argue that it is important to consider two additional factors: *complexity of product description* and *asset specificity*. Let's take a closer look at what these terms mean. When a higher amount of information is needed to describe aspects necessary for an economic transaction (or when a product is complex, like a business insurance policy), there is higher "complexity of product description" associated with that product. In contrast, in a stock trade, while the underlying asset might be complicated, the information needed to assess a specific offer is very simple: a ticker symbol, a price, a quantity. According to Malone, Yates, and Benjamin: "Because highly complex product descriptions require more information exchange, they also increase the coordination cost advantage of hierarchies over markets. Thus buyers of products with complex descriptions are more likely to work with a single supplier in a close, hierarchical relationship (whether in-house or

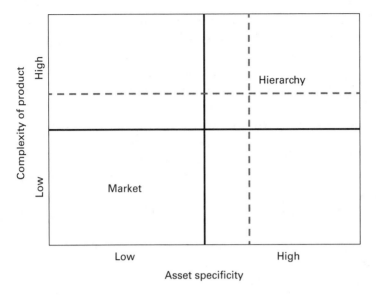

Figure 3.1
A simple schematic of the MYB framework.

external), while buyers of simply described products (such as stocks or graded commodities) can more easily compare many alternative suppliers in a market."[7]

The framework provided by MYB is illustrated in the figure 3.1. As digital technologies progress, the coordination costs associated with handling complex product descriptions through the market decrease, thus making market-based activity feasible for a larger set of activities, or shifting the vertical line of the figure upward, toward where it is depicted as a dotted line.

Next, since the idea of asset specificity will come up again later, let's spend a minute understanding it. Asset specificity measures the extent to which investments made to support a particular transaction have a *higher* value to that transaction than they would have if they were *redeployed* for any other purpose.[8] Asset specificity takes many forms: for example, if something would cost a lot to move (like coal from a coal mine located right next to a factory), we'd call it site-specific. Skills that are very company-specific (knowing how the specialized machines of a company work, knowing how a company's processes run), or assets that degrade rapidly over time (what MYB call "time specificity") are also more likely to be specific to an economic activity.

It makes more sense to organize an economic activity within an organization or hierarchy when the inputs (skills, physical attributes) related to it are *specific* to that economic activity. The second part of MYB's argument is that progess in digital technologies will reduce asset specificity in many economic activities, thus moving the vertical line in the figure to the right, and shifting a set of economic activities to the market.

Now, not everyone agreed with MYB's unilateral prediction. Several years later Vijay Gurbaxani and Seungjin Whang acknowledged that "recent advances in IT have obviously introduced a great deal of operational efficiency in the market economy by providing more efficient market mechanisms and thus lowering the associated market transaction costs," but they noted some additional tradeoffs.[9] Apart from the "external coordination costs" associated with transacting through the market, there is a set of "internal coordination costs" that hierarchies bear. These grow as the organization scales; as the management structure gets more bloated, the interests and incentives of workers are increasingly misaligned or disconnected from the broader objectives of the firm. So, inefficiency results from bureaucratic bloat.

Gurbaxani and Whang then argue that digital technologies can lower *both* external and internal coordination costs, which means the net effect can be either more or less activity within traditional organizational boundaries: "A firm may use information systems to decentralize some decision rights and to centralize others, exploiting the merits of both systems and leading to a hybrid structure."[10] Arguing against the more definitive predictions presented by Malone, Yates, and Benjamin, then, they conclude:

Previous research (e.g., [Malone, Yates, and Benjamin's 1987 publication]) has focused on the impact of IT on external coordination costs, leading to the prediction that vertical firm size will decrease as the use of IT grows. Our model shows that this is clearly one likely outcome. However, our results demonstrate the importance of developing an integrative model that also considers internal coordination costs and the corresponding role of IT. Our model provides a comprehensive description of the cost structure of a firm. Based on the model, we conclude that a firm's use of IT can result in an increase or decrease in either the horizontal or vertical dimension of firm size.[11]

In other words, MYB suggest that digital progress leads to an increase in horizontal growth, expanding economic activity beyond a firm's traditional geographic boundaries, and a decrease in vertical growth, or a reduction in the size and depth of hierarchy. Gurbaxani and Whang, however, maintain that either type of growth may be promoted by digital technologies, and that the direction or shift of economic activity cannot be clearly predicted.

So, what has transpired since? Digital technologies permeate the economy today, but the enduring changes have not moved the organization of economic activity in any one specific direction. As MIT economist Erik Brynjolfsson and his collaborators (Lorin Hitt of the University of Pennsylvania, Timothy Bresnahan of Stanford University, and my NYU colleague Prasanna Tambe, among others) have discovered in a series of studies, digital technologies hold the *potential* to dramatically improve the productivity of economic activity organized within companies, but such productivity gains only accrue to those firms (about 20% of all firms in their studies) that also invest in a series of "complementary organizational changes," like the redesign of work, an increase in performance-based pay, an increased empowerment of workers, and a flattening of the hierarchy.[12] We have also witnessed a wide range of *outsourcing* that has been enabled by digital technologies, as Dartmouth's James Quinn described in detail in his *MIT Sloan Management Review* article.[13] Today, for example, a vast majority of firms outsource all or part of their employee tech support and call-center operations, and almost all of high-tech manufacturing is done by a few giant firms based in China, Taiwan, and South Korea. Many firms, having discovered that there were high coordination costs associated with outsourcing to firms in other countries, opted for the middle ground of offshoring, moving work outside the country but often retaining it within their organization through an operating unit based in a country with lower-cost labor.

I examine the evolution of offshoring in greater detail when I discuss how crowd-based capitalism redefines work, in chapter 7. Here it is important, though, to shape our understanding of sharing economy platforms by looking at the concurrent emergence of a very specific kind of micro-outsourcing of innovative activities, under which, rather than contracting with one specific vendor to provide something the firm needs, a firm instead simply "outsources to the crowd," posting a set of challenges or requirements on a digital platform, letting the good ideas naturally bubble to the surface, and then capturing these innovations and bringing them into its production process.

One such crowd-based paradigm is commonly referred to as "open innovation"—the idea that firms can and should use external ideas as well as internal ideas in the conducting of their economic activities. The conceptual idea of open innovation is associated most closely with the work of two professors: Henry Chesborough of UC Berkeley, who introduced the idea to a mainstream audience in his 2003 book *Open Innovation*, and Eric von Hippel of MIT, who wrote the 2005 book *Democratizing Innovation* and was a lone voice in the late 1980s making the argument that customers and users outside the firm are important sources of innovation.[14] As my NYU Stern colleague Hila Lifshitz-Assaf explains in her study of open innovation at NASA, "until recently, the prevailing consensus among various streams of theoretical and empirical literature has been that innovation does and should take place within the boundaries of the firm. However, recently a new model, usually named "open" or "peer production" innovation, is challenging the permeability itself of these boundaries."[15]

An early example of open innovation emerged on the platform Threadless, described at length in a 2009 Harvard Business School case study by the HBS professor Karim Lakhani, an influential current researcher on the topic. Founded in 2000, Threadless makes printed t-shirts and some other apparel and accessories, but employs no designers. Instead, designs are created by and chosen by an online community. Each week, hundreds of designs are submitted online. The community votes on these designs. Based on the vote and other community input, about 10 designs are selected each week. The crowd then generates the candidate designs and determines the eventual successful ones; Threadless then handles production and retailing. A different early example of open innovation was within IDEO, one of the world's leading product design firms, through their openIDEO initiative that has been studied extensively by Lakhani and my NYU colleagues Natalia Levina and Anne-Laure Fayard.[16]

Open innovation is a fascinating topic with a rich body of ongoing research. It is part of a broader body of inquiry into, as Levina often points out to me, the evolution of practices that allow firms draw on resources and capabilities that lie outside the firm's boundaries. It has also given us an early glimpse into the broader, digitally enabled blurring of the boundaries between the market and the traditional hierarchy that is unfolding today. As Linus Dahlander and David M. Gann explain in their analysis of what the term "open" really means when used in open innovation, "Openness is in part defined by various forms of relationship with external actors and is thus closely coupled to a broader debate about the boundaries of the firm."[16] These authors find that this blurring takes place along two different dimensions—whether the permeation of the boundaries is outbound (the firm reveals its resources to the community) or inbound (the firm seeks resources from outside its boundaries), and whether the ensuing transactions involve money or are free. Each form has different benefits and costs.

This variation documented in studies of open innovation is interesting because it is a precursor to the wide range of platforms we witness as new sharing economy models blur the lines between the firm and the market. I turn to this topic in the following section.

Are Platforms a New Firm-Market Hybrid?

In many ways, one might see the emergence of the sharing economy as a natural culmination of these trends toward the "digital organization," toward outsourcing, and toward open innovation and the permeable boundaries of the firm. Thinking of it one way, the crowd has moved from simply providing ideas (open innovation) to providing actual services (crowd-based capitalism). Put differently, might one think of Uber and Airbnb as simply giant "micro-outsourcing" operations, with hundreds of thousands, and maybe soon, millions of small providers?

I believe it is more useful to think of these new institutions as a hybrid between a pure market and a hierarchy. Table 3.1 provides some dimensions associated with hierarchies and with markets, classifying four popular platforms (Uber, Airbnb, Etsy, and TaskRabbit) along each of 22 dimensions. (I return to many of these dimensions in chapter 8, showing how they may also be useful in assessing ways in which the providers to a platform are "employee-like," or whether the platforms themselves are supportive of sharing economy entrepreneurship.)

My MBA students Andrew Covell, Varun Jain, and June Khin at NYU Stern have helped me classify over a hundred sharing economy platforms using this framework. Our research suggests wide variation across different platforms. Many resemble markets that facilitate entrepreneurship, whereas others look more like hierarchies that employ contractors. Along with Airbnb, Etsy, and BlaBlaCar, labor platforms like Upwork and Thumbtack, social dining platforms like VizEat and Eatwith, the local tour guide exchange platform Vayable (founded by sharing economy pioneer Jamie Wong) are decidedly more market-like, ridesharing platforms Lyft and Uber fall somewhere in between, and focused services or labor platforms like Luxe, Postmates, and Universal Avenue bear a closer resemblance to hierarchies than the average sharing economy platform does.

Of course, this is simply one of many ways to categorize platforms. One could categorize them based on the service offered by the platform's

Table 3.1
Platforms: hierarchies, markets, or hybrids?

Feature	Airbnb	Uber	Etsy	TaskRabbit
Hierarchy-like				
Platform provides "production" financing to providers	No	Yes	No	No
Platform provides centralized mentoring	Yes	No	No	Yes
Platform facilitates peer-to-peer mentoring	Yes	No	Yes	No
Platform facilitates community groups among providers	Yes	Yes	Yes	No
Platform provides centralized customer support	Yes	Yes	No	Yes
Platform handles payment processing	Yes	Yes	Yes	Yes
Platform takes care of logistics in getting service to customers	No	Yes	No	No
Platform assigns provider to customers	No	Yes	No	No****
Platform assigns customer to providers	No	No	No	No**
Platform provides insurance, escrow, other risk-minimization	Yes	Yes	Yes	Yes
Platform provides day-to-day operational input to providers	No	Yes	No	No
Market-like				
Easy for provider to enter and exit provision	Yes	Yes*	Yes	Yes
Provider acquires or uses owned assets for production	Yes	Yes	Yes	Yes
Provider takes on complex tasks of 'managing inventory/supply'	Yes	Yes**	Yes	Yes
Provider chooses pricing	Yes***	No	Yes	Yes
Provider free to merchandize as they see fit (description, photo)	Yes	No	Yes	Yes

Table 3.1 (continued)

Feature	Airbnb	Uber	Etsy	TaskRabbit
Provider has in-person customer contact	Yes	Yes	No	Yes
Provider has virtual direct customer contact	Yes	No	Yes	Yes
New "hybrid" capabilities				
Peer-to-peer feedback systems	Yes	Yes	Yes	Yes
Transparent peer-to-peer feedback systems	Yes	No	Yes	Yes
Platform-based provider screening	Yes	Yes	No	Yes
Conduits to external trust indicators	Yes	Yes	Yes	Yes
Payment processing	Yes	Yes	Yes	Yes

*Some Uber drivers are constrained by their auto loans.
**In some cities, Uber's staff may send information to drivers suggesting when to be available and where.
***Airbnb has a pricing tool built into the platform.
****TaskRabbit makes active suggestions, and perhaps restricts many customers from browsing all available providers.

providers, the business model of the platform, the kind of product whose consumption model is altered, the industries being disrupted, or some combination of these factors. I have found three other frameworks useful in organizing my own thinking. They provide a useful additional lens through which one might understand the differences between the hundreds, maybe thousands, of entities that are and will in the future be labeled "sharing economy," "on-demand," or "crowd-based" platforms.

Gansky's "Meshy-ness" Grid
In her book *The Mesh*, Lisa Gansky lays out two dimensions along which one might evaluate a product before determining whether a peer-to-peer rental platform for it might emerge: how valuable the product is (cost), and how intensively the product is used by an owner (frequency of use). In her framework, low-use, high-value products (the bottom right of the figure 3.2) are in the "Mesh sweet spot." Why? Well, products that aren't

Asset usage

Asset value

Figure 3.2
A schematic of Gansky's Meshy-ness Grid.

used too intensively by an owner, like a car or a vacuum cleaner, have a lot of spare capacity, so the prospect of rental makes more sense. However, unless the product is sufficiently valuable, the coordination costs associated with a rental market become too high relative to the value gained from renting (or renting out). Thus, peer-to-peer rental of $30,000 cars makes sense, and of $100 vacuum cleaners less so.

Gansky's framework provides an elegant starting point for assessing how likely it is to see crowd-based capitalism emerge for different product categories. As I discussed in the introduction, we have seen peer-to-peer rental markets emerge for cars in several countries, such as the United States (Getaround), France (Drivy), and the Netherlands (SnappCar).

By Gansky's logic, we might also expect a great deal of activity in the market for high-end luxury products like Rolex watches. In 2013, a new startup called Eleven James launched a rental service for expensive watches. Before a genuine peer-to-peer platform emerges, however, there may first need to be innovation in the insurance models for that product category. The two platforms that launched peer-to-peer car rental in the United States, Getaround and Turo, each first spent over a year working with insurance firms to craft and commercialize an entirely new insurance product, one which would cover rental from an owner to a non-owner.

One might immediately extend the Gansky framework to assess the "value of spare capacity" inherent in owned products by simply multiplying the *value of a product* with the *fraction of time it is not used* to compute the *latent rental value* of an asset, and conclude that assets that have a high latent rental value ("idling capacity value" in Botsman's lingo, or those "more sharable" in Benkler's) are ones for which peer-to-peer rental markets will emerge. Thus, even though personal residences are used intensively, even a small fraction of spare capacity leads to a high latent rental value because the underlying asset is so valuable. Airbnb's success is a testament to the potential in unlocking this latent rental value.

Additionally, much like how the *asset specificity* associated with certain commercial economic activities shapes whether they will be organized within hierarchies or markets, there is often a corresponding asset specificity that determines the value a customer gets from a product—and the higher this specificity, the less likely we are to see peer-to-peer rental markets. For example, at the same intensity of usage, the more highly customized a product is to a user (for example, a tailored bridesmaid dress), the less likely it will be rentable, and correspondingly, the fewer customer-specific investments associated with an asset (for example, a ski suit or a tent), the more likely we are to see peer-to-peer rental markets emerge. Similarly, the greater the level of product-specific learning necessary to derive value from a product, the more likely it is to remain owned rather than rented.

It is also more likely that a rental market will emerge if the latent rental value of the asset represents a higher percentage of its owner's income. We know, of course, from the "income effect" and the "wealth effect" of textbook microeconomics that people with higher incomes and greater wealth are more likely to own expensive items. However, there are certain expensive items (like automobiles) owned by people across the income spectrum. There are also expensive items owned by people who may not have an especially high income because these items have professional significance or are highly coveted. For example, independent filmmakers may often own expensive filmmaking and photography equipment that represents a very high percentage of their income. Similarly, early adopters of "creative equipment" who spend a lot of their money on new and "cool" products may purchase products like the 2013 Oculus Rift. As I discussed in the introduction, KitSplit is a peer-to-peer rental market for this kind of equipment.

Additionally, most items, even those with status appeal, transmit worth through what I refer to as "consumption value"—you get value by using your iPhone, for instance, or by wearing a Rolex. But other items have "ownership value," where the act of ownership provides value in itself because of personal significance (for example, an engagement ring or a signed first-edition of a favorite book) or because it shapes or signals one's identity (a piece of jewelry with cultural significance, for example, although identity might just as well be tied to the car one owns). A product with low ownership value is especially well suited for peer-to-peer rental.

The rate of depreciation of an asset has a complicated relationship with its rentability. On the one hand, owners of rapidly depreciating assets (like high-end apparel whose value is tied to it being from the current "season") have a greater incentive to rent them out so as to derive maximal value from them before they "perish." I expect to see a higher prevalence of rental services run by businesses (such as Rent the Runway) for such items. On the other hand, items that retain their value over time have a higher lifetime "idling capacity" and are better suited for peer-to-peer rental.

I return to the economics of peer-to-peer rental markets in further depth in chapter 5.

Botsman's Four Quadrants

In 2013, Rachel Botsman proposed a framework for organizing the "collaborative economy," laying out four broad sites of economic activity: collaborative production, collaborative consumption, collaborative finance, and collaborative education.[18] Collaborative production is concerned with the design, production, and distribution of goods through collaborative networks. By contrast, collaborative consumption seeks to maximize assets through their shared redistribution. Airbnb and Getaround are good examples. The third category involves collaborative forms of finance, such as Funding Circle and Kiva, or Bitcoin (which enables people to carry out transactions without a traditional third-party intermediary). Finally, the fourth category consists of collaborative forms of education, such as Coursera and edX, which enable people around the world to take courses at top-ranked universities whether or not they are enrolled as students, or Skillshare and Trade School, which offer alternative peer-to-peer models for gaining knowledge.

Owyang's Honeycomb

As crowd-based capitalism evolved in 2012 and 2013, Jeremiah Owyang developed an industry-sector-based classification of the different kinds of economic activity that he viewed as "collaborative." His Collaborative Economy Honeycomb provides a nuanced categorization of the sharing

Collaborative Economy Honeycomb Version 2.0

The Collaborative Economy enables people to get what they need from their community. Similarly, in nature, honeycombs are resilient structures that enable many individuals to access, share, and grow resources among a common group.

In the original Honeycomb graphic, six distinct families of startup types were represented by the inner track of hexes. In a very short period of time, this movement has expanded, as reflected in the six additional hexes on the outer perimeter.

This visual representation of the movement is organized into families, classes, and startup examples. To access a complete directory of over 9,000 startups worldwide, advance to the Mesh Directory, managed by Mesh Labs: http://meshing.it/

By Jeremiah Owyang
jeremiah@CrowdCompanies.com
@jowyang, Dec 2014

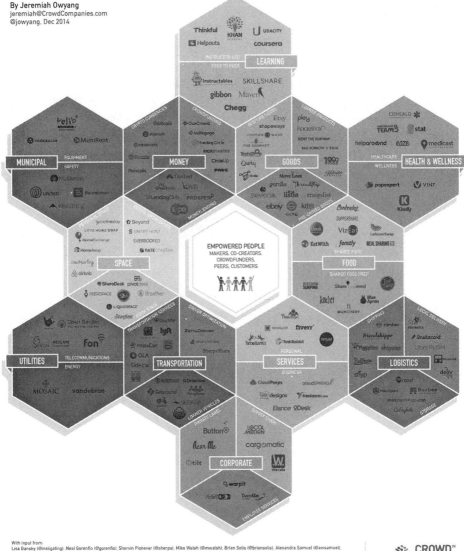

With input from:
Lisa Gansky (@insligating), Neal Gorenflo (@gorenflo), Shervin Pishevar (@sherpa), Mike Walsh (@mwalsh), Brian Solis (@briansolis), Alexandra Samuel (@awsamuel),
Bill Johnston (@billjohnston), Angus Nelson (@angusneison), Augie Ray (@augieray), Jeff Rodman (@jeffreyrodman), John Sheldon (@jsheldonus),
Jamie Sandford (@jsandford), Arun Sundararajan (@digilalarun), Jonathan Wichmann (@JonathanWich) and Vision Critical (@visioncritical).

Design by Vladimir Mirkovic www.transartdesign.com Creative Commons license: Attribution-NonCommercial.

www.crowdcompanies.com

Figure 3.3
Collaborative Economy Honeycomb.

economy in 2015 and is a useful way of keeping track of the scope and impact of this new form of organizing economic activity across different industry verticals.[19]

As I write this book, Owyang's broad categories include learning, municipal, money, goods, health and wellness, space, food, utilities, transportation, services, logistics, and corporate. However, within each of Owyang's broader categories there are further distinctions. Transportation, for example, is divided into taxi-like transportation services (e.g., Uber), car loan services (e.g., Getaround) and car optimization services (e.g., SherpaShare). In other words, for each category there are gradients that draw attention to the specificity of various sharing economy activities. Owyang's Collaborative Economy Honeycomb also clearly illustrates that as much as the sharing economy is being used to fuel pure sharing and micro-enterprises, larger corporations also embrace it.

Today's crowd-based capitalism appears to create new institutions for organizing economic activity that offer value for people across the economic spectrum both as consumers and producers. The same may be true for the new generation of decentralized peer-to-peer technologies that are the subject of our next chapter.

4

Blockchain Economies: The Crowd as the Market Maker

Think about gambling without a casino, think about stock trading without an exchange, think about real estate transactions without deeds, and think about transactions without clearing houses—that is the world we are heading into. We have just barely scratched the surface today.
—Fred Wilson, from a talk at the Collaborative-Peer-Sharing Economy Summit, New York University, May 30, 2014

In June 2015, the New York City venture capital firm Union Square Ventures (USV), well known as an early lead investor in the social media giant Twitter and the microblogging platform Tumblr, announced a $3.4 million seed investment in a new company called OB1.[1]

When the investment was announced, there was little public information about OB1. Internet searches for the company were more likely to yield discussion groups about spelling the name of the *Star Wars* character Obi-Wan Kenobi. The company's own website, a serene, detail-free, Zen-white page, offered no additional details, simply stating a promise: "Helping make trade free for everyone, everywhere."

Brad Burnham, the USV partner who led the investment, explained in a blog post that OB1 was formed to further the development of OpenBazaar, an open-source decentralized marketplace protocol. To the otherwise uninformed, a visit to the OpenBazaar website leaves one with a feeling the effort is subversive, almost sinister. "Even though the Internet is global, governments and corporations are restricting free trade," says a disembodied voice on an OpenBazaar promotional video.[2] "They collect your data and violate your privacy. They censor your transactions and take their own cut. It's time to take control back."

A look at OpenBazaar's history is hardly reassuring. It evolved from a prototype peer-to-peer market called DarkMarket developed in April 2014 by Amir Taaki, the founder of the Internet anarchist group unSYS-TEM. Taaki created DarkMarket following the shuttering of a market called the Silk Road, best known for facilitating the sales of illegal drugs, and whose founder Ross Ulbricht is currently serving a life sentence in a US prison.[3] "Like a hydra, those of us in the community that push for individual empowerment are in an arms race to equip the people with the tools needed for the next generation of digital black markets," Taaki explained to *Wired* reporter Andy Greenberg in 2014.[4]

On its website, OpenBazaar commits to "zero fees," indicating that because there are no parties in the middle of the transactions, there are no fees to pay. As Burnham further clarifies about OpenBazaar in his blog post, "There is no way for a central authority to leverage network effect market power to extract rents from the participants."[5]

At a time when most venture capitalists seem to be plowing money into sharing economy platforms that are able to do precisely what Burnham claimed OpenBazaar made impossible (i.e., "leverage network effect market power to extract rents from the participants"), why would a visible and successful venture capitalist like USV want to invest in a company aimed at furthering a technology that is not only, in a sense, "off the grid," but is also open-source and committed to "zero fees." Burnham explains further:

This begs the question of how OB1 can be a for profit business that will generate a return on the investment we are announcing today. How can a business that is consciously architected to undo network effect defensibility, one that is tearing down the walls and filling in the moats that every paper on market based competition has insisted are necessary for success ... succeed.

OB1 will offer a set of value added services to buyers and sellers on the OpenBazaar market. They expect others to provide services to the participants on OpenBazaar, and they don't expect to have any proprietary advantage over those competitors. As investors, we hope that their familiarity with the marketplace and the goodwill they generate as early sponsors of the open source project will give them an advantage but we understand they must execute very well or be left behind.[6]

Time will tell whether USV counts OB1 as a success story or not. But it's a more promising investment than it might seem. OB1 is part of a new generation of peer-to-peer systems that promise to expand the potential of crowd-based capitalism significantly over the coming years, transitioning the role of the crowd from being the source of capital and labor to actually owning and running the marketplace in a decentralized fashion. Many of these nascent systems are based on the ideas and "blockchain" technologies that power the popular digital currency Bitcoin.

And USV is hardly alone in its interest in this technology. Adam Ludwin, a partner at RRE Ventures, currently runs a startup called Chain that is also funded by the famed Silicon Valley investor Vinod Khosla. RRE, along with the venture capital firm Andreessen Horowitz, has also invested in Ripple Labs, which is building a blockchain-based market for interbank settlement. Andreessen Horowitz partners Marc Andreessen and Chris Dixon frequently express significant levels of excitement about the commercial promise of the blockchain.

These are just a few examples of a new marketplace technology paradigm that may power the next generation of crowd-based capitalism, To better appreciate the economic and social impacts of these marketplaces, we first need to understand how some of them work. The right place to start is by understanding Bitcoin.

Understanding Decentralized Peer-to-Peer Exchange

In the simplest possible terms, bitcoin is a digital currency. (I refer to the currency using lowercase "b," and the platform, technology, or ecosystem using uppercase "B.") You can acquire bitcoin by exchanging it for your dollars, euros, or yen, by providing someone with a product or service that they pay you for in bitcoin, or by "mining" bitcoin (more on this later). Your acquisition and subsequent possession of this bitcoin exists as one or more entries in a public ledger (the blockchain) in which you are identified by a secure anonymized "key." Each time you use your bitcoin, the new transaction is recorded as yet another entry in the ledger.

A lot of the attention paid to Bitcoin has focused on its success in creating currency without a government backer, about how bitcoin value measured in traditional money fluctuates a lot over time (although its exchange rate has stabilized considerably in 2015), and perhaps also about the use of bitcoin for commerce that many governments consider illegal. Instead of rehashing those topics, I focus here on thinking about Bitcoin as one of many applications of a new set of enabling technologies. I also discuss two other related applications: OpenBazaar and La'Zooz. Through this discussion, some of the key elements of the economics and technology of decentralized peer-to-peer marketplaces will become more transparent.

Bitcoin
Many of the critical pieces of a decentralized peer-to-peer market are part of Bitcoin. Let's say that you want to send your friend Clay digital money. You would ideally say something like this: "I possess at least one currency unit from prior transaction Q, and I am giving Clay one unit." This

establishes that you have the money, commits you to the transaction, and gives Clay access to the money. The physical-world equivalent would be if you were to give Clay a banknote.

Establishing a digital equivalent first requires the use of a "digital signature." Let's say that there are two unique numbers (called "keys," analogous to what goes into a lock) associated with you. One of these is known only to you, or is stored on a device you own, and is called your private key. Another, available for anyone to look up, is called your public key. If someone "locks" a message (or encodes it using a cryptography algorithm) with your public key, this encrypted message can only be "unlocked" with your private key. And vice versa—if a message is encrypted with your private key, it can only be decrypted with your public key. This allows for a simple way to create a "signature": since you are the only person who has your private key, then a message encrypted with it could only have come from you. And since your public key is public, anyone can verify that this is your signature.

Next there must be a way to prevent you from arbitrarily spending money you don't have. In the physical world, this is accomplished by making bank notes hard to counterfeit. In a system like PayPal, on the other hand, a trusted third-party (i.e., a centralized entity, or PayPal itself)—keeps track of who has how much, and updates a *private* digital "ledger" of some sort every time someone sends money to someone else.[7] Bitcoin, in contrast, uses a *public* ledger, the *blockchain*. Every user of Bitcoin has a copy of this blockchain, and it contains every single bitcoin transaction since the currency was created. When you say, "I possess at least one currency unit from prior transaction Q, and I am giving Clay one unit," Clay can verify that the message is from you by checking your signature, and he can then check his copy of the blockchain to be assured that you in fact have bitcoin to spend.

But this approach leads to a problem. Suppose you only have one currency unit to spend. Now, let's say you simultaneously send a signed message to both Clay and Emily giving them each one unit. If they both checked their current copy of the blockchain, they would find the prior transaction, it would seem like you have the money, and both of them would update their ledgers, leading to a problem down the line.

A possible solution might be to delegate maintaining the integrity of the ledger to the "crowd," as I illustrate here with this simple scenario: After both Clay and Emily receive your message and check their copies of the blockchain to see if you have the money to spend, they then broadcast the transaction to the entire network of users. This transaction then joins a list of "pending transactions," each of which will "clear" only when enough people on the network match the transaction against their copy of the blockchain and indicate that it is OK. During this waiting period it will likely be discovered that you have (perhaps mistakenly) tried to spend your unit twice.

This is sort of like writing a check in the physical world. If you hand over a personal check to someone, they now have it in their possession, but until the bank has "cleared" the check, they don't actually receive the money. In the example above, the user network (possessing individual copies of the blockchain) serves collectively as the bank.

But what's to prevent you from creating millions of identities online and "taking over" the network by controlling a majority of the user accounts? If you managed to insert fake transactions suggesting you have money to spend into a majority of the copies of the blockchain, wouldn't this allow you in effect to create "counterfeit" money?

Bitcoin solves this problem in an ingenious way: continuing to rely on a crowd-based method of clearing transactions, but artificially adding complexity to the validation process. How is this accomplished, and why does it work? Well, when a user, let's say Clay, checks the list of pending transactions and confirms their validity, Clay also has to solve an intensely challenging computational problem (the "challenge"). Solving a challenge is sort of like factorizing a big number—generating the two factors is difficult, but once you do that, verifying that their product yields the original number is easy. A Bitcoin challenge is significantly harder, but once solved, checking that the answer is correct is relatively simple.[8]

Meanwhile, Emily and others might have also validated the list of pending bitcoin transactions and, in parallel with Clay, would be trying to solve the challenge as well. If Clay happens to win (solve the challenge first), others will verify that his answer is correct, then update their blockchains with his list of validated transactions. (It actually takes a little longer than that for a set of transactions to be accepted by the blockchain, but this is a detail that is less relevant to our discussion.)

As a consequence, Clay can't simply or arbitrarily generate fake identities to take over the network and insert fake ledger entries. He'd need a large amount of computational power, and meanwhile, others are busy solving the same challenge to validate the transactions. And there's enough randomness in the challenge so that the person with the most computational power doesn't necessarily win (although having that power does have an advantage, on average.) So, while there is a risk that someone will invest way more than everyone else in computational power and start to take over the network, this is far more difficult and expensive than setting up millions of fake identities.

This leads to yet another problem, though. Computational power isn't free. What incentive do Clay and Emily have to invest their resources into solving the challenge repeatedly? Well, the "winner" of the challenge gets issued new bitcoin! (As of 2015, this reward is 25 bitcoin, worth a few thousand US dollars.) This process of validating transactions, solving the challenge, and collecting the reward is referred to as "mining" new bitcoin. Since there's a new list of transactions (or "block") to verify every 10 minutes or so, mining can translate into pretty good returns on one's investment in computational power.

Put differently, the blockchain facilitates "permissionless innovation," much like the TCP/IP protocol does for the Internet. In an early and influential 2013 blog post about the blockchain, Albert Wenger, a partner at New York's Union Square Ventures, explains the importance of such protocols:

Policy makers, however, need to understand the importance of protocols for enabling distributed permission-less innovation—that is, innovation by many individuals and startups. For instance, the hypertext transport protocol (http) is what lets a browser talk to a web server—as long as the server implements the protocol it can deliver innovative content or services to any browser. HTTP itself builds on many other lower level protocols, such as DNA and TCP/IP. Historically, protocols have emerged from either research projects or from individuals / small groups simply throwing something out that sticks. In the debate about bitcoin it is critical to understand that bitcoin has the potential to be such a protocol that enables a lot of new innovation to take place.[9]

Although the exact details of how Bitcoin works are a little more complicated than my short description in this section, a few key ideas come across: digital signatures that facilitate identity; the distributed ledger (the blockchain) that is stored on every client's device; the crowd collectively clearing each transaction; the need to make clearing transactions challenging to avoid a potential takeover of the blockchain; and the need for an incentive (some equivalent of money, typically called the "coin" that is generated from within the system) to get the crowd interested in performing the challenging work that accompanies verifying transactions.

Now, if you think about it, peer-to-peer payment is actually a fairly simple commercial application. Once you establish identity, build a system to clear transactions, and convince people that they won't lose their money, you've got enough trust to make things work. What's being transferred is uniform (money). There's no product variety to contend with. There are no physical assets involved. There's no need to discover what's available or compare prices. There's no imperative to think about how to get the physical asset from seller to buyer. There's no quality uncertainty—money is money. No complicated contracts are needed about delivery and quality. There's no business need to reveal your physical world presence or location. There's no risk associated with meeting someone unsavory.

Not surprisingly, therefore, much of the initial focus of blockchain marketplace development has been on creating new systems for trading assets that are non-physical: digital and financial assets. In a 2015 conversation I had with Adam Ludwin, the CEO of the blockchain startup Chain I mentioned earlier in the chapter, he described the blockchain as a "new database technology, purpose-built for trading assets," and sees immense potential in new blockchain based marketplaces for loyalty points, mobile minutes, gift cards, and of course, a range of financial assets. Ludwin described how many current systems for trading such assets could benefit significantly from a new decentralized marketplace. "Not that there's anything wrong with a centralized institution, but it increases costs, freezes innovation potential, and needs layers of reconciliation," he noted, further pointing out how innovation can be spurred simply by the threat of a decentralized marketplace, much like illegal peer-to-peer filesharing networks may have led to the emergence of iTunes, Pandora, and Spotify.

If one considers the history of electronic marketplaces, this initial focus on financial marketplaces is not surprising. Many stock exchanges were the early adopters of digital technologies, a decade or more before the emergence of eBay or Amazon. However, to move beyond marketplaces for digital assets and toward broader real-world marketplaces for goods and services, each of the (familiar) issues I allude to above—regarding non-uniformity, logistics, and uncertainty, among others—comes up and needs to be addressed if we hope to move toward creating serious decentralized alternatives for more complex marketplace interaction.

OpenBazaar and Smart Contracts

The OpenBazaar platform takes a first step toward creating a decentralized peer-to-peer marketplace. If you have an item for sale, you list it on the OpenBazaar client (a program or app you download to your device), along with a product description, and a price (in bitcoin). Once you confirm listing the item, this listing is broadcast to all the other clients on OpenBazaar.

So, how do you find what's available? Beyond the first critical "infrastructure" element of a distributed marketplace (i.e., the *shared ledger*), there is a second: a *distributed hash table*. For context, let's go back to the discussion in chapter 2 about the difference between Napster and Gnutella—Napster had one central index of music stored on a centralized Napster computer. In contrast, Gnutella distributed that index across the different peers on the network. While Gnutella pioneered the distributed index, the trouble with its approach was that it took users a long time to find what they were looking for; further, every time someone conducted a search, the activity would "flood" the network. And since not every peer knew about every other peer, there was no guarantee that this approach would actually find a song that was available.

A distributed hash table, the result of efforts to improve on the Gnutella method, is a more sophisticated way of indexing what's available on a distributed network. It is smarter about dividing up the index, replicating it, and distributing the information across peers, in a way that makes discovery more reliable. Today's most popular peer-to-peer file-sharing technology, BitTorrent, uses this approach. So does Facebook when retrieving your friend's photos from one of its millions of database servers.

But, getting back to OpenBazaar: if you find a product that you like you can pay for it with bitcoin. Much like PayPal, which was a critical part of making eBay work early in the evolution of peer-to-peer markets, Bitcoin provides the necessary payment infrastructure for OpenBazaar. And analogous to eBay's auction system, if the OpenBazaar price is too high for you, you can propose a new, lower price to the seller.

Once you (as the buyer) agree with the seller on a price, you arrive at another challenge. How do you ensure that you'll actually get the product you bought? This is where a third critical infrastructure element of distributed peer-to-peer markets comes in: *contracts*. On OpenBazaar, the contracts are relatively simple, using a notary as the trusted third party— and on OpenBazaar, this notary can be any other client. Once the contract is set up, you send your bitcoin payment, and these are held "in escrow." You, as the buyer, notify the seller, saying, "I've sent the funds." The seller then ships the product (and handles all the logistics). When the product arrives, you acknowledge receipt. The funds are then released to the seller. If there's a dispute, the notary acts as the mediator. (A decision by any two of the three parties—buyer, seller, or notary—releases the funds. So, for example, the buyer and seller could resolve their dispute themselves.) There's a rating system to help choose sellers, buyers, and notaries. It's a little different from what's used in a centralized market-place, and is not completely immune to manipulation.[10]

There is a more sophisticated class of contracts (called *smart contracts*) emerging for blockchain-based transactions. In *Blockchain: Blueprint for a New Economy*, Melanie Swan explains that while a traditional contract is an agreement between two or more parties to do something, in the case of a smart contract, the same terms exist, but with one exception—trust that comes from having a third-party is less important.[11] This is because the smart contract protocol can specify, as computer code, terms under which certain obligations are fulfilled, and can execute actions like send-ing a payment or deactivating a file once there is evidence of the con-tract's terms being fulfilled. (A precursor to a smart contract is the method implemented in the digital rights management system of a media store and player like iTunes, where a movie you rent is automatically deacti-vated after 24 hours.)

How does a "smart contract" manage to accomplish this? As Primav-era De Fillipi explained in her influential 2014 talk at Harvard Universi-ty's Berkman Center, the risks associated with peer-to-peer contracting can be reduced by the introduction of three new provisions: autonomy, self-sufficiency, and decentralization.[12]

Smart contracts are autonomous if after they are finalized, the initiat-ing agents theoretically never need to have contact again. Smart contracts are also self-sufficient to the extent that they are able to marshal their own resources. Finally, smart contracts are decentralized; they are distrib-uted across network nodes rather than residing in a centralized location, and are self-executing. This means that smart contracts will be applicable across jurisdictions or, in a sense, will be borderless. We may thus be inch-ing even closer toward the realization of Stanford University professor Lawrence Lessig's memorable mantra, "code is law."[13] In this respect, smart contracts would solve a dilemma that we've faced since the Inter-net's initial spread in the 1990s—transcending jurisprudence's reliance on political borders. The answer in the end, not surprisingly, is code itself.

There is reason to be cautious, however. To date, regulation through code has yielded mixed results. With the Internet came spam. Over time, we have attempted to stop spam using various different automated meth-ods, but, as Lessig himself points out, efforts to block spam have also blocked other types of information from circulating on the Internet. Code has failed, in a sense, to regulate without compromising one of the very principles upon which the Internet was founded—free speech. It remains unclear whether similar human limitations will restrict the scope of usefulness of smart contracts.

Decentralized Service Platforms

A currency like bitcoin or a marketplace like OpenBazaar gets stronger as it has more users. If you think about it, however, the early users of Bitcoin participated in the enterprise with no guarantee that their contributions of time, support or computing power would yield anything of real value. Of course, some have now been compensated handsomely, as the bitcoin they mined is worth millions of dollars. In a way, as the physicist Matan Field, a serial entrepreneur and thinker about the blockchain, explained to me in the summer of 2015, these early users added a tremendous amount of value to the system—at the margin, much more than a new user today might add—and, correspondingly, many were well compensated. Analogous to the way a venture capitalist gets compensated for risking financial capital on an early-stage company, the early users took a huge risk—but with human capital and processing power investments—and realized a big return.

But beyond the users and the folks who verify transactions, there are many other parts of the Bitcoin system that have added to its value today. People contributed to the writing of the underlying open-source computer code. Others publicized it. Others wrote user guides. Arguably, many of these stakeholders also contributed to the eventual success; but the system, although perhaps more equitable than a privately owned company, was engineered in a way that only gave the "miners" a big financial return.

This highlights another challenge facing a decentralized peer-to-peer market. In the absence of any central, third-party owning the network, how do you make sure that different peers have the right incentives to contribute appropriately, how do you make sure that the rewards match the effort and the risk, and how do you keep people motivated to sustain contributions, in effort and resources, needed to continue clearing the transactions? The presence of some sort of internally generated "coin" clearly seems integral, but how do you make it valuable, and how do you spread this value?

Co-founded in 2013 by Matan Field, Oren Sokolowsky, and Shay Zluf, La'Zooz is (as of 2015) a decentralized peer-to-peer ridesharing marketplace that takes a novel approach to this problem. (The platform is based in Israel, and the word "lazuz" means "to move" in Hebrew.)

Think about a service like Uber. Sure, there's value in the technology, but eventually, the system is more valuable to passengers when there are more drivers; and the system is valuable to drivers when there are more passengers. So a critical "input" into such a ridesharing system is user participation. Correspondingly, the users who "seed" the system with early participation are likely to be more valuable, at the margin, than those who join later.

La'Zooz has created what seems to be a familiar-looking mobile device app for ridesharing, but with a key difference: embedded in each app is a "mining app" as well, designed to encourage early participation. Here's how it works. You download and install the app. You turn it on when you are driving, and earn "zooz," the La'Zooz currency, simply by driving around with the app on. The more you drive, the more zooz you earn. You also earn zooz by inviting others to download the app. (The project leaders also sold some zooz to raise money.) Once the level of adoption in any neighborhood is sufficiently high, the ridesharing portion of the app gets activated. You can then use your accumulated zooz to buy rides, much like you'd use currency to buy an Uber or Lyft ride.

As Vitalik Buterin, an influential writer about decentralized peer-to-peer systems and the founder of Ethereum, a decentralized platform that runs smart contracts, noted in a blog post, "the idea of releasing a new currency as a mechanism for funding protocol development is perhaps one of the most interesting economic innovations to come out of the cryptocurrency space."[14] But a critical determinant of success is architecting this distribution of value right.[15] It also seems important for the manifestation of this value, the "coin," to be of continuing value as the platform grows and matures. And what's also important here is to think of the coin as not just currency, but as a store of value, like shares in a private company. The coin provides returns to early contributors—of human capital, of risky early participation, of effort publicizing the marketplace and facilitating critical mass—a new breed of purpose-driven investors.

Value Creation and Capture in Decentralized Exchange

There are a number of new forms of economic activity that new decentralized peer-to-peer marketplaces will facilitate simply because they lower transaction costs. Other decentralized systems, either independent or embedded in traditional privately owned corporations or markets, may emerge in contexts where there was previously insufficient trust for digital exchange, where the potential market was too small to attract private capital in the past, or where the blockchain lowers operating costs. Toward the end of the chapter, I'll discuss some current examples.

First, however, let's consider the broader future of decentralized peer-to-peer markets. Will the democratic promise sustain over time? Or will we see the emergence of "layers" of intermediation that represent private capital? Should we expect a trajectory resembling what followed the commercialization of the permissionless Internet, where the initial decentralized promise was followed by extensive re-aggregation and the subsequent capture of massive market value as manifested by the emergence of companies like Amazon, Google, and Facebook?

We have already witnessed the emergence of Bitcoin, a widely used peer-to-peer decentralized payment system with many users. It is instructive here to look at other fundamental capabilities that create value in any system of exchange, whether digital or not, whether decentralized or otherwise, and see what we can learn from some recent historical examples.

Attention, Search, and Discovery
As the World Wide Web blossomed in 1994, anyone with an Internet connection could publish content accessible to anyone else with an Internet connection. This massive influx of decentralized content almost immediately led to the emergence of a set of search engines and directories that facilitated *discovery*—among them, Yahoo (initially a hand-curated directory), Lycos, Infoseek, and Altavista. These search engines were able to index and organize the Web's information with a reasonable level of comprehensiveness, but were unable to provide any reliable "quality" information in an automated way. It took until 1998 and the emergence of Google before we had a good search engine for not just finding what we wanted, but for focusing us on what might be pertinent—a reliable system for both discovery and for ranking. And over the next decade—as digital information was created in smaller, more numerous, and more focused units as social media posts and microblogs—another centralized intermediary, Facebook, emerged as the dominant, human-network-mediated arbiter of discovery.

Google and Facebook have shown that immense market value can be captured from guiding discovery in a decentralized information-publishing world. Both continue to be valuable in part because what they are enabling us to discover—information on websites, information shared by other humans—is a complex "product." (In comparison, a product listing on a marketplace is relatively simple. The information about a typical product is fairly easy to describe, and prices and shipping costs are just numbers.) Besides, value placed on the same piece of information varies significantly across different end-users. Your friends' Facebook updates are far more valuable to you that those of a random person. News your friends like is more likely to be of interest to you.

It is very likely that as decentralized peer-to-peer marketplaces for the exchange of goods and services become popular, different discovery layers will follow. There are a number of search engines that specialize in finding content distributed across BitTorrent clients. BazaarBay is a search service for listings on OpenBazaar. What the first 20 years of the commercial Internet have taught us is that as *offers* proliferate—whether they are offers of information or of commercial opportunities—the critical constraint is human attention. Any service that is able to direct our attention in a manner that lets us discover what we want, quickly and reliably, is likely to be a source of value creation.

Of course, every online retailer or peer-to-peer platform today with product variety—from Amazon to Airbnb to specialized retailers—has its own search capability as well. The distributed hash tables that index the offers across OpenBazaar facilitate this form of search on a distributed peer-to-peer marketplace. But, unless all of the world's consumer commerce aggregates into a handful of such marketplaces, perhaps a worldwide, decentralized version of Alibaba's Taobao marketplace in China, it seems reasonable to anticipate that new equivalents to Facebook and Google will emerge.

Trust and Reputation

While Google was being built in Stanford's computer science department, a little-known and somewhat different search engine was being developed there as well. Called Junglee, it was a search engine for comparing the *prices* of products being listed across the tens (and sometimes hundreds) of online retailers who were springing up. In 1998, Amazon bought Junglee from its co-founders Venky Harinarayan and Anand Rajaram (both graduates from my alma mater, the Indian Institute of Technology, Madras) for a little under $200 million, and quietly retired the service, perhaps to ensure that it would not encourage too much attention being redirected to the Amazon competitors who frequently charged lower prices at the time.

Many of you may no doubt remember the other marketplace search and price comparison services that followed, most notably one called mySimon that was quite popular in 1999. However, they did little to stop the progress and eventual dominance of Amazon. Why? In part, because while people valued lower prices, they also valued other dimensions of the transaction—reliable promises of delivery, speedy delivery, and the assurance that any credit card numbers they provided were safe. And by 1999, Amazon emerged as a trusted intermediary on this front. (The company also invested heavily in logistics, something I get to shortly.) This led to the birth of the Amazon brand, and coupled with operational excellence, the dominance of Amazon in online retailing.

In chapter 2, we discussed the central role trust plays in peer-to-peer exchange. It is hard to overstate the importance of this role. Perhaps new third-party systems that facilitate a greater level of peer-to-peer trust in decentralized marketplaces will emerge, much like the different layers of the trust infrastructures from Airbnb and BlaBlaCar facilitate high-stakes intermediated peer-to-peer exchange today. For example, as of 2015, Traity, the reputation service we discussed in chapter 2, has already created a version of its service that facilitates the use of one's trust profile in a blockchain-enabled transaction. As Carlos Herrera-Yague, a former MIT computer scientist and Traity's chief scientist explained to me, this involves a set of "cards" one keeps in something akin to a Traity wallet, and which can be accessed during a transaction while preserving one's anonymity. Rather than being a completely decentralized trust system, however, this trust profile service is centralized to the extent that its use involves, in its origins, a third-party—Traity.

In the near future, however, I expect a majority of customers to continue using "brand" as the basis for their choices. Going back to chapters 2 and 3, we are reminded that today's successful platforms have invested very heavily in layering a familiar, centralized, hierarchical branded experience on top of their crowd-based marketplaces. Perhaps new brands will emerge associated with specific decentralized peer-to-peer marketplaces—and be built the way brand should be built—by creating a consistently high-quality end-user experience. But even in a decentralized peer-to-peer world, it is also likely that the trust from brand will be layered in a less organic, more capital-induced manner.

Logistics

In 1998, the retailing giant Walmart sued Amazon for infringing on its trade secrets. The charge: over the previous year, Amazon had hired about 15 of Walmart's employees, including Amazon's CIO in 1998, Richard Dalzell, who joined the company in 1997 after serving as a Walmart vice president. Walmart claimed that these former employees had leaked proprietary information about Walmart's famed supply chain manage-ment systems.

The suit was settled in 1999, but it underscored the fact that Amazon wasn't merely investing in product variety or search and discovery inno-vations like user reviews and recommendations. They were making mas-sive investments into inventing an entirely new infrastructure for inventory management, warehousing, and delivery, one that was opti-mized for a retail world in which goods had to be moved not in bulk to outlets or stores, but one-by-one to individual consumers.

Amazon's current dominance of online retailing in the United States owes much to these early investments, and to the capabilities it has built to move physical goods faster and cheaper than any of its competitors. (Thousands of other sellers now sell through the Amazon platform, lever-aging its logistics expertise and giving Amazon a slice of their profits.) Although Chinese ecommerce giant Alibaba's business model may seem more decentralized than Amazon's (at least through its primary consumer site Taobao), Alibaba has a significant ownership stake in and control over a number of its highly efficient logistics partners. Similarly, Uber and Lyft rely on systems that optimize their current pool of available drivers in real time.

Thus, although additive-manufacturing technologies such as 3-D printers will continue to increase the fraction of physical products sold as pure digital information (as we discussed in chapter 2), the need for reli-able and low-cost logistics is unlikely to go away any time soon. It seems quite likely that as peer-to-peer logistics get more sophisticated, a plat-form like Instacart may do to local commerce what Amazon did to mail-order, aggressively capturing the merchandizing and customer-relationship dimensions of local commerce while reducing neighborhood stores to little more than a distributed network of small, glorified warehouses located close to where consumers live. It is also possible that decentral-ized alternatives to the centrally coordinated peer-to-peer delivery service Deliv could emerge, adding a logistics layer to the blockchain economy. History suggests that when moving either people or products in real time, a balance between centralized control and decentralized information trumps a system built on just one or the other.

Some Challenges and Opportunities

In many ways, this new generation of decentralized peer-to-peer tech-nologies mirrors the P2P vision of Michel Bauwens that we discussed in chapter 1, and promises to create immense economic value over the coming decades. As the venture capitalist Chris Dixon wrote on his blog in 2014, Bitcoin makes activities like international microfinance, markets for computing capacity, incentivized social software, and other micropayments possible—not because we haven't considered the value of these before, but because the transaction costs were too high.[16]

There are signs that traditional businesses will embrace many of the new capabilities of decentralized peer-to-peer technologies, much like Facebook actively uses BitTorrent within its privately owned server farms. In spring 2015, NASDAQ announced plans to leverage blockchain technology to support the development of a distributed ledger function for securities trading that will provide enhanced integrity, audit capabilities, governance, and transfer of ownership capabilities. The startup R3CEV has assembled a consortium of 25 of the world's largest banks that are creating a framework for using blockchain technology in world financial markets.[17] The startup Provenance provides a blockchain-based authentication service, where, for example, you can credibly establish the provenance of a high-value item by keeping track of and being able to access every trade associated with its ownership. At the 2015 Consumer Electronic Show, IBM and Samsung demonstrated a blockchain- and smart-contract-based system that allowed an autonomous washing machine to order detergent when it ran low, and make a smart-contract-based payment when it sensed that the detergent had been replaced. A simple task, no doubt, but something that points to the promise of blockchain-based marketplaces for an Internet of (Autonomous) Things.

However, many challenges remain before we can reliably conclude that the blockchain and other distributed peer-to-peer technologies can take on significant fractions of the world's economic activity. Security concerns remain. Furthermore, a ledger that has to be distributed across every client can grow awfully large over time, and scalability of blockchain-based applications remains an open question. Payment systems like Bitcoin, because of the way they delay settlement, may need to be rebuilt to handle the real-time payments that credit cards and mobile payment systems like PayPal manage with ease today. Part of the solution to both of these challenges will come from the creation of a greater fraction of "off-the-book" transactions, but this creates a new layer of intermediation. Off-the-book transactions also create new risks. Some of you may recall Mt.Gox, the exchange that held its users' bitcoin in its own centralized Bitcoin accounts while maintaining a parallel off-the-blockchain system of keeping track of which users had how much bitcoin.

Mt.Gox ceased operations in 2014 following the 2013 loss of the equivalent of $450 million of its users' bitcoin because of what appeared to be a hacker having gained access to its Bitcoin accounts.

There are also concerns that someone who controls significantly more than 51% of the computing power being used to clear transactions (in Bitcoin's case, for example, for mining bitcoin) has the ability to alter ledger entries by "building their own chain," which, over time, will replace the true blockchain as the one that is associated with consensus. In 2014, ghash.io, a bitcoin mining pool, did attain this dominance in computing power being spent on mining bitcoin, and were in a position to launch a "51% attack" of this kind, although they were quick to reassure the community that they had no intention of doing so.

Any decentralized marketplace must also generate enough value to make the "coin" awarded for transaction-clearing activity sufficiently attractive. An alternative might be for each transaction to have a small, voluntary "commission" associated with it, and for this to be added to the payment the customer sends the provider, then shared as a reward to the "miner."[18] This would also suggest that there will be "attention" economies of scale associated with decentralized peer-to-peer marketplaces— the crowd has to notice the blockchain and care enough about it to verify its transactions and maintain the integrity of the ledger. Otherwise, what begins as a decentralized system may simply evolve into a traditional third-party platform that merely uses a glorified blockchain database.

Perhaps some of the greatest opportunity from decentralized peer-to-peer systems will come from the emerging decentralized autonomous organizations (DAOs) and decentralized collaborative organizations (DCOs) such as those that are being architected by Buterik's Ethereum and by Field and DeFillipi's Backfeed. Such organizations posit a holistic model for organizing economic activity in a decentralized manner. Perhaps these will allow the kind of decentralized, distributed ownership and control of the "platform cooperatives" that I discuss in chapter 8.

One might wonder what realistic possibilities exist for organizations that seemingly exist embedded only in computer code. However, as Buterik points out about decentralized protocols in general, "On the one hand, much like Bitcoin itself, they are in a very clear way 'backed by nothing.' On the other hand, they actually have quite a powerful backing underneath, and one that is difficult to unseat."

What is this backing that Buterik refers to? As he notes in an *Ethereum Blog* post in April 2014, "It is important to first understand that, in the space of tech companies and especially social networking startups, a large number of them are literally backed by almost nothing but social consensus." He then goes on to explain:

Theoretically, it is entirely possible for all of the employees at Snapchat, Tinder, Twitter or any other such startup to all suddenly agree to quit and start their own business, completely rebuild all of the software from scratch within months, and then immediately proceed to build a superior product. The only reason why such companies have any valuation at all is a set of two coordination problems: the problem of getting all employees to quit at the same time, and the problem of getting all of the customers to simultaneously move over onto the new network.

In the abstract, this may seem like a flimsy justification for why tech companies are valuable; when thinking about something that represents billions of dollars of value, one naturally expects that value to be backed up by something tangible like physical resources or government force, not just some ethereal instantiation of the fact that it's hard for large groups of people to suddenly move from one social configuration to another.[19]

"Fortunately," concludes Buterik in the blog post, "we still have many decades to go in seeing exactly how the decentralized protocol ecosystem is going to play out." It looks like an interesting future indeed.

II

Effect

5

The Economic Impacts of Crowd-Based Capitalism

With Napster, a computer became sighted, it could speak and it could listen. It could say, "I have this music on my hard drive," and report that up to a central index. Fanning didn't increase the capital spending on music infrastructure, he increased the capital impact.
—Clay Shirky, from a talk at the Collaborative-Peer-Sharing Economy Summit, New York University, May 30, 2014

In 2001, the 100 or so residents of Gigha, a small island located off the coast of Scotland, collectively bought out their entire island, including its 47 cottages, 4 farms, a hotel, quarry, wind farm, and 54-acre garden, for £4 million. Gigha, which had peaked in population in the 1700s, had been in decline since the Industrial Revolution—however, since the residents banded together to co-own the island through a development trust, things have been looking up. Others have started to move to the island. In 2003, one such new arrival was California native Don Dennis.

For less than the average price of a three-bedroom apartment in Manhattan or San Francisco, Dennis purchased Achamore House, a 14,000-square-foot structure, once home to the laird of Gigha. This home, purchased from the development trust, had enough additional space to house his bed-and-breakfast, as well as his evolving microbusiness of creating flower essences sourced from orchids he grew.

A decade later, in 2013, Dennis needed a small-business loan to scale his business. Perhaps inspired by the "peer collective" approach of his fellow islanders, Dennis listed to borrow on Funding Circle, the UK-based peer-to-peer lending platform.[1] His company, The Flower Essence Repertoire, was issued a loan of £18,000—an amount sourced from 266 funders. The process of obtaining the loan was simple and transparent, and the subsequent investment infused capital into the local Gigha economy.

The Isle of Gigha might appear to be an unusual first setting for a chapter on the global economic impacts of crowd-based capitalism, but, in many respects, Dennis's story illustrates some of the forms of economic activity frequently associated with the sharing economy. Dennis is a global entrepreneur, albeit on a very small scale; his fortunes depend on access to massive digital platforms for promotion, for sales, and for funding. His choices reflect a balance between local impact and global reach. The "cooperative" model reflected in Gigha's development fund is receiving renewed attention as a potential form of participative sharing economy ownership. That Dennis can operate a successful business from a location so remote that its population had nearly vanished by the turn of the 21st century is also significant.

In a sense, Dennis represents a new generation of entrepreneur—a successful owner of a "microbusiness" engaged in a somewhat unusual endeavor, perhaps purpose-driven and certainty well off the beaten track, but still decidedly capitalist, market-dependent and privately owned.

Before we discuss the broader economic principles powering crowd-based capitalism, let's consider a few more examples. I've focused quite extensively thus far in the book on sharing economy "poster child" companies like Airbnb and Lyft. So that you can appreciate the variety of new economic activity that is on the horizon, let's look instead at crowd-based businesses being powered by other peer-to-peer platforms.

First, let's consider the range of scale of the more than a million entrepreneurs on the retailing platform Etsy. While many Etsy sellers make as little as a few thousand dollars per year on the platform, at least a few report six-figure annual incomes, like Yokoo Gibran whose hand-crocheted scarves became popular enough to yield her more than $140,000 one year.[2]

Gibran became an Etsy seller because she saw the platform as a potential way to facilitate a better life pursuing something she was passionate about. Before she became an Etsy seller, she worked nine-to-five at a copy center. Describing her transition from full-time employment, she notes: "There was a point when the amount of hours spent at my place of employment began to actually reduce the amount of total income being earned through my 'secret projects' on a then relatively unknown site called Etsy.com."

Gibran is one of dozens of sellers featured on a section of the Etsy website blog called "Quit Your Day Job."[3] Other blog stories include those of Satsuma Street, who worked for seven years creating special effects for big-budget Hollywood movies, Sara Barrett, who left a corporate design job, and Mike Schmiedcke, who transitioned from being a software engineer to building and selling furniture.

Unlike small businesses of the past, while the entrepreneurship of many Etsy sellers may be "micro," their reach is "macro"—the platform makes them global businesses instantly. As Althea Erickson, Etsy's global director of public policy pointed out in a 2014 interview, "You know, when you talk about facilitating trade for small businesses, people tend to focus on helping small companies break into new markets, and develop distribution channels and all of that. But what we find with our sellers is they're already in a global marketplace. There are buyers all over the world that are buying their goods."[4]

Gibran continues to sell on Etsy as I write this book, and scaled up her business by working long hours, but that's not the only growth path on Etsy. ThreeBirdNest, which specializes in women's apparel items and accessories with a bohemian look, reported sales of close to $1 million annually, according to an Etsy blog writer.[5] The company's founder, Alicia Shaffer, processed anywhere from 150 to 1,200 orders per day, but unlike Gibran, who at one time reported crocheting up to 13 hours per day to meet her orders, Shaffer now employs over a dozen sewers and offshores the production of some of its items to keep up with demand. More importantly, she "graduated" from selling on Etsy in late August 2015 to running ThreeBirdNest as an independent small business. Alicia now sells through wholesale channels as well as a dedicated web site, as the brand expands its product line and supplier base.[6]

A similar range of provider scale exists on the car-sharing platform Turo (founded as RelayRides). Like Airbnb, which enables people to list their own homes for short-term rental, Turo enables people to rent out their personal cars to their peers. Unlike Getaround, whose cars on-demand are rented by community residents who need a ride for a short periods, Turo focused in 2015 on travelers who might need a car rental when visiting a new city—it's a peer-to-peer version of Hertz rather than a crowd-based Zipcar. Like Airbnb, most Turo "providers" simply rent out their own primary car while it's not in use, or make some money off a second vehicle. But like Airbnb, there are also exceptions. In 2013, a Turo member named David learned about the platform and decided to rent out a truck he was about to sell. The experience was positive enough for David to start using Craigslist to purchase other vehicles to list for rent on Turo. As of 2014, David had six vehicles and, sharing his story with a Turo blogger, he reported earning a couple thousand dollars per month from his microfleet.[7] To deal with the challenges of parking this fleet without a dedicated lot, David uses SpotOn—a sharing economy company like JustPark that connects people in need of parking spots to people with under-utilized parking spaces.

Is the small fleet of cars and trucks David rents out a threat to Hertz? Perhaps not yet, but his microbusiness, which he hopes will soon be able to cover his monthly housing costs, is having an impact on his local economy. David is now buying used vehicles, hiring a local mechanic to maintain his fleet, and sharing some of his profits with people who have parking space to spare.

This trend of growth in small-scale enterprise has been noted in many countries. For example, a 2015 study from the Royal Society of Arts indicated that microbusinesses (businesses with nine employees or less) account for the greatest share of employment in some of the fastest-growing industries in the United Kingdom, including education, computer programming and personal services.[8] Similarly, the 2009 study by Dane Stangler and Robert Litan from the Kaufmann Foundation showed that about two-thirds of job creation in the United States in 2007 came from young firms, further noting that "Indeed, without startups, net job creation for the American economy would be negative in all but a handful of years." Furthermore, the number of non-employer firms, incorporated businesses that do not employ anyone and are essentially businesses-of-one, has grown dramatically in the United States, from about 18 million in 2003 to over 23 million in 2013.[9]

These examples underscore at least four important general economic impacts that our shift to crowd-based capitalism is likely to have: (1) an increase in the *impact of capital*; (2) changes in consumption driven by *greater variety* and different models of access; (3) a shift in the nature of *economies of scale* and *network effects* that characterized industrial economies; and (4) a *democratization of economic opportunity* that promises inclusive growth.

The examples also illustrate another central point of this chapter. The motivations for people engaging in crowd-based capitalism are not always purely monetary. This suggests a need to focus not just on economic growth as measured by income and dollar value of output, but on economic development more broadly defined.

I have organized this chapter in the following way. I start by expanding on this need for better measures of economic progress, with the caveat that I am neither the first person to point this out, nor am I the first to note that progress induced by digital technologies exacerbates measurement problems we've always had. Despite their shortcomings, I believe it is nevertheless essential to understand how the effects of this ongoing transition look through the lens of traditional economic measures like gross domestic product (GDP). So next I discuss four key drivers of economic impact—changes in the impact of capital, changes in consumption driven by greater variety and different models of access, changes in economies of scale and network effects, and the promise of inclusive growth—in the broad context of crowd-based capitalism. I conclude with a deep dive into one specific slice of the sharing economy—peer-to-peer rental markets—and, based on the research I have done with a former NYU doctoral student, Samuel Fraiberger, provide a template for how one might rigorously analyze the long-run effects of different facets of crowd-based capitalism, on economic growth, consumer well-being, and inequality.

The Trouble with GDP

Each of the stories I started this chapter with illustrates ways in which peer-to-peer platforms are already transforming financing, production, distribution, and service delivery around the world. Where we conduct commerce (and with whom) is changing, as is our approach to building capital. There's a new meld of local and global emerging.

Granted, traditional sources of borrowing are still orders of magnitude larger than Funding Circle and its US counterparts Lending Club and Prosper. While these peer-to-peer lending marketplaces likely won't put banks out of business, they will reduce their margins by bringing greater transparency and efficiency into the aggregation and matching of distributed financial capital with its recipients. As Funding Circle CEO Sam Hodges noted in a 2015 interview, "With marketplace and peer-to-peer lending, the difference is transparency. On the one hand there are small businesses looking to borrow. On the other hand, there's a wide range of investors. As a marketplace, there is no incentive to charge more or less, thanks to data-driven underwriting. This leads to a clearing price that is fair to the borrower with sufficient returns."[10]

Peer-to-peer financial markets will also increase the number of individuals who make part of their living as commercial lenders and investors. More importantly, they may permit an entire range of people who might not otherwise have access to a small business loan to start developing new and innovative businesses. This inclusion could have an equalizing effect over time. Additionally, much like Airbnb, which has not put hotels out of business but has created variety for travelers and options for people who may otherwise find it too expensive to travel for long periods of time, platforms like Funding Circle may be best understood as diversifying and expanding an existing economic model rather than replacing it.[11]

Of course, these platforms are also changing consumer behaviors along the way. Uber, Lyft, and Gett reduce traditional taxi use because they've made the service more convenient and less expensive, and because they've created more variety through their shared services. Along with Getaround, they are poised to change consumer habits even more radically by enabling people to consider on-demand car rental and access as a viable alternative to owning personal vehicles, taking us closer to the world of widespread technology-enabled "shared mobility" that the UC Berkeley professor Susan Shaheen envisions and has been conducting research about over the last 15 years.

The challenge, of course, is finding ways to measure the impact of these different changes, which include economic effects, qualitative changes in consumer habits, and other improvements in people's economic lives. Do our established models for measuring economic impacts measure up?

It's helpful to start by assessing the commonly used measure of economic activity, the GDP, a measure of consumption and production calculated through the prices of all goods and services produced in an economy. In essence, GDP captures the "sold value" of production of final goods in the economy by subtracting intermediate forms of consumption, thus providing a clear net picture of economic activity.[12] It focuses on aggregate variables—the total sum of money spent on goods and services, or the total sum of incomes paid out to households, or the total sum of expenditures. While not perfect, these combined approaches provide a useful picture of the overall health of traditional economies.

While GDP remains a key metric for making fiscal and monetary policy decisions, a number of shortcomings of GDP as a measure of economic health are well known. First, GDP is an aggregate measure. It provides no evidence of how income or consumption or wealth is distributed. Large changes in inequality may not be represented in the GDP's averages or aggregate statistics. Second, GDP doesn't fully capture the extent to which economic growth can, at times, have a negative impact on quality of life. Increasing traffic congestion also increases gas consumption, which adds to GDP, but the long-term impacts of traffic congestion are generally not positive—they lower commuters' quality of life by extending their workday and compromising their work-life balance. Third, since GDP is only focused on market measures, nonmarket activities (e.g., unpaid domestic labor, do-it-yourself repairs. and various forms of bartering and exchange) also typically go unmeasured. Correspondingly, if previously nonmarket economic activities like carpooling, childcare coops, supper clubs, and apartment barters start to become commercial, GDP may overstate changes in economic activity. Fourth, GDP is, in a sense, blind to the *quality* of spending—spending on education or healthcare and spending on gambling are treated the same, with no regard for the impact these very different types of spending might have on future growth and well-being. Indeed, quantity rather than quality is the focus of the GDP, which means quality-of-life improvements often slip under the radar. Fifth, since the GDP does not take finite resources into account, spending that is unsustainable (e.g., spending on coal, oil, or gas and other nonrenewal resources) are not adequately captured. On a related note, other externalities, such as pollution and overcrowding, are also overlooked in GDP measures.[13] And finally, GDP does not capture changes in "consumer surplus," a point I explain in greater detail in the next section of the chapter.

The shortcomings of the GDP are by no means news, even if they become increasingly salient with the rise of the sharing economy. As a result, there are already at least a few alternative measures proposed. The World Bank's Human Development Index seeks to measure broader social indicators (e.g., educational attainment and health) and standards of living (like leisure time). The UK Office for National Statistics has adopted the Measures of National Well-being and now releases a dashboard of indicators on a quarterly basis that seek to capture economic impacts that extend the limited measures captured by the GDP. The Better Life Indicator of the Organisation for Education Cooperation and Development (OECD) takes into account additional factors, including civic engagement and work-life balance. A more radical shift in thinking is represented by the Social Progress Index, which replaces economic metrics with social and environmental ones. Here, basic human needs, such as nutrition and access to basic medical care, water, sanitation services, and safety, are weighed alongside other factors including sustainability, human rights (e.g., freedom of assembly), tolerance (e.g., for immigrants) and access to higher education.

Additional Measurement Challenges in the Digital Economy

The digitization of the economy exacerbates some of these shortcomings with GDP. Consider the example of measuring the economic impact of search engines like Google. As search engine use has become widespread, consumers have become increasingly empowered—they can make better choices with access to superior information, a larger number of markets, and up-to-date feedback and reviews on products. However, part of the higher quality of one's consumer experience is often realized as an intangible "better product fit" or by an increase in what economists call "consumer surplus," which, loosely speaking, measures the difference between the maximum amount the consumer would be willing to pay for a product or service and the actual amount paid. Thus, a big fraction of Google's impact on the economy isn't captured since changes in consumer surplus are not reflected in the GDP.

This point has been noted about digital markets more generally. While a conventional brick-and-mortar bookstore may hold 40,000 to 100,000 books, Amazon offers access to over 3 million books. The same expansion in variety holds true for music, movies, electronics, and myriad other products. Furthermore, since Amazon uses several recommender systems to help promote products, it is not just variety but "fit" that has increased.[14] Capturing the economic impacts of enhanced variety and automated word-of-mouth promotions, however, is difficult, since once again, what has changed is primarily the quality of the consumer experience. As Erik Brynjolfsson, Yu (Jeffery) Hu, and Michael Smith argue in their study of consumer surplus in the digital economy, these benefits may be particularly difficult to measure because different consumers are impacted to varying degrees. "In effect, the emergence of online retailers places a specialty store and a personalized shopping assistant at every shopper's desktop. This improves the welfare of these consumers by allowing them to locate and buy specialty products they otherwise would not have purchased due to high transaction costs or low product awareness. This effect will be especially beneficial to those consumers who live in remote areas."[15] Analogous increases in consumer surplus were documented by Anindya Ghose, Rahul Telang and Michael Smith in their 2005 study of electronic markets for used books.[16] These effects are exacerbated by a wide variety of recommender systems that use machine learning algorithms to better direct consumer choice. As Alexander Tuzhilin and Gedas Adomavicius document, such systems are ubiquitous in digital markets.[17] It is natural to expect similar challenges when, for example, trying to encompass the different economic impacts of increased variety and fit from Airbnb, or increased convenience from Lyft, or Dennis's increased access to financing on the Isle of Gigha.

A number of studies over the last 15 years have documented changes in consumer surplus that digital technologies create. More recent thinking has started to introduce an additional dimension—of *human capital gains* that arise from digitization. In this regard, the research of my NYU colleague Prasanna Tambe is particularly instructive. Tambe's work with Lorin Hitt of the University of Pennsylvania points to an intriguing new hypothesis: that part of the returns from digital technologies are often captured by a firm's *employees* in the form of human capital that may be task specific rather than firm specific, and which diffuses to other firms when these employees switch jobs. These findings add a third possibility—beyond showing up in production numbers and as consumer surplus, part of the returns from digitization come from imparting transferrable, task-specific human capital to a firm's workers. This is intuitively appealing—it seems natural that employees will gain from their firm's IT investments and serve as a conduit by which the returns from these investments are "spread" across firms.[18] As a greater fraction of economic activity is conducted by individuals who either have more fluid relationships with firm-market hybrids like Uber, Airbnb, and Etsy, or are building expertise as small-scale entrepreneurs like David from RelayRides, quantifying these labor economic impacts of digitization gets increasingly complex. I discuss some related measurement challenges in chapter 8.

There are also effects from the "localization" of exchange that may have distributive implications. For instance, a seller on Etsy may buy raw materials from a local craft store rather than buy these inputs wholesale. In a traditional marketplace, such a retailer would sell materials to hobbyists but not necessarily to other small businesses. In parallel, because microentrepreneurs often work on a very small scale, the distribution of returns may even out between small retailers and large wholesalers, but there may also be losses in economies of scale.

Even more complex is the question of how to measure the affective gains of the sharing economy. When I spoke to Airbnb CEO Brian Chesky in 2015, he alluded to one such non-financial benefit: "Hospitality is really the idea of making somebody feel like they belong; it's about welcoming somebody." Chesky added that Airbnb is "not necessarily completely changing people, but we're changing a little bit of their mindsets." As Chesky further explained, "I myself have changed as a person because of Airbnb—not because of the business but because of the actual service. I find myself caring for people more. Because when somebody's in your home, they're completely vulnerable. You have to take care of them. Taking care of and hosting people is a deeply important thing."

Four Key Economic Effects

If a peer-to-peer platform is in fact changing our mindset—changing our attitude toward others in a positive way—how do we capture such affective impacts? The answer to this question is unlikely to come from us economists. Nevertheless, there is little doubt that the expansion of crowd-based capitalism further reinforces the need to extend our measurement of economic impacts in ways that include indicators not well captured by GDP.

Meanwhile, however, there are a few broad, traditional economic impacts that we can expect. In what follows, I outline four of the most notable impacts that I anticipate.

Altering Capital "Impact"

Whether it is the asset capacity (Botsman's "idling capacity") from peer-to-peer rental markets, labor supplied through markets like TaskRabbit, Handy and Spare5, or financial capital through a lending platform like Funding Circle—everything else being equal—tapping into "spare capacity" may increase economic productivity.

For instance, a host with a spare room has more than an empty room—he or she has an asset that is not being used at full capacity. With Airbnb, the host is able to turn a small amount of extra space into a source of income, and in this sense, tap into excess capacity by making the most of the space. Similarly, with the Spare5 app, time once spent on the bus commuting to and from a full-time job can be channeled as an economic input by using your smartphone to tag images or respond to surveys from the Spare5 business community. And, when small lenders redirect money from their personal savings accounts and lend it to small businesses through Funding Circle, they potentially increase the economic impact of their financial capital.

I think of each of these examples as an increase in the "impact" of existing capital, assets or labor.[19] A digital precursor to this increase in impact we see unfolding on sharing economy platforms was explained with characteristic clarity by Clay Shirky during a keynote address he gave at the Collaborative-Peer-Sharing Economy Summit that I hosted at NYU in May 2014. Explaining how "in the digital world, the great precursor to the sharing economy was Napster," Shirky went on to illustrate:

In the 1990s, the common goal of the American music listening public was to be able to participate in something that was being called "The Celestial Jukebox";

every song available, one song at a time. Sean Fanning, the inventor of Napster, realized the hard work for the Celestial Jukebox has already been done. All of the world's music has been digitized, one CD at a time. Someone buys it, they rip it and they have the MP3s on their hard drive. That enormous volume of work that had already been done. But that enormous volume of fixed capital infrastructure was not yet an aggregate; it was not yet a collection. Computers on the networks were blind, they were mute and they were deaf. These were disconnected nodes.

What Fanning did with Napster was solve that problem. He didn't solve the storage problem, he didn't solve the transportation problem, he didn't solve the digitization problem—he just solved the indexing problem. With Napster, a computer became sighted, it could speak and it could listen. It could say, "I have this music on my hard drive" and it could report that up to a central index at which point other machines could listen and talk about what music they had and they could negotiate a transfer.

Shirky then went on to summarize his point: "Fanning didn't increase the capital spending on music infrastructure, he increased the capital impact."[20]

Perhaps the most striking pool of underutilized capital exists in the United States in its automobiles. Americans spend about one *trillion* dollars annually purchasing new and used vehicles, and the capital stock of vehicles is worth a few times more than this. (To put this amount in context, the 2015 GDP of the entire US economy is about $17 trillion.) However, as I note in the introduction, the rate at which these automobiles are utilized is distressingly low. For example, figure 5.1 shows the distribution of how intensively residents of California used their automobiles in 2009. The horizontal axis charts the intensity of usage (so for example, a usage intensity of 5% means you are using your car 5% of the time, or a little over an hour per day), and the vertical axis charts the percentage of cars in California at that level of usage. As illustrated, most of the population actually uses an owned car less than 10% of its life, which means that a vast majority of cars are parked on the street or in a garage for over 90% of their lives. (As I point out in the Introduction, this seems true in Manhattan as well.) And Californians actually use their cars more intensively than the average US resident does.

We may not need to wait for self-driving cars to see a digitally induced economic revolution in the auto and transportation sector. The range of new peer-to-peer models—Uber to get a driven car on-demand, Lyft to see who else is driving your route, Getaround to see whose car in your neighborhood might be available for you to drive by yourself, BlaBlaCar to get a ride to another city—have already started to increase the impact

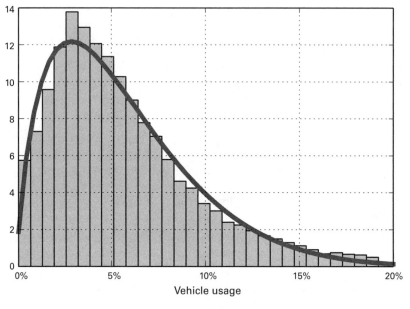

Figure 5.1
Vehicle usage in the United States (compiled from NHTS data as of 2009).

of the global automobile stock. The emergence of well-funded, agile regional players like Didi Kuaidi and Ola in the world's fastest growing consumer markets promises an impact even more profound for the user base that is not yet deeply entrenched in their auto ownership behaviors. It is possible, as Bhavish Aggarwal, the youthful co-founder and CEO of Ola suggested to me in 2015, that of the hundreds of millions of the newly minted Indian middle class who attain an income level that allows them to consider buying a car over the coming decade, many will "leap-frog" the inefficient ownership phase entirely, instead entering the automobile usage market directly as on-demand consumers.

In a series of recent talks, the economist Robert Gordon from Northwestern University has lamented the slowdown in US productivity growth and, in particular, the absence of clear evidence that the digital revolution of the last two decades has had a significant impact on the growth rates of total factor productivity. A now-famous slide from one of his recent articles is replicated in figure 5.2.[21]

Total factor productivity (TFP) increases when on average, over time, more output is produced with the same inputs—physical capital, financial capital, and labor. An increase in productivity in turn increases the

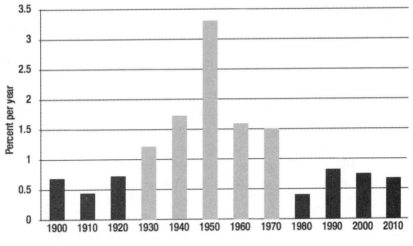

Figure 5.2
Growth rate of total factor productivity for each ten-year period (i.e., for the decades ending 1900 to 2010).

rate at which an economy grows. As platforms expand beyond increasing the "capital impact" of digital goods that Shirky spoke of, and move toward increasing, over the next couple of decades, the impact of labor, financial capital, and especially physical capital, this particular effect of digital technologies will quite possibly expand into much broader swaths of the economy, such as real estate, transportation, energy, healthcare, and labor of myriad forms.

Put differently, the promised increases in TFP growth from the digital revolution may not be a myth, as Gordon worries. Rather, they may simply have been waiting for the enabling forces of crowd-based capitalism to arrive before they showed up in the national statistics.

Economies of Scale and Local "Network Effects"

A recurring theme of technology-enabled economic progress over the last two centuries has been creation of progressively greater *economies of scale*—cost advantages that business enterprises get as the amount they produce grows. Put simply, traditional economies of scale are said to occur if one's average costs go down as one produces more. These advantages can stem from being able to spread a "fixed cost" (like the building of a factory) over a larger volume of unit. They can come from the increased specialization of labor that is possible for larger firms. (If you're doing a smaller and smaller slice of work repeatedly, the logic goes, then you can do it more efficiently, an idea perhaps best represented by Henry Ford's assembly lines.) They may also come from "learning by doing"— an increase in efficiency that comes from learning how to use equipment better, or from workers getting more proficient at what they do over time.

The documenting of economies of scale dates back to Adam Smith's observations about the division of labor in pin manufacturing in the 18th century; for a couple of centuries after that, economies of scale were typically driven by supply-side improvements. You were able to beat a competitor with sheer scale because you could incur higher fixed costs, or because you were able to lower your variable cost per unit. Since the 1980s, however, economists have documented a growing evidence of what Hal Varian and Carl Shapiro christened as *demand-side economies of scale*—that is, an increase in the value of a product as its usage grows.[22] This effect—when more usage of the product by any user increases the product's value for *other* users (and sometimes all users)—is also often called a network effect.[23] Silicon Valley investors widely covet network effects in a business model since they are often predictive of a "winner take most" market like those enjoyed currently and in the past by Microsoft, Facebook, and other technology titans.

Let's discuss, in sequence, how the move toward crowd-based capitalism might affect each of these kinds of economies of scale. At first, it might seem like a move away from a few giant corporations and toward millions of micro-entrepreneurs would cause the loss of many of the economies of scale that 200 years of progress have yielded. After all, can an Airbnb host ever produce short-term accommodation more efficiently than a specialized group of professionally trained hotel employees working as highly optimized teams in dedicated real estate? Wouldn't a giant factory in China always have cost advantages over the makers of wooden toys in Brooklyn?

The answer seems to be both yes and no. We will undoubtedly lose some of the production benefits of scale and specialization as we shift the organization of economic activity into the crowd. However, some of these gains from scale will be less relevant because the need to make large, fixed investments diminishes. You don't have to build hotels if you can tap into the idling capacity of homes. In some cases, you don't need a massive factory if you have access to a sophisticated 3-D printer. In a sense, the entire cost curve may shift down, even if the slope increases.

Additionally, many economies of scale will be preserved and redistributed by the platforms themselves. The dissemination of "learning by doing" may not occur within a hotel's organization or on the factory floor, but instead, through the networks of makers who sell on Etsy, or through Airbnb host communities and "guilds," either directly by the company through events, training, and capabilities embedded into the platform, or in a more grassroots fashion.

The actual changes will vary across industry and across country, and it will be many years before we understand on which side these competing forces balance out. But it's fascinating: there's a real chance that the economic models of crowd-based capitalism may actually be able to distribute production across millions of smaller providers without having to sacrifice significantly on the gains from scale that 20th-century organizations enjoyed.

In contrast, it seems unequivocally clear that demand-side economies of scale will become more prevalent as crowd-based capitalism gathers steam. A particular kind of network effect—the two-sided network effect—governs many economic aspects of platforms. As Thomas Eisenmann, Geoffrey Parker, and Marshall Van Alstyne explain in an influential *Harvard Business Review* article:

With two-sided network effects, the platform's value to any given user largely depends on the number of users on the network's other side. Value grows as the platform matches demand from both sides. For example, video game developers will create games only for platforms that have a critical mass of players, because developers need a large enough customer base to recover their upfront programming costs. In turn, players favor platforms with a greater variety of games.[24]

An ambitious project on the emerging platform economy, led by Peter Evans from the Center for Global Enterprise, is gathering data about scale and interaction from across hundreds of different platforms, and will no doubt shed further light on their economics over the coming decade.

Meanwhile, my own research suggests that the nature of these two-sided network effects varies in very significant ways across different sharing economy platforms. The differences have primarily to do with the *local* nature of the sharing economy that we discussed in the first half of the book. Let's first consider the example of Etsy. Much like eBay, buyers gain value from having access to more sellers, and sellers favor the platform as it signs on more buyers. It doesn't really matter much where the buyers and sellers are. If I'm a buyer in New York, another seller located in Los Angeles is pretty much as valuable as another seller located in Minneapolis.

Contrast this, however, with the network effects associated with Uber. Granted, as more drivers join the Uber platform in New York, this increases the value of the platform for users in New York (as wait times go down); correspondingly, as more users sign on to be passengers, this increases the value of being an Uber driver (you're likely to earn more money each hour because there are more potential fares). However, the benefits of these network effects are *highly localized*. Most Uber users only care about the quality of service in their *own* city. A thousand new Uber drivers in Los Angeles do nothing for the wait times of passengers in New York. The process of creating supply is therefore far more painstaking, market by market.

What does this mean? Well, the demand-side economies of scale in such a platform would not naturally lead to one global "winner," but instead, to one or more winners in each local market.[25] And each local market is therefore also more contestable. It would be hard for Etsy's sellers who retail only phone cases, or for those who live only in New York, to peel off and start their own marketplace without losing a tremendous amount of their potential demand. In contrast, it is completely conceivable that all of Uber's drivers in New York could collectively switch to a different platform (or start one of their own), eventually taking all of the demand with them.

Now let's contrast the network effects of Uber with those enjoyed by Airbnb. Again, this is a market in which supply has to be built out market by market, in thousands of different cities and towns. But the "network" benefits from hosts in Paris extend far beyond the Paris consumers. This is because unlike local transport, short-term accommodation is sought primarily by *travelers* rather than by local residents. You favor a platform that can get you accommodation anywhere in the world, rather than one that specializes in one city. Thus, on the Airbnb platform, network effects are more resilient.

In a sense, the "fractal" structure of the network effects in both these examples makes their economics more complex than those of traditional two-sided markets, potentially making them either stronger or weaker. As I discuss in chapter 6, there are a number of new regulatory challenges raised by the emergence of the sharing economy. One that I do not discuss relates to the question of market power. This is because deepening our understanding the nature of these new network effects, or asking the question framed by Professor Maurice Stucke when he spoke at a June 2015 Federal Trade Commission panel about regulating the sharing economy—"Do I have the analytical tools to assess what the impact would be?"—is critical before determining whether these new economies of scale will lead to market power worthy of antitrust scrutiny.[26]

Increased Variety = Increased Consumption

The sharing economy creates new consumption experiences of higher quality and greater variety. It is thus very likely that, rather than merely substituting old forms of commerce with new digitally enabled ones, new economic activity will be enabled. Put differently, we grow the pie, rather than simply carving it up differently.

Consider our now-familiar example, Airbnb. Hotels deliver a wide range of accommodation options. However, there are many dimensions of the hotel experience that are standard: hotel rooms are located in hotel buildings; with few exceptions, hotel rooms come with a bed, television set, and private bathroom; they, for the most part, accommodate up to two people; and the more expensive the hotel, the more amenities one can expect to receive. By contrast, on a peer-to-peer platform, accommodations may or may not be housed in actual buildings (tents and trailers are also an option), one may or may not have a bed (airbeds and sofas may also be rentable), and the relationship between price and amenities is far more variable. And the variety is even greater when one considers sites beyond Airbnb. Couchsurfing offers spare couches; OneFineStay offers luxury homes within what otherwise resembles a white glove, full-service experience; Debbie Woskow's LoveHomeSwap offers vacation rentals; Kozaza offers traditional Korean homes; China's Tujia offers corporate apartments, and India's Oyo offers a range of hotel-like and alternative options.

One might expect this increase in variety to shift demand away from traditional hotels. Some hotel industry advocates indicate this may be happening. In an August 2015 PBS interview, Vijay Dandapani, the president of Apple Core Hotels, a chain of five hotels in midtown Manhattan, and a leader of the Hotel Association of New York, claimed that Airbnb's impact was already visible. "[Occupancy] rates have not gone back to where there were, pre financial crisis, despite the fact that tourism has gone up," he asserts.[27]

But the empirical evidence of such a shift, at least as of 2015, is mixed at best. A study by Georgios Zervas, Davide Proserpio, and John W. Byers about Airbnb's impact on the hotel industry in Texas document a relatively low rate of substitution: a 10% increase in Airbnb listings is associated with a 0.34% decrease in monthly hotel room revenue, with slightly higher levels in Austin.[28] Zervas and his colleagues also note additional dimensions of differentiation in the Airbnb offer, since they are able to operate in locations where hotels typically do not exist.

Airbnb's own data documents this point across a variety of cities. For example, as illustrated in figure 5.3, showing activity for Manhattan,

Most Airbnb guests stay outside main hotel areas throughout NYC.

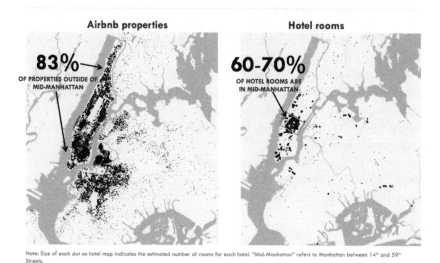

Note: Size of each dot on hotel map indicates the estimated number of rooms for each hotel. "Mid-Manhattan" refers to Manhattan between 14ᵗʰ and 59ᵗʰ Streets.

Figure 5.3
The geographic footprint of Airbnb listings in New York City.

about five out of six Airbnb listings in New York are outside midtown Manhattan, which is home to about two out of three hotel rooms.

Brian Chesky sums it up well: "As we've grown, hotels' occupancy has grown as well. That's what I think is going to happen with hotels. I'm pretty close with some hotel executives; they don't seem to be overly concerned." Indeed, as Alison Griswold from *Slate* magazine documents, the hotel industry in 2014–15 enjoyed their highest-ever levels of occupancy and average daily room prices.[29]

The same is not true of Uber and Lyft's impact on traditional taxicabs. The key difference is that, rather than being merely a differentiated service, Uber and Lyft also display higher quality across the board on most dimensions that customer value, except perhaps the ability to hail a car on the street. This does not negate the point I'm making—the increase in variety will increase consumption. However, the impact on the incumbents is likely to be negative more rapidly. Indeed, taxi drivers (most of whom in larger cities do not own their cars or "medallions") switch to Uber every day; we have already seen evidence of a drop of about 30% in the price of a New York City yellow cab medallion.[30] And in July 2015, Evgeny Freidman, the largest owner of yellow cab medallions in New

York, filed a petition to put many of his medallion-owning companies into bankruptcy.[31] And the eventual impact of on-demand transportation will likely be on the automobile industry as a whole, accelerated by autonomous cars becoming a mass-market commercial reality over the next decade. A significant fraction of consumer spending on automobiles will shift to a growing variety of on-demand mobility services.

Industrial organization economics teaches us that as product variety increases, people will consume more rather than less. This is partially the case because people who previously were not consuming are able to do so, or to do so more often (and in the case of accommodations, for longer periods of time in a wider variety of locations). It is also because, theoretically, as variety increases, the "fit" between someone's ideal product and what's available in the market improves, and this increases the price people are willing to pay on average. And as Andrey Fradkin has shown us using his research at Airbnb, improvements in search and ranking technologies make it progressively more likely that a host and guest will actually match and transact on the platform.[32] The resulting increases in consumption will drive economic growth, even measured as traditional GDP. On this front, it seems quite clear that the dramatic increases in quality and variety brought by crowd-based capitalism are bound to accelerate, rather than slow, the growth of the economy.

The Democratization of Opportunity

In summer 2014, a book titled *Capital in the 21st Century*, Thomas Piketty's treatise into the persistence of inequality over the last two centuries, was at the center of discussion in both academic and Silicon Valley circles. At the core of Piketty's book is a simple argument: inequality persists because the returns on capital (r)—whether invested financial capital, or the sort of entrenched wealth of property and other types of physical investments (i.e., the type of capital that the sharing economy promises to increase the impact of)—are persistently higher than the overall rate of growth (g) in the economy, while the rate of growth of wages is roughly the same as this overall rate of growth g. As Piketty concludes, "The inequality $r > g$ implies that wealth accumulated in the past grows more rapidly than output and wages. This inequality expresses a fundamental logical contradiction. The entrepreneur inevitably tends to become a renter, more and more dominant over those who own nothing but their labor. Once constituted, capital reproduces itself faster than output increases. The past devours the future."[33]

Said another way, rich people see their returns grow at the rate r, while most people who don't own substantial property or have large bank accounts or investment portfolios see their returns grow at the lower rate g. Thus, inequality grows over time. Given this scenario, Piketty goes on to ask, "Can we imagine a twenty-first century in which capitalism will be transcended in a more peaceful and more lasting way, or must we simply await the next crisis or the next war (this time truly global)? Can we imagine political institutions that might regulate today's global patrimonial capitalism justly as well as efficiently?"[34]

Piketty's own solutions favor more traditional and predictable redistributive interventions (like higher global taxes). However, it may well be the case that the sharing economy is already turning the tables, even if slightly, by expanding the population that enjoy "r" rates of growth.

Let's return to the example of Funding Circle in the United Kingdom: it enables everyday investors—perhaps a college student with a few hundred pounds or a retiree with a few thousand pounds—to make investments in small businesses that would typically only be the purview of a bank. Investors don't need a sophisticated understanding of the stock market to invest, and they don't need any special software to make their investments. Funding Circle's online platform is as easy to use as Airbnb or Etsy, and user communities provide a rapid education into how to assess potential borrowers.

In a sense, with little additional infrastructure, Piketty's "renters" can begin to experience the other side of the coin by making money through investing or owning rather than laboring. A similar effect can be anticipated as Etsy expands beyond its 1.5 million sellers. Again, on a very small scale, people once relegated to laboring for others are assuming new roles and occupying new locations in the established economic equation, transcending from being people who receive wages to people who own capital. Over a million Airbnb hosts now own most of the capital that would have been concentrated in the hands of the shareholders and franchisees of a hotel chain. In other words, these changes are expanding the fraction of the population that have the "r" kind of growth in their returns rather than the "g" kind, and are doing so in a way that favors people traditionally not on the high end of the wealth spectrum.

In general, the picture that this paints is of *inclusive* growth. After all, while there are some exceptions, people who choose to Airbnb a spare room, lend on Funding Circle, or rent out their car on RelayRides are generally people who have less rather than more capital. They may not be poor but they certainly aren't part of Occupy Wall Street's fabled 1%. Some of the people who seek an education on Coursera in the future may be those that were excluded from gaining a traditional high-quality four-year college degree. The traditional gatekeeping mechanisms that have prevented many of these people from moving from worker to owner or worker to investor are loosened.

Over time, a greater percent of these new "microentrepreneurship" opportunities that empower individuals previously constrained by employment at traditional corporations may evolve into enterprises larger than sole proprietorships, much like ThreeBirdNest's business did. Brian Chesky has told me that he and his co-founder Joe Gebbia used to call hosting on Airbnb "training wheels for being an entrepreneur." We will have to wait a few more years to find out if providers on Airbnb, Etsy, Lyft, and Getaround are more likely to start successful larger companies (although the first two Airbnb hosts, Brian and Joe, clearly have already). But as the lines between producer and consumer blur, it certainly seems clear that great potential exists to expand the fraction of the population that owns wealth-producing assets.

A Deep Dive into Peer-to-Peer Rental Markets

The economy is a complex system with many moving parts. I have outlined four broad anticipated impacts, but we need a more careful analysis of different changes and sectors in order to more precisely quantify the long-run economic impacts of the sharing economy.

What would this kind of detailed analysis look like? To shed light on some of the more "micro" effects of crowd-based capitalism, I now turn to one specific segment of this economy—peer-to-peer rental markets—and specifically, to the analysis and results of research I have done with my colleague Samuel Fraiberger developing a new dynamic economic model of peer-to-peer Internet-enabled rental markets for "durable" goods—assets that last a long time, and are thus more likely to have idling capacity.[35] Part of my goal in this section is also to convince you that we need careful, systematic studies of different sectors of the economy before we can decide whether crowd-based capitalism is good news or bad news. (Of course, as you may have already discerned, I am one of the optimists.)

Before diving in to what Fraiberger and I found, it may be helpful to take a more systematic look on the surface: let's assess the key economic effects that occur when consumers have access to a new marketplace in which they can rent from other consumers or supply them with excess capacity.

Think about your own experience owning a durable good like a car or a dining table. It provides value to you over an extended period of time.

In a world with no "frictions," that is, in a world where you could buy or sell instantaneously and without regard to transaction costs, you might freely adjust your ownership at any time to match your current needs, buying a Porsche when you feel like taking a drive down the beach, and then selling it and buying a minivan later that day to pick up your kids from soccer. In practice, of course, this isn't possible because durable goods are "illiquid"—you can't just simply buy and sell them instantly. There are significant and large transaction costs associated with buying and selling. As soon as you buy a car, it loses a lot of its value. Once Room&Board delivers that table to your home, its resale value is instantly a lot lower than the price you paid for it.

As a consequence, what do we end up doing? We purchase and keep durable goods until they have depreciated sufficiently to make replacement worthwhile. What does this mean? Since we can't buy and sell physical goods seamlessly based on our immediate needs, we're matching our desires to our eventual usage quite imperfectly. Your car is probably newer than what you need when you buy it (although it's fun to have a new car, of course), but probably "too old" for you right before you sell it (most of us don't sell our cars the instant they aren't new enough, we use them until they're a good bit older than our ideal). You also end up "stocking up" on capacity—for instance, a dedicated vehicle on demand in your garage, available exclusively for you 100% of the time. Even though you don't actually need access to that minivan 24 hours a day, owning it is the only way you can use it when you need to pick up your kids from soccer practice. This leads to low utilization.

Consider another example: camping equipment. You might buy a tent, camping stove, and sleeping bags in anticipation of camping with your family. Perhaps, you'll use the equipment once in a lifetime or once a year or once a month in the summer, but the rest of the time, the equipment is lying around, idling capacity in your storage unit or garage.

The introduction of peer-to-peer rental markets changes things to some extent. Now you have simultaneous access to products of differing kinds and ages for short periods of time. In other words, if peer-to-peer rental markets become more ubiquitous, you can rent a tent and other camping equipment rather than own the equipment, and you'll be able to choose which vintage of equipment suits your needs and budget. Or you might remain an owner and rent your tent out when you're not using it. Sure, there are still transaction costs—you have to find what you need and go and pick it up from someone—but these are far lower than the costs associated with buying and selling.

Another change caused by peer-to-peer rental markets is induced in part by differences in what we earn, as well as what we like, across the population, and across time. When people switch to consuming through a peer-to-peer automobile rental market like Getaround, one person's low utilization day can be matched with another person's high utilization day, and the former can become a supplier to the latter. If enough people are members, a point in time when you need money more acutely and are thus inclined to rent out that snazzy Tesla could easily match up with a time when someone else is looking to spend on the enjoyment of driving a cool car. Second, whereas ownership often posed barriers to usage (for example, not everyone can afford to own a car, and only a smaller fraction can afford a good car), a peer-to-peer rental market increases the population that has access to any form of "car usage."

Analogously, peer-to-peer rental markets introduce new levels of adaptability and flexibility that enable people to take new economic risks. If that expensive asset—be it a car or a $1,000 dress—has the potential to be rented out and to become a source of income (not just an object that is simply depleting steadily in value as it sits in your closet or on the street outside your house), you also may start to purchase items of higher value. Simply put, something you can earn money from is something you are likely willing to pay more for. This introduces the possibility that some people might "buy up to rent out." This could increase purchasing in certain luxury markets.

Of course, our model wouldn't be realistic unless it took the varied costs associated with renting into account, on both the supplier and the renter sides. In the case of automobiles, depreciation costs, which represent about 40% of the lifetime costs of ownership, will change. After all, if one rents out one's vehicle in a peer-to-peer market, the increase in mileage decreases the vehicle's resale value and lowers the age at which one might get rid of the vehicle. Similarly, if one rents out one's personal dwelling space on Airbnb, the increase in wear-and-tear could lead to higher maintenance costs, or more rapid depreciation of the property's value. Said another way, goods will be used more intensively, and as a result, they might need to be replaced more actively. So even though there may be fewer owners, these owners will be buying more frequently because, in a sense, they are "spending" the capacity of their asset more rapidly.

This effect of peer-to-peer rental is exacerbated by what economists call "moral hazard." While it may be a stereotype, there's some truth to the fact that renters don't always care for property as well as its owners do. Think about how you treat a rental car relative to how you treat your own car. You don't have a long-term commitment. Further, you are acquainted with your own assets whereas renters may not be, which might cause additional wear and tear from unfamiliarity. Thus, despite a variety of technological advances for monitoring and the emergence of sophisticated online reputation systems, moral hazard cannot be fully mitigated. As a consequence, peer-to-peer rental markets will affect the expected lifetime of an asset and increase transaction costs incurred during resale, both from increased usage and potentially less careful use.

A critical final consideration is convenience. When you own a good, you have access to that good all the time. This user experience, while expensive, is immediate and instantly on-demand. In contrast, when you rent through a peer-to-peer market, you sometimes can't access what you want when you want it. Although the popularity of peer-to-peer rental platforms has been growing rapidly, their reach and liquidity are still limited. There are still barriers to access. A car may not be available for rent when you need it on-demand (numbers from our research on Getaround in 2013 and 2014 suggested that requests were fulfilled about 70% of the time), and correspondingly, there is no guarantee that you will actually get a customer for your Airbnb or Getaround listing when you list it for rental.

The discussion above illustrates why we need systematic economic analysis to uncover the eventual effects of changes induced by the sharing economy. There are lots of different things happening in tandem, and economic models help us understand what happens when all of these changes are occurring in parallel.

For our eventual analysis Fraiberger and I used data from about two years of peer-to-peer car rental demand generously provided to us by Getaround for our research. We combined this with data from a variety of sources—the Bureau of Labor Statistics, the National Household Transportation Survey, and the National Automobile Dealers Association (the folks who provide *Blue Book* values) to "calibrate" our models, which allowed us to create the virtual laboratory of sorts that we use to make projections about the future.

So what did our analysis reveal? How will peer-to-peer rental markets impact the economy over time? Well, we found that ownership and consumption patterns change quite significantly, shifting the population significantly away from ownership. However, even when everyone in the economy has access to peer-to-peer rental markets, the shift away from ownership is gradual. As I noted earlier in this chapter, it seems likely that different existing markets will be differently impacted; the Boston

University study on Airbnb's impact on the hotel industry in Texas revealed that while lower-end hotels have been impacted, higher-end hotels have not. Similarly, we find that a peer-to-peer car rental market lowers prices in the used car market.

Next, and perhaps most saliently, our models project massive gains in consumer surplus, on the order of tens of billions of dollars annually in the United States alone. Most strikingly, lower-income households will enjoy these gains disproportionately. In many ways, in light of our discussion earlier in the chapter, this projection of inclusive growth seems natural. But it helps to understand why a little more precisely.

First, as anticipated, peer-to-peer rental markets "include" lower-income consumers who were unable to drive cars because they couldn't afford to own them. Second, the consumers who switch from owning to renting are more likely to be lower income, because these are the consumers who are attracted to the idea of saving the large annual costs associated with owning (see figure 5.4 for an example of low-to-high-income rental proportions in a San Francisco neighborhood). Higher-income consumers, on the other hand, tend to stay owners for the convenience of immediate access, even those who don't use their cars too much.

Third, the consumers who supply to the rental market are also disproportionately below median income. It's easy to understand why. There's some cost associated with becoming a sharing economy provider, and the potential earnings you anticipate have to be worth your while. Higher-income owners are less likely to take the trouble to become suppliers, while lower-income owners value the additional earnings more. In a survey we did of Getaround suppliers, we also discovered that the casual suppliers—folks earning just a couple of hundred dollars a month—tended to treat these earnings as extra disposable income, while the more active suppliers had started to use this money for basics like rent, groceries, and car payments.[36]

While our projections are for the future, a quick glance at the 2014 patterns of supply and rental on Getaround in San Francisco reveal that there is a much higher concentration of activity in those areas of the city with lower average income levels. This pattern, illustrated in the figure, is consistent with our long-run projections. Overall, our findings strongly suggest that the sharing economy holds great potential to address some of the economic disparities in today's economy, democratizing access to a higher standard of living, and to do so by growing rather than suppressing markets.

Figure 5.4
Lower-income neighborhoods in San Francisco are more active users of peer-to-peer car rental.

I've ended this chapter with a focus that is primarily on the "demand" side of the sharing economy—the economic impacts of increasing capital impact, the variety of products and services on the market, and the ease with which these products and services can be supplied and accessed. In chapter 6, I continue on this theme, examining the key regulatory issues that are raised by new consumption models, with a focus on consumer protection. Also, while discussing the potential for increased empowerment and a shift away from employment and toward entrepreneurship in this chapter, we haven't really looked comprehensively at all the different changes that these economic impacts of crowd-based capitalism might induce in the labor market. This will be the focus of the chapters 7 and 8.

6

The Shifting Landscape of Regulation and Consumer Protection

Societies that get "stuck" embody belief systems and institutions that fail to confront and solve new problems of societal complexity.
—Douglass C. North, from his Nobel Prize Lecture, December 9, 1993

When Airbnb's cofounders were developing their peer-to-peer accommodation platform, hotel regulations were the least of their worries; Chesky, Gebbia, and Blecharczyk were plugging holes in their air mattresses, making breakfast for strangers, writing code, and stuffing and selling boxes of "Obama O's" and "Cap'n McCain's" cereal in order to raise money.

But as Airbnb's growth accelerated—2013 saw them more than double their host numbers—the office of the New York state attorney general Eric T. Schneiderman, fresh on the heels of a successful effort to purge online platforms like Yelp of their fake reviews, turned its attention to providers on platforms like Airbnb. Things came to a head in October 2013, when Schneiderman subpoenaed Airbnb, demanding that the company turn over host data for the more than 225,000 New Yorkers using the platform.

By 2013, cities around the world were grappling with the regulatory challenges raised by sharing economy platforms like Airbnb. The United States Conference of Mayors issued a resolution that summer in support of the economic potential of the sharing economy, and Brooks Rainwater, the director of research at the National League of Cities, was beginning to formulate a broad inquiry into how city governments of varying scale might balance opportunities with the right regulatory approaches. Airbnb was already in negotiations with a wide range of local governments to come up with viable ways to ensure hosts were paying local taxes on income earned. Schneiderman's request for access to the company's host data, however, was about more than taxes.

At the heart of the dispute was a little-known "illegal hotels" law, championed by the state senator Liz Krueger and the state assemblyman Richard Gottfried, which outlawed New Yorkers living in multiple-unit dwellings from subletting their abodes for less than 30 days. This was not an archaic throwback to the days of illegal tenements; the law was passed in 2010, well after Airbnb started to gain traction.

Legally, what this meant was that residents could still be Airbnb hosts so long as they were present in their apartments—there was no restriction on renting out a spare bedroom or couch. Additionally, owners of free-standing homes were not restricted in any way. However, the new law struck at the heart of what was appealing about Airbnb's service in New York to visitors: being able to rent someone's entire apartment in a real city neighborhood for a few days when you visited, rather than paying for a high-priced hotel room in the more commercial and touristy down-town and midtown areas.

There are numerous subtle legal and human aspects that shaped the evolution of Airbnb's interaction with the attorney general. Some of the key events played out as follows. Airbnb responded to the request by issuing a public statement in which the company reiterated its commit-ment to work with, not against, local governments. While acknowledging that there may be a few "bad actors" abusing their platform to operate illegal hotels, Airbnb argued that it was unfair to penalize thousands of hosts acting in good faith in order to stop a small number of illegal hotel operators and slumlords that were never part of the Airbnb vision. In a statement posted on the Airbnb site on October 6, 2013, David Hant-man, their global head of public policy at the time, assured hosts that "in the days ahead, we'll continue our conversations with the attorney gen-eral's office to see if we can work together to support Airbnb hosts and remove bad actors from the Airbnb platform. We are confident we can reach a solution that protects your personal information and cracks down on people who abuse the system."[1]

But by 2013, thousands of New Yorkers had also already invested thousands of dollars in new bedding, towels, and guest room furniture to become the quasi-innkeepers of the city. Thousands of others had also started to rely on Airbnb as an inexpensive way to accommodate out-of-town guests in their own neighborhoods. In many respects, in a very short span of time, Airbnb had become part of New York.

One Airbnb host, known only as Mishelle, started a petition through the newly formed sharing economy collective action platform Peers.org, one she promised to deliver to Albany in person. As part of her petition, she wrote:

The reason this is happening is because of a poorly written law originally designed to stop slumlords from running illegal hotels with dozens of rental apartments. As a New Yorker just trying to pay my bills, I don't understand why they think I'm a slumlord. Let's remove any confusion. I've created a petition to fix the law once and for all. We're not slumlords. After ending a career in the military, I decided to return to school and complete my degree in Public Policy. Renting a room has been instrumental in helping me transition back to civilian life. It's helping me achieve my dreams by providing me with a source of income that makes it possible for me to focus my energy on preparing for a new career where I can help people through better public policy.[2]

Mishelle's "Save Airbnb in New York: Legalize Sharing" campaign eventually received over 200,000 signatures (far beyond the initial goal of 20,000), and the campaign's grassroots feel and widespread publicity added credibility and texture to Airbnb's own responses. To many, the campaign drove home the fact that Airbnb's hosts were not slumlords. As signatures on the petition grew, the face of Airbnb hosts became clearer. Although there were indeed hosts who were renting out multiple units in a hotel-like manner, it turned out that a majority of Airbnb's hosts represented a remarkable cross-section of New Yorkers from all five boroughs and from neighborhoods that rarely benefit from the city's tourist industry, from grandmothers in Harlem to hipsters in Williamsburg to families on Staten Island. Most appeared to be regular people attempting to make a bit of extra money in a city where paying one's rent or mortgage is often a struggle even if one has a full-time job.

Not all of the reaction to the attorney general's action was in support of Airbnb. Although many New Yorkers appreciated the extra money they could make hosting on Airbnb, and others liked the flexible short-term accommodation options it allowed, many others objected because their neighbors were letting strangers into their buildings in a way they worried would make their residential environment feel less safe. Others were concerned that Airbnb rentals might further restrict an already constrained residential rental environment if landlords or enterprising New Yorkers started renting out units on Airbnb instead of allowing them to be rented by long-term residents.[3]

A coalition of legislators and homeowner associations called "Share Better" launched in 2014 to generate grassroots opposition to Airbnb. The organization's website proclaims: "Far from being a harmless service where New York City residents can share their homes with guests to the City, Airbnb enables New York City tenants to break the law and potentially violate their leases, it exacerbates the affordable housing crisis in our neighborhoods, and it poses serious public safety concerns for Airbnb guests, hosts and their neighbors."[4]

In May 2014, Airbnb agreed to hand over anonymized data on its New York City users, but only after a judge ruled that Schneiderman's initial subpoena to access information on hosts across the state was too broad. Shortly thereafter, Schneiderman and his office issued a report, "Airbnb in the City." This report indicated that between January 2010 and June 2014, a significant fraction of Airbnb stays and revenue in New York City were from hosts with three or more properties. (However, additional data shared with me by Airbnb's New York City Manager Wrede Petersmeyer in December 2015 indicates that the fraction of stays and revenue from hosts with three of more properties was significantly lower between November 2014 and November 2015. The same data has been shared with city council members and the press.)

After the report was issued, Airbnb, upon request of the attorney general, sent a summary of housing laws to its New York City hosts. For example, they let hosts know that it is "illegal to host paying guests for less than 30 days unless a permanent resident of the apartment (like the host or the host's roommate) also stays in the apartment during the guest's stay."[5] The summary also advised New York City hosts to consult their own lawyers in order to determine the legality of their specific rentals.

The evolving situation involving Airbnb and New York State provides an interesting microcosm of many of the regulatory issues I discuss in this chapter. State and city government resistance to Airbnb in the United States, both in New York and beyond, persists as I am writing this book. In mid-2015, San Francisco's city authorities released a study suggesting that Airbnb was reducing affordable rental housing significantly. Airbnb responded with its own study by Anita Roth suggesting the impact was negligible. (My own view, which I discussed in a *New York Times* op-ed, is that, as of 2015, factors like rent control and population growth are the primary contributors to the shortage of affordable rental housing in San Francisco.) The level of acrimony toward Airbnb from the hotel industry is captured well by the statements made by Vanessa Sinders, Senior Vice President and Head of Government Affairs of the American Hotel and Lodging Association (AHLA), at a 2015 Federal Trade Commission meeting to discuss the sharing economy, where she noted: "Right now, there is an unlevel [sic] playing field that is compromising consumer safety, endangering the character and security of residential neighborhoods across the country, and changing the housing market in some negative ways." In summarizing some of the opposition to Airbnb, she then went on to say "Airbnb is making a substantial amount of its revenue off of illegal hotels and those that are doing this as a business. These are not mom-and-pops. ... These are not students making ends meet. They are rogue commercial interests."[6]

These ongoing conflicts tell us how complicated things can get when the impact of digital technology moves out of virtual space and into real physical spaces. The attorney general's and AHLA's objections to Airbnb highlight the extent to which regulations—in this case, the regulations that govern the hotel industry, as well as housing in New York City—struggle to accommodate the complexity of the sharing economy. True, there are a handful of bad actors who convert apartments into full-time hotels using the platform. And, much like the power sellers of eBay, they may have accelerated the platform's early growth, although Airbnb has generally been publicly opposed to this practice. David Hantman, Airbnb's global head of public policy at the time, spoke at the same Federal Trade Commission meeting and clarified the company's position: "We are also not talking about rogue hotels, or defending rogue hotels, or a law passed to do anything other than punish rogue hotels. We are talking about trying to get a law that allows people to do this once in while, and we can't get that done."[7]

Of course, Airbnb is just one of many peer-to-peer platforms whose activities create new regulatory challenges. Uber and Lyft have faced regulatory pushback in a wide variety of cities looking to enforce taxi licensing laws. In particular, given its global footprint, Uber's regulatory battles and their outcomes have been especially intense and varied. In 2015, its low-cost UberPop service has been banned in Paris and Berlin, and the platform shut down its entire service in Spain at the end of 2014, its UberX service in Seoul in March 2015, and its entire service in New York's East Hampton in June 2015. In April 2015, Dutch investigators launched a criminal investigation into Uber for providing "illegal taxi service" in violation of a court order. Meanwhile, the Brussels mobility minister has set out a plan to legalize Uber in Belgium by 2016, while in the United States, California and Virginia have enacted new laws legalizing Uber.

Etsy has a different yet equally important set of challenges. Some Etsy makers enter the platform with well-established businesses. But, similar to most Airbnb hosts, the majority of Etsy sellers open their storefronts on the site as a hobby, investing only a bit of extra time and energy with the desire to make some spare cash. Naturally, these micro-entrepreneurs are not equipped to deal with different federal and state industry regulations and may not even be aware that these regulations exist. It also seems likely that if most of the micro-entrepreneurs who populate peer-to-peer platforms like Airbnb and Etsy were aware of industry regulations, they may never have pursued their small business ideas in the first place. Regulations, therefore, might create standards that sometimes make sense on a large scale but prove insurmountable to on a small scale.

Should the microentrepreneurs using peer-to-peer platforms—for example, someone selling handcrafted toys on Etsy or someone renting out their spare room on Airbnb—be held to the same standards as a major toy manufacturer like Mattel or a major hotel chain like Hilton? If so, who should be held accountable for meeting these regulations—the owners of the platforms, the microentrepreneurs using the platforms, or both? Is there a way to build trust and protect consumers while not placing insurmountable restrictions on microentrepreneurs?

Compared to their predecessors like Google and Facebook, this new generation of platforms has had to gain sophistication with government relations very rapidly in order to survive. Some of the methods we've seen them use are quite novel and, in a sense, crowd-based in their own right. For example, in July 2015, Uber engineered a sophisticated campaign in New York City to fight a proposed cap on their provider numbers that was supported by Mayor Bill de Blasio. A key part of the campaign was the addition of a "de Blasio" button to their app, which illustrated, perhaps in a nonscientific way, how a customer's wait time might be altered by the proposed cap (see figure 6.1). (Uber won that battle.)

Similarly, in November 2015, Airbnb announced that it would facilitate the formation of a new kind of "guild," launching a campaign that would create 100 home sharing clubs in 100 cities that could better channel the political power of its over 4 million users. The emergence of ways in which the consumer voice can be rapidly aggregated and harnessed as a force in a regulatory debate—a manifestation of the "new power" Jeremy Heimans and Henry Timms explain so compellingly in their December 2014 *Harvard Business Review* article—seems like a good development in general, since, in a sense, it gives consumers a seat at the regulatory table alongside the corporate lobbyists, government officials, and labor collectives.[8]

In parallel, many platforms have injected expert and experienced talent with into the mix quite early, ranging from David Plouffe and Ashwini Chhabra at Uber, David Hantman and Chris Lehane at Airbnb, and David Estrada and Joseph Okpaku at Lyft to Althea Erickson at Etsy and Padden Murphy at Getaround. The platforms also make active use of high-powered lobbyists like Bradley Tusk and James Capalino. In many

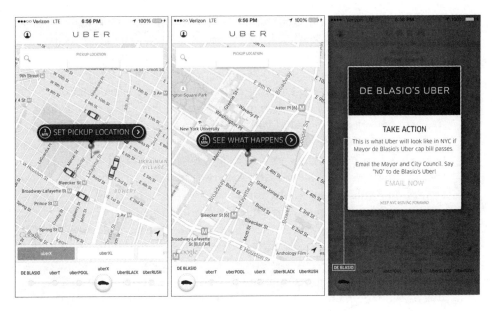

Figure 6.1
The "de Blasio" button, part of 2015 Uber campaign to fight a proposed cap on providers.

ways, the government stakeholders are in favor of this approach, because, as one city official put it during a 2015 San Francisco conversation I participated in, "It's so much easier to have a conversation with someone who actually understands how government works."

But why is this level of expertise necessary? *Because the sharing economy creates new ways of providing familiar services that are traditionally often highly regulated, regulatory conflict is to be expected.* The level of importance being paid by government to this conflict is captured well by the fact that in May 2015, two US representatives, Eric Swalwell (D-CA) and Darrell Issa (R-CA), founded a bipartisan Sharing Economy Caucus to facilitate discussion leading to congressional action, a caucus that had numerous members of Congress interested and engaged by the end of 2015.

How do we then create a robust regulatory infrastructure that prepares us for a commercial world in which the lines between personal and professional are blurring, in which the scale of providers varies dramatically, from multibillion dollar hotel chains to occasional Airbnb hosts, in a way that preserves individual freedom, consumer safety, doesn't let the 6% harm the 94%, and doesn't impose a crippling burden on city and state governments?

To answer this complex question, I will argue in this chapter that regulation, often interwoven with the provision of trust, doesn't always have to originate with the government. In other words, history reveals that regulation can take on myriad forms, governmental and otherwise. I will give you a feel for how trust in economic exchange has evolved over time, why regulations matter, and how the sharing economy poses a challenge to existing regulatory models. I will also explain three emerging models—peer regulation, self-regulatory organizations, and delegated regulation through data. I believe these models hold the most promise for a regulatory future that is best aligned with society's interests.

Eventually, peer-to-peer platforms may provide a basis upon which society can develop more rational, ethical, and participatory models of regulation—models in which users and providers are equally invested and responsible for enacting the regulations in question. Despite some regulators' fears, the sharing economy may not result in the decline of regulation but rather in its opposite: both an increase and a diversification of regulation. But what regulation looks like is also bound to change.

Why Regulation Still Matters

We hear the word "regulation" a lot (you've seen it over a dozen times in this chapter already), and it often conjures up images of government bureaucracy slowing progress. But it is important to understand that overall, the world is a safer and more reliable place because regulations exist. Generally, regulations are instruments used to implement social and economic policy objectives. Expressed another way, they are legal and administrative mechanisms designed to encourage economic activity. Why do we need these mechanisms? Because often, market practices produce inefficient, inequitable, or insufficient outcomes. Economists refer to this as "market failure." Regulations are implemented to correct market failure. For example, if monopolization of a market by one firm raises prices in a way that harms consumers, regulatory action may correct this by supporting new competition and in turn diversifying the market. Other more common motivations for regulation include protecting consumers from potentially harmful corporate actions, and ensuring public safety.

As an economist, I take a specific view on the purpose of regulation, one that others may find narrow. This chapter will therefore not do justice to the rich body of competing theories of regulation, ranging from the substantive and political procedural approaches to alternative private interest theories and a variety of institutionalist perspectives.[9] I will instead focus on the "regulation as an intervention to correct market failure" approach, viewing the challenges raised by the sharing economy through this lens.

As platforms like Airbnb, Lyft, Getaround, and Etsy disrupt old economic systems rooted in firm-to-consumer interactions and individual ownership, we are witnessing myriad regulatory issues. These issues, discussed in my 2015 *University of Chicago Law Review* paper that I coauthored with Molly Cohen, include new solutions to old forms of information asymmetry, new and old "externalities," and an increasingly blurred boundary between professional and personal modes of exchange.[10]

Information Asymmetry: When One Party Knows More than the Other
Most forms of peer-to-peer exchange are characterized by asymmetric information—knowledge relevant to the intended exchange that is possessed by one trading party but not by the other: for example, a passenger who enters a taxicab may not know the qualifications or intentions of its driver, or a hotelier knows more about the quality of her short-term accommodation than a potential guest does. Similarly, a borrower knows more about her creditworthiness than a lender does. These and other forms of information asymmetry can lead to a lower level of economic activity than society might find desirable. Part of this could be due to uncertainty about quality—I'm not going to get into a taxi unless I'm sure the driver is reliable and won't rip me off. Or information asymmetry can lead to the situation of "adverse selection": if there's no good way of distinguishing between lower and higher quality providers, then a customer is likely to be willing to pay, on average, a price commensurate with the value they'd get from an average quality provider. Noticing this, the higher quality providers will be reluctant to transact, since they're not getting a fair price for the higher value they deliver. This lowers the average quality in the market, further lowering the willingness of customers to pay, inducing further unwillingness to transact, and so on, until only the lowest quality providers are left, and the market either unravels, or remains, like Craigslist, on the fringes of the economy.

Furthermore, information asymmetry can also lead to "moral hazard"—because parties' imperfect information limits their ability to contract, one trading partner might display behavior that is less careful (e.g., reckless driving), of lower effort (e.g., lower levels of cleanliness), or somehow riskier than the partner otherwise would have chosen.

Prior to the emergence of Internet-enabled marketplaces, the only way to make peer-to-peer economic exchange safe was to embed the exchange into a trusting local community (a village, a family, a suburban neighborhood), or to look to the government or some other third-party certifying body to address these forms of information asymmetry. For example, safety concerns about drivers and information asymmetries about the distance or cost of a ride were alleviated in part through driver screening and metered fares by taxicab regulatory agencies.

Now, however, the mere existence of sharing economy platforms as third parties mediating these transactions means that we may have a range of new solutions to different forms of market failure. The eventual commercial success of a sharing economy platform is affected by the ability of its participants to engage in exchange. Thus, platforms have a natural incentive to try and reduce information failure that might deter people from using their services. For example, as I discussed in chapter 2, the many facets of Airbnb's online trust infrastructure allows their guests to learn about the quality of hosts from prior guests, gain evidence of a host's "social capital" via links to user profiles on platforms like Facebook and LinkedIn, and view digitally verified government IDs of providers. And this intervention doesn't end with the use of digital reputation systems. Lyft, independent of any regulatory requirements, conducts in-person driver screenings that also include criminal background checks and an assessment of driving history. Similarly, as of July 2013, Airbnb employed 300 people in its customer-service unit, and 50 of them were dedicated to promoting trust and safety.

Externalities: When Others Bear the Consequences of My Actions

The choices of a buyer or provider in a peer-to-peer transaction may impose costs on (or result in benefits to) others. These "externalities," the costs and consequences an individual's choices impose on others, may not be taken into account when the individual makes his or her choices. Sometimes these are positive spillovers analogous to the network effects I discussed in chapter 5. For instance, my adoption of Facebook makes it more valuable to my friends, and the Airbnb guests in a residential neighborhood help its local restaurants. But sometimes these spillovers are negative. The use of coal by a factory might reduce its costs but causes environmental damage. An additional taxicab on the road creates congestion and lengthens travel times for other drivers. A noisy Airbnb guest in an apartment building might impose costs on the other residents.

Keeping track of these externalities is challenging. Airbnb rentals are much more difficult to track than hotel rooms (e.g., a specific neighborhood may suddenly become home to a high concentration of Airbnb rentals but the availability of these rentals may fluctuate at different times of year), so it can be difficult for a government regulator to capture the costs and consequences in question, whether they be negative or positive.

Furthermore, sometimes the set of people affected by one's actions is local (the people in the neighboring building aren't affected by a noisy Airbnb guest), while in other cases the impacts may be more global, as in the case of pollution. This is an important point, one I return to later in the chapter.

Blurring of Boundaries between the Personal and the Professional

We have always been free to lend our apartments to friends and family, pick up others we know from the airport, loan money to friends starting new businesses, or make meals for friends. These are considered "personal" undertakings, unlike running a hotel, driving a taxicab, being a professional investor, or running a restaurant, and we undertake them having none of the additional oversight, licensing, screening, taxation, or training expected of providers who conduct these activities as a full-time occupation. This balance seemed reasonable when peer-to-peer exchange remained personal, and even when it was commercial but on the fringes, mediated by personal networks and sites like Craigslist. However, today's sharing platforms have brought these informal exchanges into the mainstream economy, creating service providers who are "in between" personal and professional—like Airbnb hosts who rent out their apartments when they travel, or Lyft drivers who transport people commercially for a few hours a week.

This blurring of lines raises a number of new societal challenges. First, it seems sensible to balance the lower "total" risks to consumers posed by part-time providers with judiciously designed safeguards. After all, most Airbnb hosts are not professional hoteliers, a large percentage of Lyft and Uber drivers are active on the platform fewer than 15 hours per week, and only one-fifth of Etsy sellers considers their Etsy business a full-time job. Applying a regulatory regime developed for full-time or large-scale professional providers to smaller, semiprofessional providers could stifle grassroots innovation. But absent any safeguards whatsoever, new forms of market failure may occur as a consequence of the nonprofessional nature of supply.

Moreover, this blurring of lines can either alleviate or exacerbate issues like discrimination based on ethnicity. Someone who hosts on Airbnb might feel it is okay to turn away guests of a particular ethnicity with the logic of "this is my space and I'm free to do what I want with it." Of course, such behavior is illegal, and hotels know this. But because the peer-to-peer activity is mediated by a platform now, rather than occurring in the more anonymous "physical world," we also have new opportunities to right old wrongs. For example, if a particular yellow cab in New York systematically doesn't pick up passengers of a particular ethnicity, its likely to go unnoticed; on the other hand, if a Lyft driver does the same, the ensuing data trail might make it relatively easy to spot and correct.

The Evolution of Regulation: Trust, Institutions, and Brands

Although it seems like some forms of market failure are unique to the sharing economy, most are simply characteristic of the services that are now provided using a peer-to-peer platform, and in the industrial era were solved in part by government-led solutions. Zoning has ensured that noisy hotel guests or industrial plants don't disrupt quiet residential neighborhoods. Taxicab metering prevented cabbies from ripping off passengers.

But could it be that government regulations are not always the best way to regulate peer-to-peer platforms? Can we instead imagine a regulatory system that works *with* rather than against peer-to-peer platforms? In the context of this question, it is important to bear in mind that industry regulations, however entrenched they may appear today, are part of an evolving system—one that has an eclectic history.

Regulations aimed at addressing market failure have often sought to facilitate some form of trust. Some old forms of trust are being reborn through digital infrastructures in a way that might reduce the need for government intervention, and perhaps in a way that suggests we return to methods that predated governmental intervention. Here, it is useful to turn back to consider a couple of key historical examples.

A Historical Example: The Maghribi Traders

We start with the practices of the Maghribi traders who played a leading role in world trade in the 11th century. As Avner Greif illustrates in his fascinating study of medieval trade practices in the Mediterranean, competitive advantage in trade at the time was contingent on the ability of traders to ship goods without traveling with them.[11] If you could send goods but not deliver them in person, your profit would be higher. There was a key obstacle, however. In order for this model to work, you needed to establish a relationship with an overseas agent—someone you trusted enough to accept and distribute the goods on the other end of the journey and to not rip you off in the process.

Bear in mind that that in the 11th century, the possibility for corruption was significant. If your goods were lost or damaged at sea, it might take months to find out what happened, and in some cases you would probably never discover the fate of your merchandise at all. Also, at the time, money exchanged was passed from hand to hand—a practice that exacerbated opportunities for loss, since it was easier for overseas agents to accept goods, sell them, and simply claim they never arrived while pocketing all the proceeds.

As Greif notes, "In the eleventh century, the legal system failed to provide a framework within which agency relations could be organized. The court was usually unable to verify agents' claims and actions or to track down an agent who had emigrated."[12]

In an age of limited communication, weak legal systems, and no formal banking, how did people establish trust across long distances? What provisions of trust did these early merchants establish to ensure that trade could expand without an equally significant expansion of corruption? Grief suggests that a combination of reputation and self-interested community created the trust provisions that would govern the behavior of overseas agents.

A first part of the trust system involved paying agents a wage greater than any available to them elsewhere (i.e., a "premium"). The premium had distinct advantages. While agents might make money in the short run by stealing from merchants, they might not profit in the long run if the dishonest behavior led to a loss of future opportunities.

A second critical part of the Maghribi trust system was the formation of coalitions of merchants and agents; coalition members who were merchants agreed to not employ agents who had already been caught stealing from other coalition members. The presence of the coalition gave the incentive some teeth. As Greif observes: "Given a premium and the implicit contract, a dishonest agent can earn a short-run gain by cheating while an honest agent will earn a long-run gain by being paid a premium. An agent acquires the reputation of an honest agent if it is known that the long-run gain is not less than the short-run gain. The agent cannot increase his lifetime utility by cheating. The merchant will offer the agent an *optimal premium*—the lowest cost premium for which the long-run gain is not less than the short-run gain."[13]

In other words, the relationships that created advantages for successful traders were built on community trust, rather than on trust created by the involvement of government. With no government or legal support, and long before the digital mechanisms available to eBay created analogous solutions in our time, Mediterranean merchants found a viable solution to a serious problem of trust across geographic and cultural boundaries that involved community enforcement. Indeed, as Greif observes, historical records of trade from the period reveal few documented cases of corruption.

In many respects, this medieval trading community holds important lessons for the 21st-century sharing economy. In both cases, we are faced with the challenge of establishing trust provisions in markets that stretch across geographic and cultural boundaries. In the Middle Ages, merchants established trust by leveraging two factors. First, trust was built by creating a situation where one's *reputation mattered* (overseas agents known for corruption would over time fail to profit). Second, trust was built by creating *communities of shared interest* that connected reputation to economic self-interest (the formation of merchant coalitions who adopted common hiring policies and penalties meant corrupt overseas agents had more to lose).

Economic Institutions and Brand-Based Trust

A natural question arises, of course, after considering the vignette about the Maghribi traders: What other ways of regulating exchange have evolved since medieval times, and what their role is in the sharing economy? I will confine myself to a few key observations I believe are pertinent.

Much of human interaction is structured by constraints of our own devising. We call these constraints *institutions*. As the Nobel Prize–winning economist Douglass North notes, some of these are formal constraints like rules, laws, and constitutions, while others are informal constraints like norms of behavior. Collectively, they form what North calls the "rules of the game" of a society.[14] The property rights we take for granted in most modern economies today (and which have their roots in English common law) are an example of an institution.

It would seem fairly logical that institutions play an important role in facilitating economic development. (For contrasting recent perspectives on this connection, I refer you to books by the MIT economists Daron Acemoglu and James Robinson, and by the NYU Stern economist Peter Blair Henry.[15]) In general, these "rules of the game" are tremendously empowering, because they significantly expand trade possibilities. In the specific case of property rights, North and his colleague Barry Weingast note that "The more likely it is that the sovereign will alter property rights for his or her own benefit, the lower the expected returns from investment and the lower in turn the incentive to invest."[16] Similarly, the emergence of banks eased economic exchange between strangers who do not now need to share any trust-facilitating social ties.

If institutions followed communities and reputation as the basis for trust, why would we want to return to the system these new structures supplanted? Well, relying on contracts and property rights requires a reasonable level of scale for each transaction. Writing a contract is costly. So is hiring a lawyer. This makes sense when you are a business buying millions of dollars of parts. For a two-night stay in Paris, it seems like excessive overhead.

So how have we solved the trust problem for the myriad everyday transactions we engage in today? Think about each of these transactions in your personal experience. Chances are they are touched by one of both of two kinds of "institutions"—either a government regulator or a corporate brand—and you rely on one or both to establish trust.

Consider the example of food safety, one of the earliest instances (dating to ancient times) of systematic government intervention.[17] You trust that the meat you buy is safe in the US because of the existence of the FDA. But you'd also likely trust the safety of a brand you recognize rather than one you don't. You might feel safer drinking a Coke in a country whose food safety laws you aren't clear about because you trust the brand.

Similarly, you might be comfortable letting your kids ride the roller coasters at Six Flags, but you might hesitate to let them enjoy the same ride at an unbranded theme park on the side of the highway, even though the government regulations are the same in both situations.

This combination of government regulatory agencies and the brands that, pursuing a long-run profit motive, comply with these regulations and also invest in providing a consistently high quality and safe experience, are the foundation of trust in most Western economies today. And the importance of brand cannot be underestimated in today's sharing economy. We are still a population that places its faith in brand names: platforms like Airbnb, Lyft, and Uber understand this; eBay understood this when they created Power Sellers; and BlaBlaCar understands this when they place an explicit certification of trust derived from platform activity on a driver. It is cognitively challenging to process lots of information before deciding on a transaction. A recognizable brand eases this burden tremendously.

So why might we need a different trust infrastructure to emerge for the sharing economy? Well, because transferring the political and economic rules of Western market economies to market economies in the developing world has neither proven viable nor desirable, and in much the same way, transferring the political and economic rules of the industrial economy to the sharing economy is an endeavor that should be approached with some deliberation. After all, history suggests that different types of economies require different approaches to regulation. As North observes, history has also taught us at least two other important lessons. First, he notes: "While the rules may be changed overnight, the informal norms usually change only gradually. Since it is the norms that provide 'legitimacy' to a set of rules, revolutionary change is never as revolutionary as its supporters desire, and performance will be different than anticipated." Second, he notes: "Economies that adopt the formal rules of another economy will have very different performance characteristics than the first economy because of different informal norms and enforcement."[18]

Put differently, history suggests that it is neither possible nor economically viable to simply adopt existing rules and apply them to a new economy. The challenge, then, is to determine what comes next. After all, if different economies require different models of regulation, what model or models should we develop for the emerging sharing economy? Or is the genesis of the solution already taking shape on the peer-to-peer platforms in question?

Where the Sharing Economy Is Taking Regulation

Adam Thierer of George Mason University believes that the right philosophy for regulating the sharing economy is one that rejects the idea that creators of new technologies seek permission from public officials before taking their services to market. Rather, Thierer writes: "The other vision can be labeled 'permissionless innovation.' It refers to the notion that experimentation with new technologies and business models should generally be permitted by default. Unless a compelling case can be made that a new invention will bring serious harm to society, innovation should be allowed to continue unabated and problems, if they develop at all, can be addressed later."[19]

Similarly, noting that "sharing economy practices challenge regulation on a daily basis," the Yale University legal scholar Sofia Ranchordàs argues that one should approach regulations for the sharing economy from an "innovation law perspective" so long as the activities that are being conducted do in fact fall under a reasonable definition of innovation. The "experimental" nature of innovation, Ranchordàs highlights, is of particular importance: "While innovation is an evolving and a trial and error process, regulation is traditionally characterized by the stability and continuity of rules. Therefore, regulators often delay innovation by fitting innovative services in existing legal categories and failing to update the extant legal framework to the current state of technology." As Ranchordàs puts it, "Can you share and innovate by the book? You can, but first someone has to write the book."[20]

In this section, I discuss some issues central to shaping this new "book" of regulations. As new business models conflict with the rules governing older ways of providing familiar services, we have already, de facto, returned to a model of trust built on community consensus and gained reputation. As April Rinne points out in her early (2012) analysis that draws parallels between the sharing economy and microfinance, "In microfinance, your reputation substitutes for credit history (because the latter doesn't exist)." She further notes, "You're banking on an individual's trustworthiness within society, rather than her material assets, as the best indicator of whether she can and will repay a loan. As a result, social standing among peers—especially within tight-knit communities—is built over time and reigns supreme. Similarly, in the sharing economy this kind of social fabric and "trust barometer" can be created thanks to new technologies."[21]

This reliance on digitally created community trust—and in particular, user-generated reviews—is not simply a feature of peer-to-peer platforms like Airbnb or eBay but has already permeated the economy at a larger scale. My NYU Stern colleagues Anindya Ghose and Panagiotis Ipeirotis have established, in a series of research studies, how user-generated reviews on Amazon play a critical role in shaping economic outcomes.[22]

Such online user-generated reviews can also affect brick-and-mortar businesses. In the past, one might have chosen a restaurant based on its Zagat ratings but in the 21st century, Yelp has eclipsed Zagat. And customers are not the only ones to use such reviews. At the 2013 United States Conference of Mayors, Greg Fisher, the mayor of Louisville, described to me how the city's department of health uses Yelp as a leading indicator to trace food-borne illnesses, sending health inspectors to restaurants where they see Yelp accounts of people falling sick. This kind of crowd-based monitoring can complement traditional regulation, especially when reputation and public opinion are effective catalysts for detecting deficiencies in, and inducing enforcement of, regulations already on the books.[23]

Besides, on peer-to-peer platforms, user-generated reviews are but one of many signals about a potential provider that a potential customer gets. Furthermore, they are tightly integrated within a platform built by a third-party institution that also mediates the eventual transactions. This introduces the possibility that someone other than the government can be called on either to define or enforce the rules.

Relying on user reviews and other digital signals means trusting platforms that naturally profit from the exchanges in question. But doesn't this create a conflict of interest? Not always. Because the reputation of a platform is directly related to the quality of the transactions it helps mediate—much like the reputation and profitability of the brands we trust are tied to their commitment to high quality and sufficient safety—the self-interest of the platform is often aligned with that of society, and the platform is thus often invested in ensuring that the exchanges it facilitates do not succumb to market failure.

The trick is to identify those dimensions of risk where the incentives of the platform and the incentives of society (or of consumer protection) don't diverge, and those where the risk of divergence exists. For example, ensuring that hosts advertise their quality accurately seems well aligned with Airbnb's profit motive, while ensuring that guests do not make too much noise when staying in an Airbnb might be less aligned.

Moving to the next point, peer-to-peer platforms often offer a greater variety of transactions than traditional industrial-economy providers. This stems from the blurring of personal and professional practices and, as I discuss in chapter 7 on the future of work, the rise of the new generalists. For example, before platforms like Airbnb existed, travelers had limited choices. With Airbnb and similar platforms, the entire landscape of short-term rentals has changed. From a regulation perspective, this poses new and difficult challenges. Should someone be able to rent out a hammock? What risks are posed by renting out a tree house? Are there nationally recognized safety standards governing such structures? If so, how does one enforce them? In other words, peer-to-peer platforms make one-size-fits-all solutions more difficult, if not impossible, to execute using a government-only approach.

Finally, and on a related point, because the vast majority of peer-to-peer providers are either moonlighting (e.g., a lawyer renting out a cottages on Airbnb or an actor driving a Lyft on a part-time basis) or at least working independently, the scale is often quite small, as discussed in chapter 5. For example, over 90% of Airbnb hosts are occasional hosts, two thirds of Lyft drivers drive less than 15 hours a week,

EatWith or Feastly hosts prepare far fewer meals than a restaurant, and most Etsy sellers work on a scale that will never come close to competing with large-scale manufacturers producing comparable products.

Is it reasonable to hold these occasional providers to the same standard as a commercial provider? Of course it is, you might say, safety is safety, and we can't compromise on it. But the truth is, we compromise already, and we always have compromised. Regulations are important because they provide necessary protections—they are in the interest of the common good—but we also know that regulations come at a cost to society. For example, restaurant inspections and kitchen hygiene standards add to the costs of both the provider and the government. Perfect food safety could be accomplished by stationing an inspector full-time in every restaurant to inspect every item of food. But such a system would simply be too expensive. The taxes needed to support this kind of system would be really high. Restaurant food would become really costly (and perhaps a little creepy), and in this extreme and fabricated scenario, the industry would collapse.

This is why we make tradeoffs—New York City, for instance, only sends inspectors into restaurants from time to time, balancing the cost of someone falling sick with the cost of running the inspection infrastructure. Perhaps it is beneficial to focus government resources on higher-volume restaurants, since the probability of and cost of contaminated food for these establishments is higher for society.

To take this argument to its conclusion: if you are now dealing not with a restaurant feeding thousands of people a month, but with a supper club that hosts half a dozen dinners a month, perhaps the intensity of health inspection needs to shift as well. Expecting anyone who hosts dinners on VizEat, EatWith, or Feastly to have a kitchen that measures up to city health codes isn't just impractical in a way that will kill the nascent industry of shared home-provided meals; it isn't consistent with the way in which we have historically made the tradeoff between the cost of something going wrong and the cost of preventing it from happening. We may need what SideCar CEO Sunil Paul calls "safe harbors" for the sharing economy. And the continued presence of the health regulator provides an entity of last recourse in case something goes wrong, something that, as I discussed in a *TechCrunch* interview in 2012, is always an important role for the government.[24]

So where do we stand? We clearly don't want to abandon regulations entirely. However, there are a wide variety of regulatory "entities" that

Figure 6.2
The many facets of trust in the sharing economy.

have governed trust, safety, and the prevention of market failure in the past, and in our economy today. Government regulatory entities are just one in a spectrum of forces that facilitate trust. (See figure 6.2 for other examples.) For the sharing economy, the regulatory frameworks we develop need to be well suited for the unique aspects of exchange they facilitate. The scale, variety and technology are different. There is little value in trying to retrofit old regulatory regimes onto the new models.

Future Regulatory Models

As I've emphasized throughout the chapter, it seems inevitable that over time new regulations and even new models of regulation will emerge—and inevitable as well that while we try in vain to retrofit existing government rules developed for an industrial economy for the sharing economy, we will have many formal and informal regulatory systems operating simultaneously. Over time, the idea that peer-to-peer platforms are eroding regulations may prove entirely unfounded.

But as the number of independent commercial providers scales well into the millions in many industries, clinging to existing forms of government enforcement would create an immense regulatory burden. In contrast, a few new forms of regulation hold particular promise in shifting much of this burden to other stakeholders. Three of these models are *peer regulation*, *self-regulatory organizations*, and *delegated regulation through data*.

Peer Regulation

The idea of peer regulation can conjure up images of a dystopian world where everyone's neighbor is a potential spy. But if you think about it a little, peer regulation can represent an equitable way to regulate from within, one that is cost-efficient for society and leverages learning-by-doing in a way that is well suited to the scale of peer-to-peer. The equitable aspect of regulation, in part, has to do with the difference between inspectors masquerading as peers (which might be thought of as peer monitoring), and peers creating standards for each other. To appreciate the difference, consider the following two examples.

In Berlin, anyone can walk on to a bus or subway without paying. To ensure that people do pay, however, the system also employs plain-clothed inspectors of all ages. What this means is that on Berlin's bus and subway system, everyone from the elderly woman sitting across from you to the guy who looks like he plays in a punk band is a potential regulator. While tourists often risk riding on Berlin's subway for free, most Berliners would never dare take a free ride and risk a 40 euro fine and, worse yet, the humiliation of begin dragged off the subway by someone who looks like a kindly grandmother or barista from the local coffee shop. The citizens who choose to work as inspectors gain a basic wage and commission for issuing fines. Citizens who don't work as inspectors are more likely to always have proof of fare because they understand that everyone is a potential inspector.

While the system works, however, is it not really a method of peer regulation. After all, the city's transportation commission, not peers, are making the rules and setting the fines and simply using people who look like peers to carry out the regulatory work.

By contrast, consider the type of self-regulation that is built into a platform like Airbnb. While there are no official inspectors on the platform, the platform's review system, which now includes two layers of reviews (public reviews that are visible to other travelers and private reviews that are only visible to hosts), does serve a regulatory function. If a rental is consistently subpar, the reviews will indicate a problem. However, the platform, which now also welcomes private reviews, is more generative than most rating systems. Visitors have the option of supporting a host by giving them a high review but still offering tips, suggestions, and critiques privately. In theory, this means that new hosts can continue to grow their microbusinesses while gaining feedback that will help them improve the service they are offering over time. And the entire system is driven by peers and with peers' best interest in mind. In short, in the absence of suitable government regulations as Airbnb emerged, peers set standards and worked collectively to ensure they were met.

An advantage of this model is that no single benchmark needs to apply to every rental. If someone is renting out a sofa in an artist studio for $50 per night, their visitors will likely be different than the visitors who opt to rent out a luxury condo in a doorman building for $400 per night. The market doesn't demand that the standards applied to the sofa in the artist studio be on par with the standards applied to the luxury condo. Correspondingly, the "regulators"—the peers opting to stay in these very different types of spaces—are also different. In essence, platforms can support myriad context- and customer-specific standards within a single regulatory framework.

One might consider taking this form of peer regulation up a notch with a blend of the two systems we have just discussed—by formalizing a role for expert providers to play in making sure that new or novice providers are up to snuff. I discuss this kind of formalized "peer regulation" as one example of a more general system, a self-regulatory organization.

Self-Regulatory Organizations

Think about a different form of peer regulation—partnership between a city health regulatory agency and a consortium of social dining platforms. This hypothetical consortium might creates a system where active providers on these platforms volunteer to become some combination of "educators" and "inspectors" in exchange for an incentive provided by the platforms, perhaps receiving some training from government health inspectors and with some oversight of standards by the government. The expert providers will likely have better "close to the ground" information and knowledge than the government health inspectors, the platforms can benefit from an expansion of their business without the threat of regulatory action, and the system experiences an overall increase in safety and quality, while weeding out those few providers who probably shouldn't be on the platform in the first place. This example is one instance of what I'd call a *self-regulatory organization* (SRO).

Given its history and diversity, it not surprising that the term "self-regulation" defies simple definition or categorization. But a key clarification is in order: *a self-regulatory organization is not the same as the absence of regulation, or an entity policing itself.* Rather, it is the defining, the enforcing, or both, of regulation by parties other than the government. Self-regulatory systems vary widely based on their levels of voluntariness, accountability, enforcement, and governmental intervention, but generally SROs are privately run with limited governmental involvement. Unlike trade organizations, which promote the well-being of an industry, SROs are meant to police an industry by formulating regimes of collective rulemaking in which entities come together to develop, monitor, and, at times, enforce standards to govern the behavior of members.

Much like the merchant communities described in Greif's account of the Maghribi traders, other formal merchant and craft guilds emerged in medieval times, imposing strict rules regarding their members' wages, tools, technology, quality, and prices. These early examples of communal self-regulation of public goods are encouraging because they suggest that self-regulation is a natural part of economic development. Today, SROs continue to exist but are more often associated with professions than trades. The American Medical Association, the National Association of Realtors, and bar associations serve to regulate, respectively, doctors, realtors, and lawyers. These modern SROs have significant enforcement and compliance capabilities and even quasijudicial authority due to their ability to audit and penalize members. SROs in the 21st century span a range of other industries, from financial services and nuclear power to chemicals and cotton.[25]

The success of SROs has been mixed. As Cohen and I discuss at length in our 2015 paper, there have been some notable successes, like the Institute of Nuclear Power Operations (INPO), and some perceived failures, like the Financial Industry Regulator Authority (FINRA), although, in considering whether FINRA is a success, one might argue that after more than 80 years of self-regulation, US capital markets are still among the most efficient in the world.

Looking through a range of examples, Cohen and I identify four factors that may prove integral to establishing workable SROs within the sharing economy. First, an SRO must establish credibility early on through its performance. Second, self-regulatory actors must demonstrate strong enforcement capabilities. Third, SROs must be perceived as legitimate and independent. And finally, an SRO must take advantage of participants' reputational concerns and social capital.[26]

The state of California has pioneered a self-regulatory approach for one sector of the sharing economy, through the creation of Transportation Network Companies (TNCs) in 2013. As described in detail by Catherine Sandoval, the commissioner of the California Public Utilities

Commission (CPUC), at the 2015 Federal Trade Commission workshop about the sharing economy, this represents an interesting partnership between government and sharing economy platforms. Here's how it works. The CPUC has defined a set of standards that drivers of smartphone-based point-to-point urban transportation vehicles (taxis) need to conform to. But rather than taking on the burden of ensuring that the hundreds of thousands of Lyft, Uber, and Sidecar drivers across the state are compliant, they have instead delegated this enforcement responsibility to the platforms. A platform needs to register as a TNC, and is then responsible for ensuring all drivers that get business through its platform are compliant.[27] There are clear advantages to the taxpayer, since government overhead is minimal. Besides, the platforms have excellent enforcement capabilities (if a driver is noncompliant, they are simply disconnected from the application and can no longer get any business).

Returning to the example of Airbnb: while no comparable state-wide government-sanctioned solutions have emerged in the United States, different self-regulatory systems are already playing a large role in the functioning of the market, and the platform is doing well with regards to credibility and reputation. The systems are recognized as important by both hosts and renters, and they work. Furthermore, a number of countries, most notably, France, have passed laws clarifying or legalizing the subletting of one's primary and secondary residences for short periods. The most notable of these is "Bill ALUR," a national law passed in March 2014 clarifying that wherever you live in France, you can rent out the home in which you live, without having to ask permission from your local city hall.[28] (This was especially notable given that Paris, the most visited city in the world, is also home to the highest number of Airbnb hosts, over 40,000 as of May 2015.

When it comes to altering behavior to minimize the impacts of certain externalities, one might also consider involving a growing number of co-op associations, condominium boards, and homeowners associations (for brevity, I will refer to all of these as "HOAs"). Homeowners and renters have a continuous, high-bandwidth relationship with their HOA; these organizations are credible, can monitor compliance, and possess robust enforcement capabilities. Perhaps, over time, this will lead to some buildings and communities becoming Airbnb-free, while others can advertise themselves as Airbnb-friendly, a grassroots alternative to zoning for an economy in which the lines between personal and commercial are increasingly blurred.

Data-Driven Delegation

Consider a different problem—of collecting hotel occupancy taxes from hundreds of thousands of Airbnb hosts rather than from a handful of corporate hotel chains. The delegation of tax collection to Airbnb, something a growing number of cities are experimenting with, has a number of advantages. It is likely to yield higher tax revenues and greater compliance than a system where hosts are required to register directly with the government, which is something occasional hosts seem reluctant to do. It also sidesteps privacy concerns resulting from mandates that digital platforms like Airbnb turn over detailed user data to the government. There is also significant opportunity for the platform to build credibility as it starts to take on quasigovernmental roles like this.

There is yet another advantage, and the one I believe will be the most significant in the long-run. It asks a platform to leverage its data to ensure compliance with a set of laws in a manner geared towards delegating responsibility to the platform. You might say that the task in question here—computing tax owed, collecting, and remitting it—is technologically trivial. True. But I like this structure because of the potential it represents. It could be a precursor for much more exciting delegated possibilities.

For a couple of decades now, companies of different kinds have been mining the large sets of "data trails" customer provide through their digital interactions. This generates insights of business and social importance. One such effort we are all familiar with is credit card fraud detection. When an unusual pattern of activity is detected, you get a call from your bank's security team. Sometimes your card is blocked temporarily. The enthusiasm of these digital security systems is sometimes a nuisance, but it stems from your credit card company using sophisticated machine learning techniques to identify patterns that prior experience has told it are associated with a stolen card. It saves billions of dollars in taxpayer and corporate funds by detecting and blocking fraudulent activity swiftly.

A more recent visible example of the power of mining large data sets of customer interaction came in 2008, when Google engineers announced that they could predict flu outbreaks using data collected from Google searches, and track the spread of flu outbreaks in real time, providing information that was well ahead of the information available using the Center for Disease Control's own tracking systems. The Google system's performance deteriorated after a couple of years, but its impact on public perception of what might be possible using "big data" was immense.

It seems highly unlikely that such a system would have emerged if Google had been asked to hand over anonymized search data to the CDC. In fact, there would have probably been widespread public backlash to this on privacy grounds. Besides, the reason why this capability emerged organically from within Google is partly as a consequence of Google having one of the highest concentrations of computer science and machine learning talent in the world.

Similar approaches hold great promise as a regulatory approach for sharing economy platforms. Consider the issue of discriminatory practices. There has long been anecdotal evidence that some yellow cabs in New York discriminate against some nonwhite passengers, a claim that seems consistent with analysis done by Benn Stancil when New York Taxi and Limousine Commission started to release anonymized trip data (see figure 6.3).

There have been similar concerns that such behavior may start to manifest on ridesharing platforms and in other peer-to-peer markets for accommodation and labor services. For example, a 2014 study by Benjamin Edelman and Michael Luca of Harvard suggested that African American hosts might have lower pricing power than white hosts on Airbnb.[29] While the study did not conclusively establish that the difference is due to guests discriminating against African American hosts, it raised a red flag about the need for vigilance as the lines between personal and professional blur.

One solution would be to apply machine-learning techniques to be able to identify patterns associated with discriminatory behavior. No doubt, many platforms are already using such systems. In a September

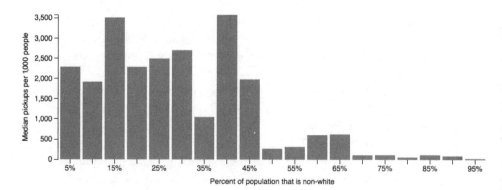

Figure 6.3
How taxicab usage varies with racial composition of neighborhood in New York City.
Source: Mode Analytics.

2014 panel discussion I participated in at the Techonomy Detroit conference, the moderator, Jennifer Bradley of the Aspen Institute, asked Task-Rabbit's president Stacy Brown-Philpot whether the platform had "flags or protections or things that could alert you to discrimination in the system or bad actors." "We do. We have a data science team that we run [to] constantly to make sure we're flagging and alerting human beings to actually go through and look at it," Brown-Philpot replied, "and we actually track data on what drives somebody to select a tasker, and you can see all their pictures so you know what they look like, and the most important thing is a smile. That's it."[30]

Data science holds tremendous promise as a way to detect systemic forms of discrimination, often difficult to identify on a case-by-case basis during face-to-face interaction, but which may be brought to light and addressed with data analytics. For example, Lyft and Uber would quite easily be able to detect and flag in real time the patterns of passenger accepts and refusals that might correspond to discriminatory behavior on the part of their drivers.

But why leave this for the platforms to volunteer to do if they so choose? Rather, there is the opportunity to delegate the enforcement of a range of different laws to these platforms, perhaps asking for audited records of compliance in exchange.

A more radical alternative, one that has been proposed by both Nick Grossman of Union Square Ventures (whose blog, the Slow Hunch, paints a fascinating picture of regulation in the digital economy), and by influential tech blogger Alex Howard, is to mandate that the platforms hand over actual operational data to city and state governments, who can then use the data to regulate. I prefer my idea of data-driven delegation to this alternative approach of "mandated transparency," since it raises fewer familiar privacy concerns and poses lower risks of leaking competitively harmful information. There is precedent to this approach—publicly traded corporations are, in some sense, also regulated in a delegated way. They provide audited summary evidence (through their filings with the SEC), rather than being asked to provide raw operational data for a regulator to use in confirming compliance. Correspondingly, leaving the data inside the platform's own systems, while mandating its use in regulation, seems far more efficient.

As sharing-economy SROs—whether platforms themselves or third-party associations that emerge—establish a track record of credibility and enforcement and gain legitimacy as partners in regulation, they can then perhaps be called on to help invent self-regulatory solutions to social issues that are especially difficult to address by centralized governmental intervention. One might imagine a variety of societal objectives being achieved in part by the platforms applying machine-learning techniques to their data to detect patterns, or integrating some notion of social responsibility into the design of their software systems. This approach of data-driven delegation can yield far more expansive regulating through data alternatives than are feasible with complete transparency, and it suggests promising opportunities for self-regulation—ones that are appropriately reflective of the interesting meld of a decentralized marketplace and a centralized institution that sharing-economy platforms represent. Put differently, the sharing economy might offer innovative approaches to not just its own regulation challenges, but to unresolved regulation challenges that predate its emergence.

There are numerous other regulatory issues related to the sharing economy that I have not covered, but which perhaps should form the basis for future writing. New privacy issues are raised as digital platforms hold increasingly granular information about our real-world exchanges. Of course, mobile operators have had granular information about our physical space movements for many years now, and credit card companies about our real-world transactions. Further, I have not addressed issues of liability and insurance. I believe that peer-to-peer insurance represents an extremely exciting area of business growth. I have not discussed how "smart contracts" that blockchain-based exchange make feasible might extend the reach of traditional or new institutions deep into the digital domain.

I have also not yet examined another critical area of regulation that has taken center-stage in 2015: the regulation of *labor* in the sharing economy. I turn to this topic in chapters 7 and 8.

7

The Future of Work: Challenges and Controversies

Many people blithely assume that the critical labor-market distinction is, and will remain, between highly educated (or highly skilled) people and less-educated (or less-skilled) people. But this view may be mistaken.
—Alan S. Blinder, "Offshoring: The Next Industrial Revolution?"
Foreign Affairs (March/April 2006)

Over the past decade, labor lawyer Shannon Liss-Riordan has success-fully fought for the rights of employees as diverse as baristas, janitors, and exotic dancers. In 2014, she took on a new fight—this time on behalf of Uber drivers she alleges are being incorrectly classified as contractors rather than as employees.[1]

The workers suing Uber maintain that the platform wants the cost advantages of working with contractors while simultaneously maintain-ing the control of working with employees. According to Liss-Riordan, the performance of Uber drivers is "managed" based on user ratings, and they receive guidelines from city managers directing them toward high-demand areas on a daily basis, so one might argue that they are some-what employee-like. But as I discussed in chapter 3, Uber drivers are also microentrepreneurs who own their vehicles and pay for their own gas and repairs while building their transportation microbusinesses. Indeed, there is a long history of taxi drivers operating as independent contrac-tors in the United States.

Uber maintains that it is a technology company that simply provides a platform for drivers to connect with customers in the same way that Airbnb helps hosts meet vacationers in need of accommodations. The Uber driver population also seems to not see full-time employment as the Holy Grail. In a survey conducted in June 2015 by SherpaShare, a pro-vider of financial services to sharing economy providers, two out of three Uber drivers indicated that they viewed themselves as independent con-tractors to the platform rather than as employees.[2]

As this book goes to press, the case, involving 160,000 Uber drivers, is still underway. In March 2015, Edward M. Chen, a California judge, rejected Uber's request for a summary judgment, which would have effectively enabled the case against Uber to move forward without a full trial. In his conclusion, Judge Chen wrote:

The application of the traditional test of employment—a test which evolved under an economic model very different from the new "sharing economy"—to Uber's business model creates significant challenges. Arguably, many of the factors in that test appear outmoded in this context. ... It may be that the legislature or appellate courts may eventually refine or revise that test in the context of the new economy. It is conceivable that the legislature would enact rules particular to the new so-called "sharing economy." Until then, this Court is tasked with applying the traditional multifactor test.[3]

And, in December 2015, the court certified the case as a class action. In a parallel class-action suit brought against Lyft, Judge Vince Chhabra echoed a similar sentiment, but perhaps more strongly, when he wrote: "California's outmoded test for classifying workers will apply in cases like this. And because the test provides nothing remotely close to a clear answer, it will often be for juries to decide."[4] A related June 2015 decision by the California Labor Commissioner went against Uber, ruling that a specific driver was an employee and entitled to business expense reimbursements, a decision Uber is currently appealing.

The judges' reactions suggest that established tests to determine what constitutes employment may no longer hold in the sharing economy. New labor definitions are needed for a world of crowd-based capitalism. As the case against Uber reveals, however, this future has arrived well in advance of the policy needed to support it. According to a study done in collaboration with Intuit by Steve King of Emergent Research, there are already 3 million on-demand workers in the United States alone, a number he projects will grow to over 7 million by 2020. The on-demand grocery-shopping platform Instacart has also faced lawsuits from its workers; in July 2015 it opted to switch some of them to part-time employment. The same month, the labor services platform HomeJoy ceased operations, citing impending labor lawsuits as a reason why its business model was no longer viable, while Luxe and Shyp announced that their workers would henceforth be part-time or full-time employees. While TaskRabbit and Handy maintain a contractor relationship with their providers, other platforms like ManagedByQ and Alfred employ their providers full-time, and their CEOs, Dan Teran and Marcela Sapone, have frequently argued the advantages of full-time employment over an independent-contractor relationship.[5]

And policy makers have started to take note. In a June 2015 speech, Virginia senator Mark Warner called for federal policy makers to take action, later laying out elements of a plan in a *Washington Post* op-ed.[6] In a July 2015 campaign speech, Hillary Clinton noted both opportunities and challenges:

Many Americans are making extra money renting out a spare room, designing websites ... even driving their own car. This "on demand" or so-called "gig economy" is creating exciting opportunities and unleashing innovation, but it's also raising hard questions about workplace protections and what a good job will look like in the future.[7]

As I write this book, Warner, his deputy chief of staff Kristin Sharp, and his team continue to lead the conversation about a legislative agenda to prepare the United States for this ongoing workforce transition. Additionally, at an October 2015 labor conference hosted by the White House, President Barack Obama discussed ways of protecting the new workforce in an hour-long town hall discussion he moderated with Michelle Miller, the co-founder of coworker.org, after highlighting the opportunities created by the future of work heralded by platforms like Uber, Lyft, and TaskRabbit in an earlier keynote speech.

But what exactly do these opportunities look like? On one side of the argument, there are the Liss-Riordans of the world who may consider the future of work—at least as it is currently unfolding in the sharing economy—as a near-certain race to the bottom. Among the most vocal proponents of this view is the former labor secretary and University of California professor Robert Reich. Asserting that a better name for the sharing economy would be the "share-the-scraps economy," Reich posits: "Customers and workers are matched online. Workers are rated on quality and reliability. The big money goes to the corporations that own the software. The scraps go to the on-demand workers."[8] In this dystopian view of the future, work will be defined by low wages, the elimination of benefits, and high levels of job insecurity. People will work longer hours for less money, income will be fragmented, the safety net will be a distant memory, and work environments will have less ideal and less carefully monitored conditions.

On the other hand, there are sharing economy enthusiasts who see the future world of work as one defined by increased flexibility, fluidity, innovation, and creativity. In this utopian future, individuals will be empowered entrepreneurs who take control of their own destinies on an unprecedented scale. Innovative new products and services will flow from platforms that are gateways to innovation or, as Lisa Gansky engagingly described them in a 2013 conversation with me, "finishing schools for entrepreneurs." Average workers will work fewer hours on a more flexible schedule from wherever they want and make more money doing work that they choose. Stephane Kasriel, the CEO of the labor platform Upwork, explained the draw of making a living on-demand at a September 2015 World Economic Forum panel: "The younger generation really aspires for this kind of career. They don't want the nine-to-five job, working with the same employer, needing to be on-premise. They like the flexibility, they like the independence, and the control they have."[9]

Of course, both camps will eventually be right to some degree. Neither the doomsday predictions nor utopian projections will likely ever be fully realized. Whether or not the sharing economy proves detrimental or empowering to workers in the long-term, whether we see "empowered entrepreneurs" or "disenfranchised drones," will be contingent on a number of factors—factors that businesses, workers, and consumers will determine to varying degrees, that will be shaped by policy choices we make over the coming decade, and that will be explored at length in this chapter and the next one.

"Freelanceability," Offshoring, and Automation

It seems likely that the sharing economy will convert some of what is corporate and government employment today into different forms of flexible and freelance work. In order to understand what sectors might see a greater level of labor transition due to this wave of digital disruption, and why, it is first helpful to link the transition to on-demand work with two other narratives that have dominated discussions about labor and technology over the last couple of decades. Since the 1990s, there has been a significant growth in the prevalence of offshoring. More recently, there has been a persistent focus on—and in some cases, panic about—digitally-induced automation.

Offshoring

Offshoring refers to the practice of a company using an internal labor force that lives in a country different from where that company is located. Over the past few decades, a growing number of jobs have been offshored. Often, the motivation for offshoring is to lower costs; sometimes it is also to tap into a new pool of talent. Furthermore, there are sometimes tax advantages to offshoring. As a recent study by Shu-Yi Oei and Diane Ring highlights, the regulatory ambiguity that occurs when slotting sharing economy work into existing categories can lead to analogous tax compliance and enforcement gaps on sharing economy platforms.[10]

For many reasons it is hard to find accurate numbers capturing the exact magnitude of offshoring. Some of these reasons shed light on comparable measurement challenges we can expect as the sharing economy grows. While some jobs can be tracked (e.g., full-time credit card call center positions relocated from the United States to India), other jobs are more difficult to track because it is not jobs per se but rather specific components that are being offshored. For example, as work itself changes, and is increasingly fragmented into hundreds of tasks that are staffed on platforms such as Upwork and Fiverr, it is nearly impossible to measure what percentage of the work in question is being offshored.

That said, there are two things we can reliably believe. First, only some jobs have the ability to be offshored. Second, highly offshore-able jobs only account for a small fraction of the US job market. Both of these points are made with great precision and thought in the work of the Princeton economist Alan Blinder.

Blinder's position is that offshoring represents a new epoch of work that has not yet reached its peak. Just as earlier generations witnessed a move from agriculture to manufacturing and later from manufacturing to services, we are now in an epoch where at least some types of work are no longer location bound. While manufacturing jobs were already being offshored several decades ago, we are now witnessing the offshoring of a new category of jobs—service industry jobs. The movement, Blinder argues, is driven by three factors: the development of digital platforms that enable companies to recruit and monitor workers around the world, technological changes that enable workers to serve customers in any location, and the entry of highly populated countries, including India and China, into the global economy.

The impact on the US labor market has been significant. But it is important to bear in mind that only some forms of service work lend themselves to offshoring. As Blinder observes, "It is critical to distinguish between two very different sorts of services … *personally delivered* (or just "personal") and *impersonally delivered* (or just "impersonal"). The first category encompasses a bewildering variety of jobs, ranging from janitors and childcare workers on the low-wage end to surgeons and CEOs on the high-wage end. Similarly, the second category includes both low-end jobs like call center operators and high-end jobs like scientists."[11] What's key, Blinder maintains, is to focus *not* on a job's skill or the educational credentials required to do the job but rather on whether the service in question can be delivered electronically over long distances without compromising quality.

As it turns out, while some jobs fall into this category, most do not. Indeed, in a study that used four different approaches to assess the vulnerability of common occupations, Blinder and his colleague Alan Krueger concluded that the fraction of jobs that were offshore-able varied quite widely across industry, with consistently higher fractions in finance and insurance, and lower fractions in accommodation and food services. Overall, Blinder and Krueger report: "Each estimate represents a non-trivial minority of all jobs, roughly comparable to the shift from manufacturing to services between 1960 and now. In other words, the shift toward service offshoring is a potentially dramatic labor market transformation."[12]

Notably, as Blinder's findings also reveal: "Contrary to conventional wisdom, the more offshorable occupations are not low-end jobs, whether measured by wages or by education. The correlation between skill and offshorability is almost zero."[13] Many highly skilled and well-compensated jobs are *just as vulnerable* to offshoring as jobs held by people in low-skilled and poorly compensated occupations. No level of skill or education can insure one from the impact of offshoring.

In other words, offshoring, according to Blinder, may be both less widespread and more universal than often assumed. The same may hold true for how "freelanceable" a job is. We have already seen "on-demand" freelance marketplaces emerge for a range of professions. Postmates offers simple delivery on demand. TaskRabbit and Thumbtack provides plumbers, event planners, and electricians. The platforms Pager and Heal get you a doctor on demand. Universal Avenue offers a sales force on demand, and HourlyNerd gets you a consultant with an MBA.

And what if offshoring, as Erik Brynjolfsson and Andrew McAfee suggest, is only a way station on the road to automation?

The Second Machine Age
Like offshoring, automation is by no means new. The quest to automate simple human tasks has occupied scientists and engineers for centuries. By the late 19th century, machines were being used to automate the tabulation of data gathered in the US national census. By the 1920s, automated switchboards controlled many of the incoming and outgoing calls at Bell Telephone.

In the 1960s, Herbert Simon characterized decision making in terms of a continuum of programmability, predicting that computers would replace programmable organizational functions, leaving humans to handle the nonprogrammable tasks, especially those involving interpersonal communication and judgment. Simon's predictions have materialized in part today, with information-processing infrastructures of increasing complexity becoming programmed and available as modules that handle entire processes from order taking to fulfillment, inventory, and customer support. All of these functions previously required more active intervention by human beings.

Thus far, as the machines eliminated some jobs, they created others. However, it is possible that we are now entering a new era of automation in which the rate of previously human-performed work now done by machines may outpace the rate at which these machines create new jobs. A November 2015 McKinsey and Company study indicates that "as many as 45 percent of the activities individuals are paid to perform can be automated by adapting currently demonstrated technologies."[14]

Looking deeper into the future of work, Erik Brynjolfsson and Andrew McAfee in *The Second Machine Age* argue that although computers have been transforming work, economics, and everyday life for several decades, we have finally reached a pivotal moment—a moment when we are grappling with the "full force" of digital technologies.

The Second Machine Age builds on a book by the economists Frank Levy and Richard Murnane about the human–computer tradeoff in the labor market.[15] Levy and Murnane examine, in detail, what tasks computers perform better than humans, and what tasks humans perform better than computers. They draw a broad conclusion—that computers have inherent advantages in tasks like rule-based decision making and simple pattern recognition, but digitization makes two kinds of tasks (complex communication and expert thinking) more valuable—and prescribe that humans acquire the skills that enable them to take on jobs involving such tasks.

McAfee and Brynjolfsson argue however, that computers are in fact on the verge of surpassing humans at some of the tasks that Levy and Murnane contend humans would continue to dominate. They cite the 2011 victory of IBM's Watson computer in *Jeopardy*, the coming of age of the autonomous automobile, and the emergence of the iPhone's Siri as early indicators of this eventuality. As McAfee and Brynjolfsson explain, "We mean simply that the key building blocks are already in place for digital technologies to be as important and transformational to society as the steam engine. In short, we're at an inflection point—a point where the curve starts to bend a lot—because of computers. We are entering a second machine age."[16]

Before writing *The Second Machine Age*, Brynjolfsson and McAfee wrote a shorter book with the same theme, *Race Against the Machine*. As their thinking evolved from the first book to the second, the authors became decidedly more optimistic about this second machine age. "We're heading into an era," they contend, "that won't just be different; it will be better, because we'll be able to increase both the variety and the volume of our consumption." What they mean is not simply that we will consume more but consume differently: "We also consume information from books and friends, entertainment from superstars and amateurs, expertise from teachers and doctors, and countless other things that are not made of atoms. Technology can bring us more choice and even freedom."[17]

However, the optimism in Brynjolfsson and McAfee's *The Second Machine Age* is tempered toward the end with caution. They note that that as digital computing leads to increased automation, there will be at least some have-nots:

Technological progress is going to leave behind some people, perhaps even a lot of people, as it races ahead. As we'll demonstrate, there's never been a better time to be a worker with special skills or the right education, because these people can use technology to create and capture value. However, there's never been a worse time to be a worker with only "ordinary" skills and abilities to offer, because computers, robots, and other digital technologies are acquiring these skills and abilities at an extraordinary rate.[18]

If one takes Brynjolfsson and McAfee's predictions at face value, the future appears to be one where automation will increase at a previously unprecedented rate, consumers will experience increased choice, but many workers (with the exception of those who are particularly well positioned to thrive in the digital age) risk being rendered obsolete. As they further argue, "The better machines can substitute for human workers, the more likely it is that they'll drive down the wages of humans with similar skills. The lesson from economics and business strategy is that you don't want to compete against close substitutes, especially if they have a cost advantage."[19]

This emphasis on "special skills" is of particular interest because many economists assume that the ability to harness the benefits of digital technologies is something predominantly available to highly skilled workers. This is consistent with research on technology and wages well summarized in David Card and John E. DiNardo's hypothesis of *skill-biased technical change* (SBTC): that "a burst in new technology causes a rise for the demand for highly skilled workers that in turn leads to a rise in earnings inequality."[20] A number of measurement techniques have evolved from this research, focused primarily on examining the rates of substitution between skilled and unskilled labor and the ensuing impacts on the relative productivity of different skill groups across different industry sectors.

In contrast, as I demonstrate throughout this book, sharing economy platforms have an impact on the work prospects of people across the occupation spectrum, from computer scientists and consultants to household cleaners and cab drivers. In this respect, just as offshoring may be occupation blind, as suggested by Blinder, so too may the labor impacts, both positive and negative, of the sharing economy.

The New Digitally Enabled Workforce

While offshoring and the rise of the second machine age continue to profoundly restructure the economy, neither phenomenon fully captures the changing nature of work in the 21st century. Beyond the fact that businesses are no longer restricted to hiring people in their geographic vicinity, and in a growing number of instances can opt to program tasks that once required human workers, the present landscape of labor is also marked by myriad other notable changes: the proliferation of marketplaces, the emergence of new generalists, the increased immediacy of labor supply, the emergence of task economies, and the rise of invisible work.

New Marketplaces

As we have discussed earlier in the book, a growing fraction of economic activity is being organized through marketplace-like platforms. A frequent concern associated with such marketplaces is that they will depress wages as more qualified workers flood restricted markets, and as transparency and competition drive down the price of labor to the textbook ideal of "perfectly competitive markets."

In figure 7.1, I compare the wage rates of providers on a large US-based labor platform across a range of professions to the corresponding wage rates for those professions that have been complied by the United States Bureau of Labor Statistics (BLS), the most comprehensive source of data about wages in the United States. The figure illustrates the contrast in San Francisco in the summer of 2015; in collaboration with Marios Kokkodis, a former NYU colleague and current professor at Boston College, I have been periodically performing this comparison across different cities in the United States. (So, for example, wages for online plumbers in New York are compared to the BLS averages for plumbers in New York.)

Our findings have consistently suggested that workers can generally expect to earn more per hour getting their freelance assignments through

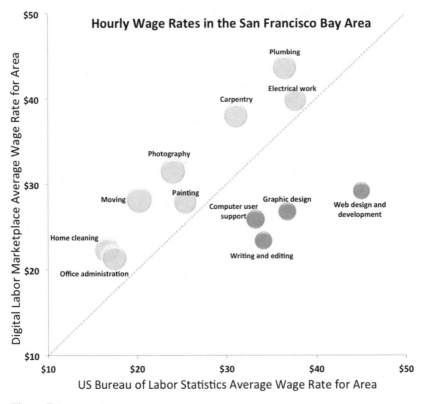

Figure 7.1
Wage comparison in San Francisco, summer 2015.

a digital labor market than by seeking it through traditional channels, even after they pay the platform its commission. A study by Hall and Krueger (2015) documented a similar difference between the average hourly earnings of Uber drivers and taxi drivers.

These findings form an instructive starting point to explore why the emergence of new marketplaces isn't necessarily bad news for the workers who choose to provide services through them. A closer look at the data, however, suggests that this on-demand wage premium is not uniform across occupations. As illustrated for a sample of the most frequently listed occupations, while many have significantly higher wage rates, workers in others are making less per hour than the national averages.

What explains the difference? Well, first, most services offered on a marketplace like Handy or TaskRabbit require the provider to be geographically collocated with the customers. Until Brynjolfsson and McAfee's robots get really sophisticated, it is likely that a plumber has to be in the same town or city as the bathtub being unclogged. Thus, while the launch of a labor platform in a city might cause small initial increase in the availability of cleaners and repair persons, as more people with full-time jobs decide to do a bit of home cleaning or plumbing on the side, the platform is not yet in the business of training or certifying new workers. TaskRabbit's arrival in a city, for example, does not result in a sudden surge in certified electricians or a flood of new plumbers into that city. Rather, it makes it easier for the city's existing electricians and plumbers to find people in need of their services, and it gives these customers a greater number of choices beyond their neighborhood plumber.

A number of individual factors explain why some on-demand workers get paid more than others, including experience levels, geography, and whether the platform certifies them as being a superior provider or not. However, for an occupation as a whole, what seems to matter most is whether the worker needs to be present at the actual geographic location where the work is being requested. For example, someone can be a web designer or copy editor from anywhere, but location matters for a plumber or carpenter.

Although the supply of workers in professions that require supply–demand collocation is not significantly affected by the presence of an online marketplace, a likely demand effect is that more people now seek these services when they need them (rather than, for example, leaving that bathroom drain unsnaked because of the $300 quote from the plumber down the street). What expands, therefore, is the market rather than the number of available workers in these fields.

Put differently, new marketplaces increase ease of access. The demand for many of the popular occupations in today's on-demand marketplaces is partly discretionary. When it becomes simpler to find a reliable home cleaner or high-quality photographer, a greater percentage of human needs translate into actual demand for labor, because it is more feasible for people to find the providers they are looking for. There's also a better alignment between what they want and the service or provider they eventually find.

Thus, when a new electronic marketplace comes to town, there's no reason to always expect lower wages because of a sudden increase in the supply or workers. But what might explain the *rise* in wages? Well, the assertion that new marketplaces will result in perfect competition and depress earning levels focuses on one older aspect of economic theory while ignoring a different aspect that has gained a great deal of attention in the last 40 years: that of "information asymmetry." As I defined and discussed in chapter 6, sharing economy platforms can reduce many forms of information asymmetry. The predictions of economic theory are that such reductions will increase, rather than reduce, wages over time.

Let me explain the consequences of information asymmetry, and in particular, the effect of "adverse selection" further by appealing to the example of used car markets that George Akerlof famously used in his Nobel Prize–winning work. In Akerlof's model, there are two kinds of used cars—those of high quality, and those of low quality (the "lemons"). Suppose that prospective buyers have no way of determining the true quality of a used car prior to purchasing it. The price a buyer would be willing to pay would then be somewhere between the value of a high-quality car and the value of a lemon. (If the buyers are risk averse, this price would be lower than the average of the two values weighted for their relative frequency.) However, seeing that the price they can command is lower than the value of their vehicles, high-quality sellers then exit the market, leaving just the lemons in the market. Less trade takes place than is desirable.

Now consider the introduction of vehicle inspections. Buyers now have greater "quality transparency"—they are able to get a clear idea about whether any candidate vehicle is actually as good as advertised. Sellers of higher quality cars can get a price closer to the fair value of their product. Buyers start to trust used car markets more, people trade cars more often, the economy grows, and more importantly, the average price and the average quality of used cars goes up, not down.

Thus, the presence of Upwork, Handy, and TaskRabbit, and in particular, their screening process and review systems, plays a role somewhat analogous to vehicle inspections in the used car example. Prospective consumers of services can now get a better sense for the quality of different service providers, relying on assessments that come both from the crowd and from experts. More of them will seek these services than in the past. Better providers have an incentive to provide more since they can charge an hourly rate closer to the value of their service, and also because poor performance can restrict future work opportunities if it leads to a negative review visible to prospective customers.

Furthermore, in the long run, a greater level of wage transparency can have additional benefits for workers, and not just for today's geospecific service-oriented peer-to-peer platforms. For example, a platform like Upwork exposes both users and providers to industry norms. Someone who visits the platform hoping to find a qualified person to write corporate copy at 1-cent-per-word will soon discover that the qualified writers simply do not work at that low a rate. New designers, programmers, and writers on these platforms also gain insight into wage rates for colleagues at different points in their career (for example, a young scribe will quickly learn the going rate for US-based proofreaders, editors, and writers, and how experience and compensation line up).

As a result, workers breaking into the industry can set rates in accordance with industry standards in the country from which their demand originates, and workers in lower purchasing-power parity countries might end up realizing their skills are worth more than they thought. In this way, decreased information asymmetry across providers may counteract some of the negative impacts of increased global competition, although whether it will negate them entirely in the long run remains an open question.[21]

New Generalists

For most of the past 500 years, and specifically since the advent of industrialization, we have observed progressively greater specialization in our economies. We witnessed this initially as manufacturing became increasingly compartmentalized in the 19th and early 20th centuries. Shoe heels, for instance, could be manufactured in one shop and attached to uppers in another shop. Over the last century, other professions ranging from medicine to education have seen a rise in specialization as their science became increasingly complex. General medicine gave way to a growing number of sub-specialties. The teacher charged with teaching all subjects to students in grades 1 through 12 in a single schoolhouse has evolved into increasingly specialized schools organized by age, level, potential, and subject. Across fields, one's economic success became increasingly contingent on specialization.

With sharing economy platforms, however, we are witnessing an interesting revival of the generalist. The blurring of lines between the personal and the professional, and between formal work and casual work, creates a range of opportunities for non-specialists. A lab technician can easily moonlight as an innkeeper by renting out a spare room on Airbnb. Likewise, as I discussed briefly in a 2015 National Public Radio interview, aspiring actors who have set themselves up to expect to make part of their living doing on-demand work between acting gigs can just as easily tap into the new platforms to find work snaking clogged drains or shuttling people from place to place. An accountant with a hidden passion for jewelry making can set up shop on Etsy to make a bit of extra money as a maker (and perhaps even balance her own books). In short, sharing economy platforms are enabling a move away from specialization by allowing a growing number of nonspecialists—empowered by the capabilities of sharing platforms—to provide market-grade services.

In many ways, this trend follows the transition predicted by Michael Hammer in his highly influential 1990 *Harvard Business Review* article "Reengineering Work: Don't Automate, Obliterate." At the time, Hammer argued, "Many of our job designs, work flows, control mechanisms, and organizational structures came of age in a different competitive environment and before the advent of the computer. They are geared towards efficiency and control. Yet the watchwords of the new decade are innovation and speed, service and quality."[22] Hammer further preached the value of "generalists" rather than specialists: a vision of that was realized in part through the radical restructuring of work that played out over the decade after his article was published.

But in many respects, what is happening in the sharing economy today exceeds even Hammer's bold vision of a reengineered future workplace. While Hammer recognized that everything about work would need to change—job design, organizational structures, management systems, anything associated with work processes—his vision continued to place organizations at the center of the economy. "Big, traditional organizations," Hammer maintained, "aren't necessarily dinosaurs doomed to extinction, but they are burdened with layers of unproductive overhead and armies of unproductive workers."[23]

The shift we're seeing today is more extensive. Alongside the reengineering of work predicted by Hammer, we are seeing the dismantling of centralized workplaces as more and more business operate without a headquarters and without a pool of permanent workers, opting instead to build enterprises by drawing on workers who are brought in to complete specific projects or tasks. In parallel, as I discussed in chapter 5, these sharing economy platforms embed capabilities that lower the specialization requirements for many professions—in some ways, akin to the way franchising operations do for many businesses.

Immediacy of Labor Supply

Work was once relegated to work hours. Depending on the profession, work happened during the 12-hour shift or 8-hour workday. Today, work can take place in increasingly microscopic units, in increments as short as a minute or two. The new marketplaces spawned by the sharing economy are allowing us to tap into labor supply in a much more granular and efficient way.

As an example, consider the on-demand work platform Spare5. Spare5 enables people to complete small tasks on their mobile devices in exchange for a fee. Americans spend an estimated three hours per day using their smartphones. While part of the time is spent completing required tasks (e.g., ordering groceries or paying bills using an online banking app), a quick survey of people in line at a Starbucks or riding the bus during rush hour reveals that most of those three hours are spent doing less-necessary and "unproductive" things like playing Candy Crush or Fruit Ninja.

Spare5 takes that "spare" 5 minutes (or more) one currently spends playing video games or browsing social media and turns them into money-making moments. The tasks, which range from photo tagging to completing surveys, are simple tasks (and at times boring), but nevertheless necessary in a technology-centric society.

In theory, companies benefit by tapping into the time of skilled and knowledgeable workers and workers benefit by recuperating lost time (e.g., the time they are currently wasting as they commute to and from work, or sit in the waiting room of a doctor's office or in the lobby of a community center where their child is taking swimming lessons). In a nutshell, labor efficiency is increased not by extracting more out of existing employees but rather by foraging for lost moments of time that can be turned into work. Of course, this may come at a social cost: if we're spending all our spare time digitally scurrying between microtasks, we may sacrifice valuable leisure, negating some of the work-life balance benefits that being a microentrepreneur affords.

Task Economies
In the past, hiring thousands of workers to carry out small tasks wasn't feasible because of the high administrative costs of such a structure. Today, smaller and smaller tasks can increasingly be outsourced with minimal transaction costs to crowds of workers connected to digital platforms. An early example of this form of "taskification" can be seen in the popular Amazon's Mechanical Turk, which connects millions of workers around the world to customers who have broken down projects into simple tasks with compensation ranging from a few pennies to a couple of dollars.

One might wonder if a platform like Amazon's Mechanical Turk, which seems to be, like Spare5, largely used for simple tasks like image tagging and survey responses, can make a dent in how the vast majority of the economy's productive work is done. For example, will we see complex consulting projects or sales activities being broken down and offered on these platforms for people to contribute to in their spare time?

Granted, the scope of work that can be done on the microtask platforms we have discussed seems limited. However, HourlyNerd, a platform backed by the Mavericks owner and "Shark Tank" investor Mark
Cuban, brings a TaskRabbit-like marketplace to management consulting.
Sweden-based Universal Avenue is creating a marketplace that allows a
user to tap into a sales force on demand. Enterprise software like that
built by WorkMarket will make it easier for companies to tap into these
on-demand task marketplaces and integrate them into their corporate
workflows.

An especially compelling example comes from a recent prototype,
built by Devin Fidler of the Institute of the Future, called iCEO, "a virtual
management system that automates complex work by dividing it into
small, individual tasks."[24] Fidler's system demonstrates how the complex
work we typically associate with senior managers can be instead done by
software that parcels tasks to workers on oDesk, Elance, and Amazon's
Mechanical Turk workers. For example, iCEO was given the project of
creating a 124-page research report for a Fortune 50 client. As Fidler
describes it:

We spent a few hours plugging in the parameters of the project, i.e. structuring
the flow of tasks, then hit play. For instance, to create an in-depth assessment
of how graphene is produced, iCEO asked workers on Amazon's Mechanical
Turk to curate a list of articles on the topic. After duplicates were removed, the
list of articles was passed on to a pool of technical analysts from oDesk, who
extracted and arranged the articles' key insights. A cohort of Elance writers
then turned these into coherent text, which went to another pool of subject
matter experts for review, passing them on to a sequence of oDesk editors,
proofreaders, and fact checkers.

iCEO routed tasks across 23 people from around the world, including the
creation of 60 images and graphs, followed by formatting and preparation.
We stood back and watched iCEO execute this project. We rarely needed to
intervene, even to check the quality of individual components of the report as
they were submitted to iCEO, or spend time hiring staff, because QA and HR
were also automated by iCEO. (The hiring of oDesk contractors for this project,
for example, was itself an oDesk assignment.)[25]

As work is divided into ever-smaller units or specific tasks, organizations can thus choose to dedicate a full-time employee to do more work
like they have in the past, or to hire one or many part-time contractors to
carry out the work that would have once been carried out by a full-time
employee. The advantage to organizations of the latter approach is that
there's more scope to make sure tasks are completed when they need to
be completed without keeping workers idle on the payroll. In addition,
hiring, recruitment, and compensation can take place outside of regular

work hours because sharing economy platforms that match contractors to organizations are "on" all the time. As the matching of work to skills gets increasingly automated, this also enables organizations to more easily work with contractors in different time zones.

Invisible Work

As we move into an economy where work is decomposed into tasks done around the world, performed in people's spare time or through on-demand platforms, and services are provided by freelancers working through multiple platforms or offered by generalists who may be specialists in something else, our systems to keep track of how much employment there is in the economy start to get seriously challenged. For most of the second half of the 20th century, most Americans worked a single profession at a time, as a full-time job. If they lost that job, they were out of work until they found another full-time job. In today's economy, being employed or unemployed is becoming increasingly difficult to measure as microentrepreneurship, multiple gigs, freelance work, and fluid self-employment muddle traditional definitions and measures. Senator Warner, talking about changing nature of the workforce in a video interview with *USA Today*, reflected on the attitudes of his three daughters, all in their 20s: "When you meet people in that generation," he said, the opening question "is not 'where (do) you work?' It's 'what are you working on now?'"[26]

As a growing number of individuals no longer conform to the 20th-century ideal of "having a job" and as more employees become microentrepreneurs in their spare time, the line between losing and gaining "jobs" becomes increasingly difficult to measure. How then do we measure employment in the sharing economy?

A natural question in the United States is whether the unemployment numbers being collected by the Labor Department are sophisticated enough to capture these changes. Consider someone who used to work a full-time job but is now unemployed and drives an Uber or provides services on TaskRabbit. If that person reports this new work for profit in a response on a BLS survey, they would continue to be counted as employed. However, the numbers reported by the BLS don't capture the additional "employment" or "work" generated by *underemployed* people who were already working at least an hour a week (like a software contractor who now also does Lyft on the side). Additionally, the BLS surveys don't fully capture people who contribute to the sharing economy while holding regular full-time jobs (an investment banker who rents out her apartment periodically on Airbnb, a doctor who creates and sells handmade items on Etsy on the side).

As I discussed at length in 2013 with Emily Badger, a reporter at the time with *Atlantic Media*, part of the challenge also lies in how people who do these activities think of them. Survey questions that ask about your "job," your "main job," your "other job," or your "business" may lead people in the sharing economy to under-report what they're up to simply because they don't think of their activities in those terms. As I explained to Badger, "A knitter on Etsy thinks she's selling the products of her 'hobby.' A driver on BlaBlaCar thinks he's taking gas money to drop people off while he's already on his way from Munich to Hamburg. And an Airbnb host doesn't quantify how many hours she spent last week 'hosting' tourists from Chicago. Clearly, we need to rethink the way we add up all the work that is being done in the economy."[27]

There's more to it than rethinking the way we count. Just as the impacts of the sharing economy have proven difficult to fully capture using existing economic measures, such as the GDP (discussed at length in chapter 5), creation of work in the sharing economy cannot be easily understood using established employment measures. We also need to develop metrics that take into account job quality, income stability, and work-life balance. A full-time job that requires a long and expensive daily commute may in fact be less desirable than two part-time jobs carried out from home. Measuring this by using existing metrics is difficult. Whatever new metrics are developed, one thing is clear—just as our economic measures need to take other factors into account (work-life balance, sustainability, equality), so too do our employment measures.

I began this chapter by highlighting the challenges associated with Uber's ongoing labor disputes. As I have discussed through the chapter, this is the tip of an iceberg, a much broader digitally induced redefinition of our world of work. Whatever the outcomes of these ongoing cases, perhaps the most important impact of Uber's labor dispute will be the attention it draws to deeper societal challenges that will unfold over the coming decades. We need labor policy that anticipates this ongoing transition, moves past the false dichotomy of "employee" and "independent contractor" to redefine how we categorize productive work, decouples the social safety net from full-time employment, and better supports our emerging networked society of microentrepreneurs. We also need to think hard about whether the corporate ownership structures of the 20th century are adequate for this new world of work. I discuss each of these issues in greater depth in the next chapter.

8

The Future of Work: What Needs to Be Done

The jury in this case will be handed a square peg and asked to choose between two round holes.
—US District Judge Vince Chhabria (regarding the Lyft class-action lawsuit, March 11, 2015)

There is no question that the economy is undergoing a major shift that may prove as significant as the Industrial Revolution. But change is not what is in dispute here. Rather, the key questions that remain to be answered are whether or not the change will ultimately create a better world of work, and what can we do to nudge things in the right direction.

Will the sharing economy ultimately represent the rise of the microentrepreneur—a generation of self-employed workers who are empowered to work whenever they want from any location and at whatever level of intensity needed to achieve their desired standard of living? Or will it represent the culmination of the end of broad-based and high standards of living that the United States witnessed in the 1950s and 1960s—a disparaging race to the bottom that leaves workers around the world working more hours for less money and with minimal job security and benefits?

Put another way, will the future of work be populated by successful microentrepreneurs, like David with his fleet of cars on Turo, ThreeBird-Nest's Alicia Shaffer on Etsy, and Don Dennis running his business from the island of Gigha? Or will the future be populated by disenfranchised workers who scurry between platforms as they hunt for their next wedge of piecework?

In this chapter, I highlight the labor issues central to shaping this future of work. First, I examine the current debate on the employment status of sharing economy workers and proposed expansions to the US worker categorization model. Next, I ask, how do we ensure that a social safety net is available to people whose chosen form of work is something other than full-time employment? In the long run, a universal basic income may be socially desirable, although crafting policy that shares the funding of a portable safety net among the individual, the marketplace, and the government may be more politically feasible. Third, I conjecture that platforms facilitating genuine entrepreneurship at a small scale will lead to more inclusive growth than those whose platform-provider relationship is more hierarchical, and outline over 20 metrics that might help identify the right kind of platform-based entrepreneurship. Fourth, I examine the growing interest in "platform cooperativism" and ask how feasible it will be for structures with some form of shared ownership to exist without sacrificing the economic advantages that shareholder corporations enjoy. I end with a brief discussion of "data Darwinism" and the risks associated with a world of work where opportunities are tied too closely to user reviews and ratings.

Independent Workers and Dependent Contractors

As I write this book the central labor policy question for the sharing economy seems to concern the employment status of the new, flexible workforce. Are they employees, or independent contractors, or something else? Since my training is in economics and business rather than in the law, I won't waste your time with a layperson's take on the legal nuances of whether full-time employment applies to Lyft drivers and Instacart shoppers. (As venture capitalist Simon Rothman of Greylock Partners has pointed out to me, labor law seems to be the new IP law in Silicon Valley: everyone's a little bit of an expert.) Rather, what I do in this section is frame five key issues that should shape the policy discussion as we evolve toward a more flexible model of categorizing work, a model toward which I advocate moving gradually and with deliberation, with pilots and safe harbors, so that we gather more data before making any significant extensions to the current framework.

First, the employee/independent contractor question is not new. According to Justice Wiley Blount Rutledge, quoted by Justin Fox in a *Bloomberg View* article:

Few problems in the law have given greater variety of application and conflict in results than the cases arising in the borderland between what is clearly an employer-employee relationship and what is clearly one of independent entrepreneurial dealing.[1]

As Fox points out, Rutledge is not a local judge commenting on Lyft in 2014 but rather a US Supreme Court justice deciding on the employment status of newsboys in *1944*, in a case that pitted the National Labor Relations Board (NLRB) against media giant Hearst. As US Labor Secretary Tom Perez said at a December 2015 Aspen Institute workshop about portable benefits, ambiguity in labor classification is neither a new challenge, nor one created by the on-demand economy. Worker categorization is thus a historically vexing issue, not a fresh challenge posed by the sharing economy's newly minted corporate giants.

Second, the determination of "employee" versus "independent contractor" is not algorithmic. True, the issues discussed are always about how *independent* the contractor is, and how much *control* the potential employer exerts on the potential contractor/employee. However, there are different guidelines that come from both common law and from other regulatory bodies. For example, the Internal Revenue Service, uses the form SS-8 to help make a case-by-case subjective determination, based on answers an individual provides to a series of questions organized by the following factors[2]:

a. Behavioral: Does the company control or have the right to control what the worker does and how the worker does his or her job?

b. Financial: Are the business aspects of the worker's job controlled by the payer? These include things such as how the worker is paid, whether expenses are reimbursed, and who provides tools/supplies.

c. Type of Relationship: Are there written contracts or employee-type benefits (like a pension plan, insurance, or vacation pay)? Will the relationship continue, and is the work performed a key aspect of the business?

These IRS guidelines, however, are sometimes different from those suggested by the Fair Labor Standards Act, common law, and legal precedent. In a December 2015 proposal to create an "independent worker" category, written for the Hamilton Project of the Brookings Institute by Seth Harris of Cornell University and Alan Krueger of Princeton University, the authors summarize the varied nature of the definition of "employee," illustrated in table 8.1.

Third, the true underlying issue isn't really about a desire among workers for full-time employment, but rather about a desire to obtain the benefits currently and exclusively associated with that status. As Fox notes, since the 1944 ruling—which for collective bargaining purposes categorized the newsboys as employees—workers classified as employees "now enjoy a wide variety of federal, state and local protections, from

Table 8.1
Definitions of "employee" under selected statutes

	Role of work: Is the work performed integral to the employer's business?	Skills Involved: Is the work not necessarily dependent on special skills?	Investment: Does the employer provide the necessary tools and/or equipment and bear the risk of loss from those investments?	Independent Business Judgment: Has the worker withdrawn from the competitive market to work for the employer?
Fair Labor Standards Act (Centered on degree of economic dependence on employer	YES	YES	YES	YES
Internal Revenue Code (IRC) (Centered on control	YES[a]	YES	YES[b]	YES[c]
Nationwide Mut. Ins. v. Darden (ERISA and other laws)[d]	YES	YES	YES	N/A
Common Law (From Restatement Second of Agency § 220	YES	YES	YES	YES

Source: Seth D. Harris and Alan B. Krueger, "A Proposal for Modernizing Labor Laws for Twenty-First-Century Workers: The 'Independent Worker,'" *The Hamilton Project* (Washington, DC: Brookings Institute, December 2015).
Note: "Yes" contributes to a conclusion that the worker is an "employee"; "N/A" indicates the factor is not considered under the specified law.
a. The IRS looks at the role of the work as an indicator of control—if the work is "key" to employer's business, the employer will likely have the right to direct or to control the work).
b. The IRS also specifically looks at whether the worker has a high degree of unreimbursed expenses.
c. The IRC does not use "business judgment" as a term, but does ask if the worker's services are available to the market directly.
d. The Supreme Court draws its multi-factor test from Nationwide Mutual Ins. Co. v. Darden, 503 U.S. 318 (1992).

Duration: Does the worker have a permanent or indefinite relationship with the employer?	Control: Does the employer set pay amount, work hours, and manner in which work is performed?	Benefits: Does the worker receive insurance, pension plan, sick days, or other benefits that suggest an employment relationship?	Method of Payment: Does the worker receive a guaranteed wage or salary as opposed to a fee per task?	Intent: Do the parties believe they have created a employer–employee relationship?
YES	YES	N/A	N/A	N/A
YES	YES	YES	YES	N/A
YES	YES	YES	YES	N/A
YES	YES	N/A	YES	YES

minimum-wage and overtime laws to unemployment insurance, that aren't available to independent contractors."[3]

This is an important distinction for a number of reasons, most saliently because the specter of future litigation may actually be preventing workers from getting benefits funded by the platforms. Since one of the IRS's criteria for determining whether a worker is an employee is whether that worker gets benefits, a platform that considers benefits for its independent-contractor workers as, for example, a retention strategy, or a way of attracting new workers, will shy away from this to avoid potential class-action lawsuits. This was a point made repeatedly at an October 2015 meeting of the Congressional Sharing Economy Caucus (which I discussed in chapter 6). Platforms who wish to give their providers feedback to help them do a better job, or offer them assistance in diversifying the portfolio of services they offer, worry that this could be construed as employer-like "training." Platforms that suggest how their providers might more effectively tap into higher demand pools fear that this could be construed as employer-like "management."

As I mentioned in chapter 7, it seems as if a majority of Uber drivers don't want to give up the flexibility of being independent contractors. Before you raise your eyebrows at my basing a conclusion on a quick survey run by a Silicon Valley insider, let me point you to results from the analysis done as part of a 74-page report on the US contingent workforce, done by the Government Accountability Office (GAO), an independent, nonpartisan agency that works for Congress (see table 8.2).[4]

As indicated by these findings, as early as 2005, it was clear that a vast majority of self-employed workers and independent contractors don't want an alternative employment structure. (These are the most recent numbers available through this agency.) Of course, perhaps many of

Table 8.2
Estimated percentage of workers who want a different type of employment, 2005

Would you prefer a different type of employment?	Agency temps	On-call workers and day laborers	Independent contractors	Self-employed
Yes	59.3 (+/–7.4)	48.3 (+/–5.5)	9.4 (+/–3.8)	7.5 (+/–4.9)
Depends	6.8 (+/–11.3)	6.2 (+/–7.4)	5.4 (+/–3.9)	4.0 (+/–5.0)
No	33.8 (+/–9.5)	45.5 (+/-5.7)	85.2 (+/–1.5)	88.4 (+/–1.7)

them wouldn't mind the benefits associated with being an employee, but do we really have to force this tradeoff between benefits and independence? Why should the quest for this kind of protection have to involve the Faustian bargain of full-time employment?

Fourth, many current and future labor disparities highlighted by recent press coverage as falling under the umbrella of the "sharing economy" may have less to do with the platforms themselves than with prevailing labor laws and conditions that predate the rise of the peer-to-peer platform. Granted, many of Airbnb's hosts are homeowners with extra space and time, and who are just looking to top off their retirement income; and many Etsy sellers are hobbyists pursuing a side business while raising a family. As Liz Gannes of Re/code noted about the sharing economy independent worker in her compelling "Instant Gratification" series in 2014, "Generally, these people are not a traditionally stable workforce. They are instead a flexible and scalable network of workers —'fractional employees'—that tap in and tap out as needed, and as suits them."[5]

However, this description does not apply to all sharing economy providers. Many Uber and Lyft drivers, Handy providers, and TaskRabbit taskers make a significant percentage of their living through the platforms, and the fraction of the world's workforce that fits this description will grow in the coming years. Although full-time employees can pool their individual bargaining power and take collective action, protected by the National Labor Relations Act (NLRA), the NLRA does not protect independent contractors, and current antitrust law may penalize them for doing so, a point Elizabeth Kennedy highlights using the example of independent physicians in her 2005 paper on collective bargaining for dependent contractors.[6] Further, as Ai-Jen Poo, a 2015 MacArthur Foundation Fellow, has highlighted for decades, the labor laws governing domestic workers are unfairly biased against workers relative to labor laws that cover other professions.[7]

Fifth, the current constraints of labor law will not allow a market-based solution to easily emerge. As I have already pointed out, we do not have space under the current structure to see the extent to which benefits and other protections of the platforms will naturally provide a flexible and on-demand workforce. Over the summer of 2015, as class-action lawsuits against larger platforms intensified, many sharing economy platforms—including Shyp, Luxe, Eden (on-demand technical support), and Instacart—reclassified their flexible workers as full-time or part-time employees. Perhaps, as Marcela Sapone, the CEO of Hello Alfred argues, this is well aligned with certain business models, especially those involving repeated customer interaction.[8] But it would be quite unfortunate if early-stage entrepreneurial companies were choosing a work arrangement that was suboptimal for both their businesses and their workers simply based on a fear of future litigation.

How would one relax these constraints in a manner that allows us to examine what the market will provide naturally, and what we need the government to step in and make happen? A solution many have proposed in the United States involves the creation of a third category, alternatively referred to as the "dependent contractor"[9] or the "independent worker."[10] Again, this is not a new idea. The category exists in many countries including Germany. In a 1965 article, the Canadian legal scholar H. W. Arthurs examined the legal environment around the introduction of such a categorization of workers in North America, and began by reflecting on the inherent contradiction in the term:

> Because the choice of either legal designation—"employee" or "independent contractor"—in effect prejudges the issue of their right to bargain collectively, a new term is needed: "dependent contractor." They are "dependent" economically, although legally "contractors." The ambiguity, the paradox, of their position is thus reflected in the term used to identify them.[11]

Early discussions of a "third way" for worker classification in the sharing economy came from Wilma Liebman, the chair of the United States NLRB in the first Obama administration,[12] and from Denise Cheng of MIT in her 2015 Roosevelt Institute policy paper.[13] The more detailed Brookings Institute "independent worker" proposal from Harris and Krueger in December 2015 highlights a number of legal reforms that would need to accompany such a definition. Salient among them are the need to alter antitrust law to allow independent workers to collectively bargain (as I discussed earlier); the need to make entities that use labor provided from independent workers exempt from offering minimum wage, overtime, and other hours-of-work-based worker protections; the need to allow platforms to provide workers-compensation insurance without triggering employee categorization; and the need to allow non-employer platforms (or what they call "intermediaries") to withhold taxes. The authors also propose that an intermediary pay half of the worker's contributions toward the FICA payroll taxes (as much as 13.8% of earnings, and currently borne entirely by independent contractors).[14]

Although the introduction of a third category of worker will help many sharing economy providers and will also allow today's platforms greater flexibility in providing market-based protections and benefits to their providers than is currently possible, at the time I write this book, I believe that it is important to proceed cautiously in defining the boundaries around a new category and clarifying as well the specific obligations associated with each of the stakeholders (the platforms or other companies, the providers themselves, the different arms of government). Any changes to categorization will apply not just to sharing economy workers but, potentially, to existing workers currently classified as full-time employees, affiliated with both digital intermediaries and other traditional corporations. (For example, if taken to an extreme, the "immeasurability of work hours" principle that Harris and Krueger outline could apply to a wide variety of full-time employees who have flexible work arrangements or who perform knowledge work.)

The potential for unintended consequences that could dial back progress made by decades of labor reform are significant. For example, as my colleague John Horton of NYU argues in a 2011 blog post, the idea of platforms imposing a minimum wage seems progressive, but could have the unintended consequence of "pricing" a subset of providers out of the market, thereby shifting their income streams up to the more skilled or capable providers in the marketplace. As he concludes, "This starkly highlights one of the real drawbacks of a minimum wage as social policy, which is that it might be globally progressive and yet highly locally regressive for workers on the bad side of the cut-off."[15]

In the interim, I feel it would be very useful to create a "safe harbor" for specific sharing economy platforms that would allow them to give benefits, training, insurance, and other forms of protection to their independent contractor providers without triggering a categorization of these providers as employees. We are still very early in the labor transition induced by the sharing economy. Labor laws generally last for decades, but we have very little data, gathered over just a few years, about sharing economy labor activity. Creating this kind of safe harbor may be the right action today because it allows us both time and "space" to learn what kinds of protections and benefits might actually emerge naturally as market outcomes—for example, whether platforms will in fact invest in training their providers, or use benefits to attract better providers—and what might require governmental intervention. After all, at least in the United States, a number of facets of "employee benefits," including paid maternity leave, income stability, subsidies on better than average health and dental insurance, and paid vacations, are not in fact mandated by law, but are often provided voluntarily by companies, driven by their desire to keep good talent, and to nurture it appropriately. A safe harbor will allow us to understand how correspondingly nurturing venture-backed platforms will be of their providers if given the freedom to invest in them without having to employ them full-time.

Finally, it seems worth looking at a 2005 decision by the NLRB (one that Wilma Liebman pointed me to during a very interesting conversation in early 2015) in the context of what kinds of dimensions are currently used to make this determination, as well as of how well they apply to the sharing economy.[16] The case, again, involved whether or not newspaper carriers were employees or contractors. The criteria used to reify the carriers' status as contractors were established using several dimensions. First, did the worker complete an application or a contract? (It isn't clear if filling out a Web form would constitute an application or not.) Employees are given applications to complete, whereas contractors are issued contracts. Second, are taxes being withheld? Employers withhold taxes from employees' paychecks as they are issued but contractors, who receive a 1099 from an employer at the end the year, pay directly to the government. (Airbnb is withholding hotel taxes in a growing number of cities, an administrative convenience that clearly shouldn't alter its hosts' employment status.) Third, who supplies the tools needed to complete the job in question? Employees are typically provided with the tools they need to complete a job while contractors are expected to supply their own tools. (Would the centrally provided Uber driver app, or the Airbnb/ Etsy software that every host and customer uses be considered a "tool"?) Fourth, can disciplinary actions be taken against the worker? While independent contractors may have their contracts terminated, they can't be disciplined as employees might be. (Does blocking someone temporarily from accessing a platform, or lowering his or her ranking on a recommended provider list, constitute "disciplinary action"? Every platform has the ability to do this.) Fifth, is the worker free to solicit new customers and set their own prices? Again, while contractors can solicit new customers, in most cases, employees cannot nor are they expected to do so. (I return to this point in "How Entrepreneurial Is Your Platform," later in this chapter.) Finally, who is responsible for training? While most contractors are responsible for their own training, in the case of employees, there is an expectation that training will be provided. (Does attending an Airbnb host event constitute "training"?)

If we apply these labor guidelines, or those of the IRS, to the sharing economy, it is clear we need a more fine-grained definition of a variety of other aspects of the institution-worker relationship, and not just "control" and "dependence." A lot of what is sold on Etsy, perhaps, has limited market potential if the channel were to shut down, which makes many Etsy sellers "economically dependent" on the platform. But no reasonable person would consider them employees. The different platform dimensions I identified in chapter 3, and to which I return later in this chapter (in the section titled "How Entrepreneurial Is Your Platform?"), may form one basis for a longer-run solution.

The New Social Safety Net

As we wait for a new categorization of work to take shape, we continue to journey into an economy where a larger and larger percent of the population will not seek employment as salaried workers. Important worker protections like health coverage, insurance against workplace injuries, paid vacations, a stable income, and other safeguards often provided or guaranteed by large institutional employers will need to come from other sources. This challenge was summarized well in the op-ed on the gig economy by Senator Mark Warner, which I also quoted from in chapter 7: "So these workers, even if they are doing very well, exist on a high wire, with no safety net beneath them. That may work for many of them—until the day that it doesn't. That's also the day that taxpayers could be handed the bill, which is why Washington needs to start asking some tough policy questions."[17]

In October 2015, a diverse group of individuals signed a letter proposing portable benefits for sharing economy workers. The collective was spearheaded by the Peers co-founder Natalie Foster; a former White House senior advisor, Greg Nelson; a corporate social responsibility expert and freelancer, Libby Reder; and the former McKinsey consultant Lenny Mendoza. I was a signatory, as were the Freelancers Union founder Sara Horowitz and the coworker.org founder Michelle Miller, both of whom I discussed in chapter 7. The 40 or so other initial signatories included the CEOs of Etsy (Chad Dickerson), Handy (Oisin Hanrahan), and Instacart (Apoorva Mehta); Lyft's president John Zimmer and its CEO Logan Green; the Silicon Valley icon Tim O'Reilly; the influential labor organizer and former SEIU president Andy Stern; the venture capitalists Brad Burnham, Simon Rothman, and Hunter Walk; as well as the leadership of the Aspen Institute, the Roosevelt Institute, the Institute for the Future, and a few other professors, from Berkeley, Harvard and Northwestern.

The letter set out a number of principles to guide the creation of these portable benefits. These included a call for the model to be:

Independent: Any worker should be able to access a certain basic set of protections as an individual regardless of where they source income opportunities.

Portable: A person should be able to take benefits and protections with them in and out of various work scenarios.

Universal: All workers should have access to a basic set of benefits regardless of employment status.

Supportive of innovation: Businesses should be empowered to explore and pilot safety net options regardless of the worker classification they utilize.[18]

These principles, simple and intuitive, frame the vision of a collective whose diversity of stakeholders points to a potent future for the legislative action and regulatory reform needed to realize the vision.

However, the vision, while compelling, does not address where the funding for this safety net will come from. Activists like Sara Horowitz, who founded her Freelancers Union in 1997, have been working for decades trying to create a self-funded benefits solution for freelance workers. It seems natural that the funding model might depend on how dependent the freelancers are on their freelance work to make a living. Sara's own research has shown that there is a wide variety in the nature of freelance work in the United States: while her estimates peg the 2015 count of freelancers in the United States at a remarkable 53 million, about one in four of these are "moonlighters," or people who supplement income from a full-time job with freelance work on the side, and a further 2.8 million are small business owners who employ others but still identify with the freelance worker label.[19]

As I argue in a Policy Network essay in 2014, governments will face significant challenges funding these new capital contributions to society.[20] Decoupling this safety net from full-time employment would require some adjustment even in countries where many such safeguards are paid for by the state, for instance in the Scandinavian countries that have adopted what is often called the Nordic model of the welfare state. The challenge will be even greater in countries such as the United States and the United Kingdom, where large institutional employers have a bigger hand in providing worker benefits.

Despite the obvious challenges in scaling solutions developed for smaller countries like Denmark (with a population of less than 6 million) to larger ones like the United States (with its population of over 300 million), it is nevertheless instructive to look at one particular dimension of the Nordic model, that of Flexicurity, a linguistic blend of "flexible" and "security." This model provides labor policy that allows both greater flexibility in contracting, as well as greater flexibility in job mobility, implemented through proactive job training programs; it ensures security in terms of income stability during transitions between jobs. A simple extension might instead lower income volatility between weeks or months, based on a historical average earnings stream.

A bolder possibility along these lines is embodied in the idea of a fixed monthly income guaranteed by the government. While this idea may seem quite extreme, it is a vision whose advocates range from the social entrepreneur Peter Barnes, whose book *With Liberty and Dividends for All* discusses the desirability of a universal basic income,[21] to the venture capitalist Albert Wenger of Union Square Ventures, who spoke about basic income at his TEDxNewYork talk in November 2014. In her entertaining Medium post "Silicon Valley's Basic Income Bromance," Lauren Smiley discusses the diverse base of support for basic income across a variety stakeholders in the technology industry.

The underlying idea of a basic income is really simple. Every working-age individual in a country receives a monthly check from the government. No strings attached. Although seemingly radical, the idea is closer to reality than one might imagine. In fact, a referendum will be held in Switzerland in 2016 to vote on creating a basic annual income of 30,000 francs (a little over 30,000 US dollars). In a different conception put forth by the famed German sociologist Ulrich Beck, the basic income would not be free money, but would emerge from a system under which citizens alternated between regular paid work and "civil labor."

An obvious objection to this kind of social safety net is based on a fear that it lowers people's incentive to work. However, the little evidence that we have from prior experiments suggests otherwise. In 1974, the Canadian town of Dauphin in Manitoba conducted an experiment: 30% of the town's population was given a "mincome," a minimum income, for five years. The level of this guaranteed income was lowered by between 35% and 75% (in three treatment tranches) for people who had jobs, thus varying the structural disincentive to seek employment. Despite this design, as reported in a study by the economist Evelyn Forget, the drops in the fraction of the "treated" group (the 30% receiving the mincome) who sought paid employment were relatively small (1% for men, 5% for unmarried women, and 3% for married women), and Forget further reports that the social benefits from this program seemed to outweigh any losses in labor output.[22]

At a recent New York panel discussion organized by Natalie Foster in June, Wenger pointed to the Alaska Permanent Fund as an example, and argued that an income of $1,000 per month to every working-age American would cost less than 20% of the GDP. Incentive effects aside, it seems clear that the critical challenge of getting a basic income up and running is political rather than economic, especially around the issue of how one might seed-fund it.

Meanwhile, there is precedent to suggest that a middle-ground solution involving the market is not a bad idea. For example, as corporate pension plans have dwindled in the United States over the last few decades, the 401(k) and associated programs have evolved to facilitate retirement planning. These represent a partnership between different stakeholders—individuals put aside a portion of their income each month, corporations supplement their contribution, and the government provides a tax break. I don't mean to suggest that 401(k) plans have solved the retirement problem for everyone, but merely that they represent a partnership model that has worked for some over the last decades in creating an alternative to employer-provided benefits. We may seek to create similar structures for other slices of the safety net.

Senator Warner proposes a different kind of hybrid model, the "hour bank," which would create underlying infrastructure for the provision of benefits to providers who work through multiple platforms. As Warner describes, it has been "used by the building trades for 60 years, to administer benefits for members who work for a series of contractors. It could be consumer driven in part, too—perhaps allowing customers to designate a portion of their payments to go to a fund that helps support workers."[23] Shelby Clark, a Turo co-founder and, as of 2015, the executive director of Peers.org suggests that such a model needs to have three characteristics: independent access (workers choose benefits independent of employer), innovative benefits (a safety net tailored to the reality of people working through multiple platforms), and flexible payments (allowing both the worker and one or more "employers" to share the contributions).[24]

Another possibility is for the platforms themselves to embrace the responsibility. Protecting the providers that power their profits may not simply be doing the right thing; it can also be smart capitalism. As I discussed in chapter 3, today's Internet marketplaces are not mere clearinghouses for matching and price discovery. Rather, they are new market-firm hybrids that centralize certain activities (branding, trust, payments, and sometimes pricing and customer service), while decentralizing others (supply infrastructure creation and actual service provision). Offering a branded service experience of consistently high quality requires a reliable and steady source of high quality supply from providers. This supply must be ensured by platforms that lack the typical directive authority or culture-building capabilities that traditional firms use to manage their employees. Put differently, a platform's most important economic "inputs" are its providers. Making sure they are protected, secure, and thus more focused on their provision activities makes good long-run business sense.

There is also reason to believe that provider protection will be an effective retention strategy for platforms. If collective organizing for independent contractors becomes legal, platforms must consider provider unionization. These platforms must also consider the prospect of large-scale provider migration that might accompany the creation of local cooperatives. (I discuss this in further detail later in this chapter. Also, as I mentioned in chapter 4, the latter scenario—a threat to any provider-dependent platform—is especially likely for taxi or chauffeured urban transportation platforms like Lyft and Uber, and geography-specific platforms like Instacart, TaskRabbit and Handy, where a majority of demand from each consumer is concentrated in a specific city, making network effects from global reach a less effective barrier to entry.) These risks can be mitigated partially by a worker safety net that is platform specific and creates a longer-term partnership with providers.

While it may be ideal if platforms adopted this thinking and embraced worker protection as a business strategy, it seems likely that, as has been in the case in the past, worker protections will also be contingent on the emergence of new types of worker alliances. From early guilds, which enabled artisans to gain control of local markets and realize higher prices for their work, to 20th-century labor unions, we find examples through history of workers organizing to empower themselves on both an individual and collective level under a range of economic models. Moving forward, we might expect to see the rise of new groups focused on protecting workers' interests. There is significant potential for these groups to use the "new power" of Jeremy Hiemans and Henry Timms that we have discussed in chapter 6 in a way that gives them a role akin to labor unions in the past, balancing power between the providers and the platforms. After all, in contrast to so-called old power, which was only held by a few, new power promises to be more open, participatory, and peer-driven—a resource most powerful when channeled rather than hoarded. A second scenario involves the rise of groups that more closely resemble traditional advocacy groups, like the National Domestic Workers Alliance, and whose primary mandate leads to lobbying for new labor laws. Finally, as discussed by Nathan Schneider of the University of Colorado in a 2015 *New Yorker* article, it is possible that we will witness the emergence of new guilds—worker organizations that set their own standards of service.[25] These guilds could serve a role akin to the one already played by some professional organizations (e.g., the American Medical Association), and if indeed they emerge, it seems natural to expect they will extend their role into facilitating collective action for the labor force they represent.

How Entrepreneurial Is Your Platform?

A quick comparison of Etsy's platform and Uber's platform illustrates that each has a fairly different relationship with their providers. Uber sets prices and controls merchandising; Uber customers don't choose their drivers. Yet by offering car financing to its drivers, Uber has facilitated thousands of new microentrepreneurs who now, in a way, run their own small businesses. By contrast, Etsy's sellers are more entrepreneurial in a traditional sense. While they may be dependent on the Etsy platform to reach customers and process sales, they set prices, choose and are chosen by customers, and are responsible for their own merchandizing.

In an economy of microentrepreneurship, the level of *real* entrepreneurship facilitated seems like a natural way in which one might characterize the relationship between a platform and its workforce. In chapter 3 (table 3.1), I provided a glimpse into a number of different dimensions that I use to organize my thinking about platforms. To assess whether or not a platform supports entrepreneurship, one can redeploy that framework to examine what aspects of provision through the platform resemble traditional contract work, and what aspects are more entrepreneurial. One can do this by categorizing the factors into three kinds—incubation, independence, and infrastructure (see table 8.3).

Incubation

We have seen a number of institutions that "incubate" or "accelerate" early-stage businesses emerge over the last few years. Simply put, their goal is to help get a start-up business off the ground using a process that speeds up development by providing aspiring entrepreneurs with the resources and services they need to succeed. In order to understand whether or not a peer-to-peer platform is supporting entrepreneurship, it

Table 8.3
Factors in assessing a platform's support of entrepreneurship

Incubation

Platform provides centralized mentoring

Platform facilitates peer-to-peer mentoring

Platform facilitates community groups among providers

Platform provides "production" financing to providers

Independence

Provider chooses pricing

Provider has in-person customer contact

Provider takes on complex tasks of 'managing inventory/supply'

Provider free to merchandize as they see fit (description, photo)

Provider acquires or uses owned assets for production

Easy for provider to enter and exit provision

Provider has virtual direct customer contact

Platform provides centralized customer support

Transparent peer-to-peer feedback systems

Platform provides day-to-day operational input to providers

Customers choose their providers

Providers choose their customers

Infrastructure

Peer-to-peer feedback systems

Platform facilitates the logistics of getting service to customers

Platform-based provider screening

Platform provides insurance, escrow, other risk-minimization

Platform handles payment processing

Conduits to external trust indicators

is first important to consider whether or not the platform is doing anything to incubate fledging microbusinesses.

Uber, for instance, arguably does incubate fledging business by providing financing to drivers who may otherwise be ineligible to secure an auto loan (e.g., because drivers are new immigrants without a credit history in their country of residence). Airbnb, which has a voluntary and informal training program (e.g., by inviting new hosts to meet-ups with seasoned hosts), and which more recently has started offering more formal training programs for its hosts, is also arguably incubating business by providing new entrepreneurs with the skills they need to succeed on the platform. Etsy's forums, which enable sellers to build community and draw on other sellers' expertise to do everything from troubleshoot platform bugs to gain tips on how to use social media platforms to promote their Etsy shop, also provide an example of the way in which a platform might facilitate incubation.

Independence

As illustrated in table 8.3, there are a number of dimensions to independence. Many platforms require that providers acquire or otherwise "bring" assets to the provision of their services: TaskRabbit's taskers may need to provide a vehicle, Lyft drivers and Getaround providers must own their cars, Airbnb hosts own or rent their space, and Etsy sellers must have access to their own production facilities. It may seem like all of the platforms are facilitating independence on this dimension, but that isn't necessarily going to be the case in the future—we are bound to see the emergence of centralized production facilities of different kinds, whether they be fleets of driverless Ubers or a maker space with different additive manufacturing capabilities, and we will then perhaps need to examine the extent to which the platform requires its providers to use its own centralized assets.

A second dimension relates to pricing, supply, and merchandizing. For the most part, most sharing economy platforms—TaskRabbit, Airbnb, Uber, Lyft, Getaround—allow their providers to choose when they, their assets, or their services are available. This forces providers to "learn" how to manage their inventory—whether it be when to be behind their Lyft wheel, what months to rent their Airbnb, what hours of the day to offer their Getaround rental, or what days of week to be available as a Handy provider to help people move.

There is also variation in the level of pricing control. Uber and Lyft define prices in each of their cities, while Sidecar allowed drivers to set their own prices. TaskRabbit allows home cleaners to choose their own rates, while HomeJoy used to set a flat hourly rate in each city. Airbnb offers complete pricing flexibility, but provides a pricing tool for hosts that may be based in part on a centralized revenue management approach. Etsy sellers, Getaround providers, and Airbnb hosts have to invest significantly in merchandizing (photos, copy that describes their products or properties, and so on), while Uber and Lyft drivers are not called upon to do this, although this perhaps reflects the service being offered rather than the nature of the platform itself.

Analogously, when a provider can choose its customers and vice versa, this signals a greater level of independence, since it allows the creation of provider-specific customer relationships that are more entrepreneurial and less contractor-like. Again, on this front, there is variety across platforms. Airbnb allows complete freedom for guests to choose their hosts and vice versa. (There is a "book now" alternative, but that's a choice a host can make.) TaskRabbit allows customers to choose providers, but the system restricts fairly rigidly the set of providers a customer can choose from. Providers, on the other hand, are free to accept or reject customers.

There is a delicate balance between the forms of incubation that a platform might provide, and the level of independence it allows. Airbnb strikes an interesting balance on this front. Hosts are free to rent out any space of their choosing, and have control over the "user experience" that guests enjoy. While visitors may or may not appreciate their hosts' décor, their level of cleanliness, or response time, the platform places no restrictions on what types of dwellings can be rented nor in what conditions. At the end of the day, an Airbnb host can choose to not clean and to skip the courtesy of providing clean towels and sheets, and the consequences are borne through the online feedback system.

Infrastructure

As I discussed in chapter 2, we have come a long way since Craigslist, and most of today's sharing economy platforms provide some kind of infrastructure to facilitate the commerce they enable. Most provide a variety of different forms of trust, making their "space" a safe place for providers to nurture their businesses.

A simple dimension, although one that is likely to become less important over time, is whether or not the platform in question provides the infrastructure needed to carry out financial exchanges. For example, does the platform offer a secure way to complete transactions, and more notably does the platform provide a way to carry out financial exchanges without reliance on a traditional trusted third party? Another dimension relates to whether the platform offers customer relationship management (CRM) mechanisms that aid a provider in their customer service. Airbnb provides a peer-to-peer messaging service that facilitates host-guest communication, while Uber's customer support is almost all centrally provided by the platform.

The connection becomes a little more complex when one needs to consider whether or not the platform has the potential to provide assurance and insurance both to users and providers. One might think of risk minimizing forms of infrastructure (like car insurance, host insurance, workers compensation insurance) as tied by law to employees rather than entrepreneurs, but this kind of insurance and escrow also allows the platform to become a safe place for providers to "grow their microbusiness."

Sharing Ownership in the Sharing Economy

Although less common than shareholder corporations, the cooperative ownership structure has a presence in both the US and European economies, with (as of 2009) over 30,000 cooperatives operating in 73,000 US locations, holding assets over $2 trillion, and revenues of over $650 billion.[26]

A key early advocate of this structure for the sharing economy is Janelle Orsi, a 2014 Ashoka Fellow and thought leader about law in the sharing economy. In 2010, Orsi founded the Sustainable Economies Law Center (SELC) to develop a legal infrastructure and legal expertise that would sustain worker cooperatives of different kinds.[27] More broadly, SELC focuses on interventions that will enable the widespread creation of new economic models, ranging from direct legal support to communities to drafting new legislation. She and her team are building networks of legal practitioners and changemakers with the goal of establishing a new category of case law and transactional lawyering meant to directly support new sharing economy activity. Another advocate, Chelsea Rustrum, notes in her Digital Cooperative 101 that cooperatives also support greater community development.[28]

Over the course of 2015, Trebor Scholz of the New School and Nathan Schneider of the University of Colorado have become the face of a movement calling for the emergence of "platform cooperatives," sharing economy platforms owned by their providers and funded through mechanisms other than institutional venture capital.[29] Their inaugural "Platform

Cooperativism" conference, held in November 2015, brought together hundreds of enthusiasts looking to create the next generation of organizations to fulfill the Nobel laureate Elinor Ostrum's vision of "governing the commons,"[30] and promises to seed a new wave of thinking and research about alternative ownership structures to shareholder corporations that are made possible by new Internet technologies.

In the face of this newly found optimism, it is instructive to examine why worker cooperatives have been somewhat rare in the United States. While there are some successful worker cooperatives (for example, Sunkist, formerly the California Fruit Exchange, is entirely owned by citrus fruit growers and has been since 1893), most US worker cooperatives have proven less successful and relatively short-lived. Economic theory suggests that worker cooperatives are more efficient than shareholder corporations when there isn't a great deal of diversity in the levels of contribution across workers, when the level of external competition is low, and when there isn't the need for frequent investments in response to technological change. This would explain why a worker cooperative like Sunkist has thrived since the late 19th century where other types of cooperatives have failed.

Do current industries seeing the emergence of peer-to-peer platforms share something in common with Sunkist? If one thinks about it, a worker-owned equivalent to Uber seems quite feasible. Cab drivers, after all, offer a more or less uniform service in an industry with a limited amount of competition. Once the technology associated with "e-hail" is commoditized, the potential for a worker cooperative appears to be in place, since each local market is contestable, as I discussed in chapter 5. The emergence of Swift, a platform owned by drivers, may be an early leading indicator.[31] (At least until the fleets of driverless cars take over.)

Many active participants in the sharing economy see the sharing of the wealth as a moral imperative; others suggest it makes good business sense. In a 2014 *Fast Company* article, Lisa Gansky summarized the early evolution of the sharing economy by indicating that "early companies like Uber, Lyft, Quirky, Airbnb, TaskRabbit, RelayRides, and 99 Designs garnered much visibility, but these companies were funded by venture capital, with an eye on big paydays for investors—and not necessarily for the drivers, hosts, creators, and sellers that make the companies viable." As an active investor herself, she noted, "There is nothing wrong with that approach. I myself have invested in several private companies over the years and have been a beneficiary of the process." However, in arguing for expanding, she points out: "Building business models that generate the dignity and incentives that accompany ownership enhance the resilience and value of a brand. A Sunkist-like cooperative model is one way forward. There are others. Resilient brands and marketplaces understand that retaining the high performers is key to success for any business."[32]

However, when it comes down to the reality of actually creating the cooperatives, many founders find the prospect of building a scalable business with that ownership model challenging. During a panel discussion that Juliet Schor and I participated in at the 2015 Platform Cooperativism conference Schor highlighted two specific challenges she had noticed with sharing economy cooperatives: that their value system was better thought out than their value proposition (or in other words, that they tended to focus excessively on how the wealth would be shared rather than on a compelling offer to create the value in the first place), and that she had observed significant levels of class, race, and gender exclusivity in her ethnographic research of sharing economy cooperatives.

Overcoming both of the challenges raised by Schor seems critical to the widespread success of platform cooperatives. However, the challenge I have heard mentioned most frequently is of raising money, and in particular, early-stage capital. Simply put, the model of corporate ownership naturally lends itself much more seamlessly to the raising of large amounts of capital in exchange for outside ownership.

In September 2014, I moderated a panel discussion about new ownership models for the sharing economy at the Social Capital Markets conference (SOCAP). The panelists included Orsi, Gansky, and Adam Werbach, a co-founder of Yerdle, the platform to exchange owned assets that I discussed in the introductory chapter. Werbach, a former Sierra Club president, discussed the challenges he faced looking for ways in which he could structure Yerdle as a cooperative while still preserving the ability to raise the external capital he knew would be necessary to realize his vision. While noting that he was familiar with Orsi's work, Werbach described the search for an ownership model as a challenge, noting that he was

familiar with co-op structures and had a bunch of conversations about all of the different models of doing that—and they rapidly became a swarm hole for us: really hard, no good models to point to, couldn't actually know what to do and meanwhile we were trying to build a product and organization. We found, as an option, starting up as a California benefit corporation. ... This is a part of California corporate law that allows you to set up a corporation and essentially say that your mission is your top priority and you can make a choice that would be noneconomic in favor of your mission and your directors wouldn't be able to fire you for that or your shareholders wouldn't be able to sue you for that, which is a basic protection for the organization.[33]

Werbach then went on to discuss how he raised a seed round of financing successfully, but people around him felt he would face significant challenges raising his next round of financing as a benefit corporation. Yerdle was eventually funded by the Westly Group (an investor in Honest Buildings, another benefit corporation), and has since also received additional funding from traditional venture capital investors, but his experience highlights the barriers entrepreneurs perceive to structuring themselves as anything other than a traditional corporation.

In many ways, these fundraising challenges echo those raised by OuiShare co-founder Benjamin Tincq. (See chapter 1, where I quote him at length describing how the purpose-driven philosophy of many sharing economy entrepreneurs are often subsumed by capital realities when it comes time to put their ideals into action.) For entrepreneurs like Tiberius Brastaviceanu, who is trying to expand Yochai Benkler's idea of "commons-based peer production" (also discussed in chapter 1) beyond settings like Wikipedia and Linux that rely on free labor, there are no standard ways in which one can organize and fundraise. As he told Nathan Schneider in 2014, "There's no blueprint for the kind of organization we're trying to build."[34]

However, a number of new alternative funding models are emerging that promise to make this vision of "sharing the wealth" in the sharing economy feasible. One of these, the Fairshare model from Karl Sjogren, devises a structure based on different classes of ownership shares—for founders, for people with a continuous working role, for users, and for investors—that reflects the differing contributions of these different stakeholders.[35] In many ways, the design seems like a hybrid of different co-op types and a shareholder corporation, and its philosophy is reminiscent of the different kinds of "coin" that, as I discussed in chapter 4, Matan Field of BackFeed envisages will power the marketplaces of the future. Another model, pioneered by Joel Dietz of Swarm, combines the idea of basic income with different roles in a "distributed collaborative organization to create a way of crowdfunding a cooperative structure. A third model, embodied, for instance, in the efforts of organizations like Cutting Edge Capital, aim to bring the existing "direct public offering" model into the digital age by creating online marketplaces that facilitate it. There are also many forms of traditional crowdfunding that focus on cooperatives, including the Peak Agency, and organizations like the Democracy Collaborative that connect nascent cooperatives with philanthropists, nonprofits, and foundations in their respective areas.

As experimentation with different platform cooperative models continues, a different yet familiar idea—allocating shares of platforms (that remain shareholder corporations) to providers—seems like the most pragmatic near-term path towards sharing the wealth of the sharing economy. Such "provider stock ownership programs" (PSOPs) could achieve, for platforms, the mix of joint ownership and profit sharing that employee stock ownership programs (ESOPs) aspire to implement for traditional organizations. (And the level of such ownership can be significant—in 1995, the United Airlines ESOP owned 55% of the company.) An early example of this kind of program is from Juno, a ridesharing service that has committed to ensuring that its drivers own 50% of the company's founding stock by 2026.

Data Darwinism

In March 2013, after observing a protest from Uber drivers who had been dropped from the platform after their average user rating fell below a pre-specified minimum—such protests were unusual at the time—GigaOm founder Om Malik posted a blog entry in which he wondered if we were witnessing the new world of labor unrest: "In the industrial era, labor unrest came when the workers felt that the owners were profiting wrongfully from them. I wonder if in the connected age, we are going to see labor unrest when folks are unceremoniously dropped from the on-demand labor pool."[36]

Malik's comment may seem a little tongue-in-cheek, but it was oddly prescient of what was to unfold over the next couple of years. More importantly, there was a deeper point in his post. Malik predicted the emergence of what he termed "data-Darwinism" and suggested that it will be an important social and labor issue in the years to come.

So what exactly is data Darwinism? The key idea relates to how we evaluate our providers, the workforce of the sharing economy, and how these evaluations, codified in data, could shape access opportunities for this workforce.

Consider the example of the Uber drivers of 2013 who had been dropped from the platform. It is possible that these were in fact the "bad apples" that Uber's peer-to-peer feedback systems rightly weeded out. But what if the drivers had a bad draw of customers? What if one of the drivers simply had a bad day at work, which caused a few customers to rate him or her poorly? What if customers in a neighborhood systematically didn't like drivers of a particular ethnicity, and this was the neighborhood a driver happened to be in one day. Or what if, as Josh Dzieza argued in his 2015 article "The Ratings Game," the proliferation of online feedback systems has simply turned us customers into really bad bosses.[37] A simple point emerges from Malik's post: perhaps Uber's rating system shouldn't be too quick in rushing to judgment.

But the more significant point is that one's access to opportunities today also shape one's future access to opportunities. Restaurants that get well rated early on Yelp often enjoy increased demand as a consequence of a higher perceived value, allowing them (if they are good) to build a more robust reputation over time. And as Professor Michael Luca from Harvard Business School has shown, people have a propensity to be biased by the ratings they have already seen, and rate a highly rated restaurant higher based simply on the fact that the establishment had a higher rating to begin with. Further, as Kartik Hosanagar and Daniel Fleder of the Wharton School demonstrate, automated recommender systems can amplify this bias, nudging choices presented to future customers toward those products that have enjoyed prior success, further favoring the popular over the niche.[38]

This is the *Darwinist* aspect of rating systems based on user-generated data. The strong get stronger. The fittest survive. Even though these assessments of fitness might be rather noisy.

What happens when we start to apply these product and merchant rating systems to individuals looking for work? In 2015, TaskRabbit began to present specific taskers to each potential customer rather than allowing customers and taskers to simply find each other based on requests and bids. It is quite likely that this "consideration set" is biased toward those taskers who have already built up a good reputation. Over time, a greater percent of what shapes our access to opportunity will be the "equity" from online feedback systems rather than in the credentialing provided by real-world institutions or the contact lists on our LinkedIn profiles.

As Mike Dudas, the co-founder (along with NYU Stern alum Tanner Hackett) of Button, a platform that creates more seamless interaction across mobile apps, discussed in a blog post: "This equity comes in the form of performance data that market participants create while providing goods or services to customers in a marketplace. This data can take the form of ratings and reviews, completed works, photos, and income reports. This data is at the core of systems that marketplaces use to establish trust today."[39] In such a world, a couple of slips early in one's "platform career" may have serious consequences, especially if sharing economy platforms start to become critical conduits to finding work (much like Amazon is now an essential channel for anyone selling niche products via mail-order).

As the world of work starts to rely more heavily on such data, a different barrier to access might be the inability to "take this data with you" when you want to, say, switch to a different platform or channel. Today, when you start hosting on Airbnb or Etsy, you start without any feedback. According to Dudas, there is an alternative that might be better for society:

The next step would be to allow marketplace service providers to take their data (ratings, reviews, pictures, income statements, etc.) with them if they choose to leave a specific platform or marketplace; I call this employee data portability. Employee data portability would empower workers, arming them with a strong tool for re-employment and valuable data that could be used to directly market to potential customers[40]

I began this chapter by two contrasting future worlds of work promised by the sharing economy: one of empowered entrepreneurs and the other of "disenfranchised drones." As the discussion in this chapter illustrates, we must wade into this exciting yet uncertain future prepared to grapple with a number of complex societal issues, including the reclassification of work, the funding of the social safety net, and the creation of new ownership structures.

It is important that we realize that neither future is preordained by the economic fundamentals. Crowd-based capitalism is still in its infancy. We are bound to see a mix of both futures. But the choices we make over the coming decade will determine which one dominates.

9

Concluding Thoughts

Writing a manageably sized book about a topic one is passionate about forces some tough choices, and I omitted from the discussion some topics of great interest to me. In aiming to strike a balance between practicality and prophesy, I have focused the book more heavily on the immediate future of crowd-based capitalism, rather than on the more distant future. The accommodation, transportation, and freelance labor sectors have been the earliest to see big changes induced by crowd-based capitalism, but commercial real estate, health care provision and energy production and distribution will soon follow. And the digitization of the physical will, over the coming decade, yield mass-market autonomous vehicles in the United States, Western Europe and parts of Asia, radically reshaping the automobile industry, shifting market power away from today's leading manufacturers and towards a range of technology platforms—Uber, Lyft, Didi Kuaidi and Ola, as well as Apple, Google, and perhaps even Amazon. In parallel, the additive manufacturing revolution will change how artifacts are made, shifting more and more production into the crowd. The blockchain revolution may create new global exchange possibilities we have not yet begun to conceive.

Our urban infrastructures will also be reshaped by crowd-based partnership models. Today's on-demand platforms have already produced a creative new mix of public and private transit. What Wake Forest College professor Lauren Rhue and I call "invisible infrastructure"—that is, the use of idling capacity and digital platforms to build citywide or nationwide capabilities that once required steel and concrete investment—may shape the urban infrastructures of the future. BlaBlaCar's national transportation networks, JustPark's invisible parking lots, and Airbnb's disaster-relief housing platform are early examples. The evolution of trust in society on account of people's increased participation in the sharing economy will play a key role in making invisible infrastructure feasible.

As a consequence, deepening our understanding of trust in society that is digitally mediated, as well as how the use of digital technologies changes levels of trust between people, is critically important. I hope our research with Frederic Mazella of BlaBlaCar and my NYU colleague Mareike Mohlmann, which is ongoing as this book goes to press—but which will be available via the NYU and BlaBlaCar websites in 2016—will be a first step in this direction.

City governments, in parallel, will try to become more "shareable" as they get more crowded. Over time, they are likely to realize that unlocking the true potential of the sharing economy requires a fundamentally rethinking of how they plan and govern, and fairly radical changes in our approach towards both residential zoning and the role of regulatory agencies.

* * *

Is crowd-based capitalism a passing phase, an interesting social experiment before society returns to the familiar confines of 20th-century managerial capitalism? This seems quite unlikely. In a September 2015 Project Syndicate op-ed, my NYU Stern colleague and Nobel-prize winning economist Michael Spence summarized why:

> The truth is that the Internet-led process of exploiting under-utilized resources— be they physical and financial capital or human capital and talent—is both unstoppable and accelerating. The long-term benefits consist not just in efficiency and productivity gains (large enough to show up in macro data), but also in much-needed new jobs requiring a broad range of skills. Indeed, those who fear the job-destroying and job-shifting power of automation should look upon the sharing economy and breathe a bit of a sigh of relief."[1]

* * *

The professor in me hopes that the book leaves you with a set of frameworks that give you new perspective, a critical lens through which you develop your own, deeper, understanding of this complex new world. (As Marcel Proust has told us, "The true voyage of discovery is not in seeking new landscapes but in having new eyes.")

In chapter 1, I gave you a first lens through which to consider the odd meld of the economic and the social in the sharing economy, highlighting how what we are seeing unfold has elements of both a commercial economy and a gift economy. In chapter 2, I used a technology-centric lens, drawing on an evolving understanding of digital technologies to help you think about the future of capitalism as shaped by its digital and trust determinants. In chapter 3, you encountered the lens of transaction costs, of markets and hierarchies, thinking through what kinds of institutions this blurring of boundaries between the visible and invisible hands might yield. In chapter 4, through a short discussion about the new wave of digital enablers as well as their historical precedents, I hope you have a better lens through which to view how the decentralized peer-to-peer revolution unfolds, and, despite the surrounding idealism, recognize the significant possibility for value re-aggregation by large intermediaries.

These first four chapters focused on cause. Their eventual effects are on society, on the economy, on how we regulate human interaction, and on what the future of work will look like. Chapter 5 outlines some fundamentals that can form the basis for a more informed discussion and analysis of what to expect and how to measure the eventual economic impacts. Chapter 6 imagines a new world of regulation, with a different balance between public and private players, and new digitally enabled manifestations of age-old community enforcement. Chapter 7 paints a clearer picture of what changes, beyond offshoring and automation, we should expect for our workforce, and chapter 8 equips you with an understanding of the key policy challenges these will induce in the years to come.

The complexity of this ongoing transition—part of a broader set of changes that Professor Klaus Schwab, the founder of the World Economic Forum calls the "fourth industrial revolution," may explain society's struggle to come up with a shared label for the phenomenon I call crowd-based capitalism.[2] Perhaps, like most interesting things in life, the sharing economy is shaped by its internal contradictions.

Capitalist or socialist? Commercial economy or gift economy? Market or hierarchy? Global or local economic impact? Regulatory arbitrage or self-regulatory expression? Centralized or decentralized value capture? Empowered entrepreneur or disenfranchised drone? Job destruction or work creation? Isolated or connected societies? As you may have realized by now, the answer to each of these questions in the sharing economy is "yes."

Notes

Introduction

1. See the December update of the 2012 *Internet Trends Report* at http://www .kpcb.com/blog/2012-internet-trends-update and the May 2012 report at http://www.kpcb.com/blog/2012-internet-trends.

2. https://skift.com/2016/01/31/airbnb-cto-and-3-tech-ceos-discuss-the-digital -platform-economy-at-davos.

3. Erica Swallow, "The Rise of the Sharing Economy," February 7, 2012. http://mashable.com/2012/02/07/sharing-economy.

4. Although Funding Circle is now open to US and global investing, the platform's business model is different in the United States. Most of the lenders are commercial for US borrowers, and individuals don't make aggregate small investments into a large loan. I use the sterling pound example because this model of investment is unique to the UK.

5. Joel Stein, "Tales from the Sharing Economy, *Time*, February 7, 2015. http://time.com/3687335/in-the-latest-issue-21.

6. I don't have an exact date for the onset of the Industrial Revolution, although most of what I have read suggests sometime between 1750 and 1800. See, for example, Robert Lucas, "The Industrial Revolution: Past and Future" (2004), https://www.minneapolisfed.org/publications/the-region/the-industrial- revolution-past-and-future.

7. Alfred Chandler, *The Visible Hand: The Managerial Revolution in American Business* (Cambridge: Harvard University Press, 1977), 17.

8. In "Stone Age Economics," Marshall Sahlins provides an interesting and insightful description of economic exchange as a cultural phenomenon, characterizing different forms of economic exchange during the Stone Age, and making the somewhat counterintuitive claim that these were the original affluent societies. Although some of his claims have been disputed by subsequent research, that claim itself is less important and interesting than the descriptions of models of exchange. Readers interested in a deeper history of exchange (and money) should also read David Graeber, *Debt: The First 5000 Years* (Brooklyn: Melville House, 2011).

9. I discuss a small fraction of the history of trust in economic exchange in greater detail in chapter 6.

10. I focus on the United States because, to my knowledge, its historical economic data on employment is most extensive. In Stanley Lebergott, *Manpower in Economic Growth* (New York: McGraw Hill, 1964), see his table A-4. I exclude nonpaid family workers, incorporated zero-employee businesses, and domestic workers from the charts. I am also grateful to my NYU Stern colleague, the economic historian Richard Sylla, for a highly illuminating discussion about this subject.

11. Lebergott, *Manpower*. I use data from table A-4 to compute the percentage of nonfarm workers. Again, I exclude domestic workers, unpaid workers, and zero-employee corporations. The percentage of "independent workers" in the United States workforce today depends on how you define "independent worker." It is notable, however, that the number of zero-employee firms in the US has grown rapidly in the last decade, numbering over 23 million in 2014.

12. The sociologist Juliet Schor discusses this in her essay *Debating the Sharing Economy*: "While the discourse of novelty in this sector is overrated, there is something new afoot: what I call "stranger sharing." Although there are exceptions (e.g., elite travelers in ancient Greece), people have historically limited sharing to within their own social networks. Today's sharing platforms facilitate sharing among people who do not know each other and who do not have friends or connections in common." http://www.greattransition.org/publication/debating-the-sharing-economy.

13. See, for example, Zimmer's participation in the "Wheels of Change" panel at the 2014 CityLab conference at http://bcove.me/1i8kqj02.

14. http://www.fastcompany.com/3038635/my-week-with-alfred-a-25-personal-butler.

15. Geoffrey A. Fowler, "There's an Uber for Everything Now," May 5, 2015, http://www.wsj.com/articles/theres-an-uber-for-everything-now-1430845789.

16. See TrustMan at http://www.betrustman.com. In the summer of 2015, Mazzella and I, along with others including NYU's Mareike Moehlmann, started collaborating on an academic study of why people trust each other on the BlaBlaCar platform. None of our findings are available as this book goes to press, but many will be released in 2016.

17. Cat Johnson, "The Tool Library Movement Gains Steam," January 29, 2014. http://www.shareable.net/blog/the-tool-library-movement-gains-steam.

18. Romain Dillet, "'La Ruche Qui Dit Oui' Scores $9 Million from USV and Felix Capital for Its Local Food Marketplace," *TechCrunch*, June 16, 2015. http://techcrunch.com/2015/06/16/la-ruche-qui-dit-oui-scores-9-million-from-usv-and-felix-capital-for-its-local-food-marketplace.

19. James Surowecki, "Uber Alles," *New Yorker*, September 16, 2013. http://www.newyorker.com/magazine/2013/09/16/uber-alles-2.

Chapter 1

1. http://2015.ouisharefest.com.

2. http://democracyos.org.

3. Jeremy Heimans and Henry Timms, "Understanding 'New Power,'" *Harvard Business Review*, December 2014, https://hbr.org/2014/12/understanding-new -power.

4. As of spring 2016, I am a member of OuiShare's 12-person advisory board. This is a position that involves no financial compensation.

5. Francesca Pick, "What OuiShare Means to Me," https://medium.com/ ouishare-connecting-the-collaborative-economy/what-ouishare-means-to-me -4f275d9917f.

6. For Gorenflo's description of Shareable, see http://shareable.net/about. The interview is available at http://www.collaborative-economy.com/project -updates/sharing-economy-with-neal-gorenflo-shareable. A summary is provided at http://www.shareable.net/blog/interviewed-shareables-neal-gorenflo-on-the -real-sharing-economy.

7. A collection of some of Owyang's blog posts is available at "Quick Guide: The Collaborative Economy Body of Work for Corporations (updated June 2015)," http://www.web-strategist.com/blog/2013/08/22/table-of-contents-the -collaborative-economy.

8. Arthur De Grave, "The Sharing Economy: Capitalism's Last Stand?," *OuiShare: The Magazine*, March 21, 2014, http://magazine.ouishare. net/2014/03/the-sharing-economy-capitalisms-last-stand.

9. Diana Filippova, "The Quest for New Values," *OuiShare: The Magazine*, October 27, 2014, http://magazine.ouishare.net/2014/10/the-quest-for-new-values-1.

10. Paul Romer, "Talkin' Bout a Revolution," January 2, 2015, http://paulromer .net/talkin-bout-the-revolution.

11. https://twitter.com/cdixon/status/626637369723199488.

12. Jeff John Roberts, "As 'Sharing Economy' Fades, These 2 Phrases Are Likely to Replace It," *Fortune*, July 29, 2015. http://fortune.com/2015/07/29/ sharing-economy-chart.

13. Rachel Botsman and Roo Rogers, *What's Mine Is Yours: The Rise of Collaborative Consumption* (New York: HarperCollins), xv.

14. Lisa Gansky, *The Mesh: Why the Future of Business Is Sharing* (New York: Portfolio Penguin, 2010). https://informationdj.files.wordpress.com/2012/01/ future-of-business-is-lisa-gansky.pdf.

15. Ibid.

16. Alex Stephany, *The Business of Sharing: Making It in the New Sharing Economy* (London: Palgrave Macmillan, 2015), 9.

17. Ibid., 12.

18. Yochai Benkler, "'Sharing Nicely': On Shareable Goods and the Emergence of Sharing as a Modality of Economic Production," http://benkler.org/

SharingNicely.html. First published in *Yale Law Journal* 114 (2004): 273–358, 278.

19. Ibid. This observation built on Benkler's earlier notion of "commons-based peer production," introduced in his essay "Coase's Penguin, or, Linux and the Nature of the Firm," *Yale Law Journal* 112 (2002): 369, where he discusses the peer production that characterizes, for example, open-source information projects like Wikipedia or open-source software like Linux. Benkler situates these as a third alternative to market-based and hierarchy-based forms of organizing economic activity, one that creates sufficient gains (in information and in allocation) that compensate sufficiently for the "information exchange costs due to the absence of pricing and managerial direction and the added coordination costs created by the lack of property and contract." In "Coase's Penguin," Benkler also attributes the original concept of commons-based peer production to Eben Moglen's 1999 *First Monday* article, "Anarchism Triumphant: Free Software and the Death of Copyright" (see http://firstmonday.org/ojs/index.php/fm/article/view/684/594).

20. Benkler, "'Sharing Nicely,'" 278.

21. Ibid., 343.

22. Ibid., 358.

23. Michel Bauwens, "The Political Economy of Peer Production." *CTheory* 1 (2005), http://www.ctheory.net/articles.aspx?id=499.

24. Lawrence Lessig, *Remix: Making Art and Commerce Thrive in the Hybrid Economy* (New York: Penguin, 2009), 145. Remix is also available at Creative Commons, http://www.scribd.com/doc/47089238/Remix.

25. Ibid., 146.

26. Ibid., 146.

27. Ibid., 145.

28. Ibid., 146.

29. Ibid., 152.

30. Ibid., 177.

31. There is a range of different social goals for time banking, which may include developing new businesses, providing social services, sharing expertise, providing alternative forms of juvenile justice, and providing disaster relief. For a useful overview, see Edgar S. Cahn and Christine Gray, "The Time Bank Solution," *Stanford Social Innovation Review*, http://www.ssireview.org/articles/entry/the_time_bank_solution.

32. This notion of a gift economy is perhaps what Bauwens is trying to distance from in his idea of P2P. "It is our contention that [the comparison between the sharing economy and gift economy] is somewhat misleading," he writes. "The key reason is that peer to peer is not a form of equality matching; it is not based on reciprocity. P2P follows the adage: each contributes according to his capacities and willingness, and each takes according to his needs. There is no obligatory reciprocity involved. In the pure forms of peer production, producers

are not paid. Thus, if there is 'gifting' it is entirely non-reciprocal gifting, the use of peer-produced use-value does not create a contrary obligation" (from Bauwens, "Political Economy").

33. Lewis Hyde, *The Gift: Creativity and the Artist in the Modern World*, 25th anniversary edition (New York: Vintage, 1983), xvi.

34. Ibid., xx.

35. Ibid. 70. (In *Remix*, Lessig draws extensively and explicitly from Hyde's book, especially from Hyde's detailed examples of Alcoholics Anonymous and scientific peer-review, both of which lead to his conclusion that "price is poisonous," In many ways, Lessig's 2007 conception of a "sharing economy" is synonymous with Hyde's conception of a "gift economy.")

36. Benkler, "'Sharing Nicely,'" 375.

37. Hyde describes how anthropologist Bronislaw Malinowski spent several years living on these islands during World War I, eventually mapping out how the circles associated with the flow of armshells and necklaces across people spanned many adjoining islands.

38. Hyde, *The Gift*, 24, 48, 24.

39. Benkler, "'Sharing Nicely,'" 316.

40. Hyde, *The Gift*, 47.

41. Ibid., xxi–xxii.

42. Ibid., xvii.

43. See https://www.kickstarter.com/blog/kickstarter-is-now-a-benefit-corporation.

44. http://tradeschool.coop.

45. Natalie Foster, "It's Time for CPUC to OK Ride Shares," *SFGate*, September 13, 2013, http://www.sfgate.com/opinion/openforum/article/It-s-time-for-CPUC-to-OK-ride-shares-4825997.php.

46. http://steinhardt.nyu.edu/pach/.

47. Sherry Turkle, *Alone Together: Why We Expect More from Technology and Less from Each Other* (New York: Basic Books, 2011). 1.

48. Robert Nisbet, *The Quest for Community: A Study in the Ethics of Order and Freedom* (Wilmington, DE: Intercollegiate Studies Institute, 2010), 21.

Chapter 2

1. http://minus.com/lbg98QhH9AALlU.

2. The emergence of trust systems for blockchain-enabled marketplaces may revitalize the potential of Craigslist-like marketplaces. I return to this point in chapter 4.

3. https://twitter.com/digitalarun/status/651878601177079811.

4. Kozmo's Manhattan operation was just becoming profitable when the company went under.

5. Vasant Dhar and Arun Sundararajan, "Information Technologies in Business: A Blueprint for Education and Research," *Information Systems Research* 18 (2007): 125–141, http://dx.doi.org/10.1287/isre.1070.0126.

6. Professor Dhar and I discuss many of these early consequences in detail in our 2007 paper.

7. As I write this book, this iconic example is yet to gain widespread commercial acceptance. See Folasade Osisanwo, Shade Kuyoro, and Oludele Awodele, "Internet Refrigerator—A Typical Internet of Things (IoT)," http://iieng.org/siteadmin/upload/2602E0315051.pdf. Also see Fred Butcher, "What Is a Smart Refrigerator," https://fredsappliance.com/2014/06/smart -refrigerator/ for an interesting historical overview.

8. For an overview of the drone delivery technology tested by Amazon in 2014, see http://www.amazon.com/b?node=8037720011.

9. Marc Andreessen, "Why Bitcoin Matters," *New York Times*, January 21, 2014, http://dealbook.nytimes.com/2014/01/21/why-bitcoin-matters/.

9. See Chris Anderson, *The Long Tail: Why the Future of Business Is Selling Less of More* (New York: Hyperion, 2008).

10. Jason Tanz, "How Airbnb and Lyft Finally Got Americans to Trust Each Other," *Wired*, April 23, 2014, http://www.wired.com/2014/04/trust-in-the -share-economy.

11. James Coleman, *Foundations of Social Theory* (Cambridge, MA: Harvard University Press, 1990).

12. Chris Nosko and Steven Tadelis, "The Limits of Reputation in Platform Markets: An Empirical Analysis and Field Experiment," http://faculty.haas. berkeley.edu/stadelis/EPP.pdf.

13. For an influential early overview, see Paul Resnick et al., "Reputation Systems," *Communications of the ACM* 43, 12 (2000): 45–48; and Chrysanthos Dellarocas, "The Digitization of Word of Mouth: Promise and Challenges of Online Feedback Mechanisms," *Management Science* 49, 10 (2003): 1407–1424. For a more recent discussion of their place in computer-mediated transactions, see Hal Varian, "Computer-Mediated Transactions," *American Economic Review* 100, 2 (2010): 1–10. For a study on the importance of the content in feedback text, see Anindya Ghose, Panagiotis G. Ipeirotis, and Arun Sundararajan, "Opinion Mining Using Econometrics: A Case Study on Reputation Systems," *Proceedings of the 44th Annual Meeting of the Association of Computational Linguistics*, 2007, http://www.cs.brandeis. edu/~marc/misc/proceedings/acl-2007/ACLMain/pdf/ACLMain53.pdf. For a study of the bias introduced because of the fear of retaliation, see Chrysanthos Dellarocas and Charles A. Wood, "The Sound of Silence in Online Feedback: Estimating Trading Risks in the Presence of Reporting Bias," *Management Science* 54, 3 (2008): 460–476.

14. This conception of social capital relies significantly on the writings of sociologist Pierre Bourdieu, and in particular, P. Bourdieu. "The Forms of

Capital," in J. Richardson (ed.), *Handbook of Theory and Research for the Sociology of Education* (New York: Greenwood, 1986), 241–258.

15. Sean Moffitt and Mike Dover, *WikiBrands* (New York: McGraw Hill, 2011), 5.

16. https://www.jumio.com.

17. I conduct scientific research in collaboration with Traity and its scientists.

18. A number of prior efforts have tried to aggregate such individual marketplace reputation profiles. Perhaps the most salient among these is the effort by TrustCloud (http://www.trustcloud.com).

19. Duncan McLaren and Julian Agyeman delve into these and other ways in which cities are complementary to the sharing economy in their excellent book, *Sharing Cities* (MIT Press, 2015).

20. Robin Chase, *Peers Inc: How People and Platforms Are Inventing the Collaborative Economy and Reinventing Capitalism* (New York: PublicAffairs, 2015), 4.

Chapter 3

1. Thomas W. Malone, Joanne Yates, and Robert I. Benjamin, "Electronic Markets and Electronic Hierarchies," *Communications of the ACM 30, 6* (1987): 484–497.

2. I personally recall seeing the trade of cassette tapes with recordings of Bob Dylan concerts from the Usenet (now Google) group rec.music.dylan, mediated by influential group members who provided an early form of the idea of "peer regulation" that I discuss in chapter 6.

3. While some choices made by the farmers are influenced by Whole Foods, the farmers themselves would not be considered part of the organization. For example, in June 2015, the retailer introduced a "Responsibly Grown" rating system that categorizes its produce and flowers as "Unrated," "Good," "Better," and "Best" based on assessing an array of farming practices ranging from soil health, air pollution, and waste reduction, to farm worker welfare, water conservation, and GMO use. Farmers (especially those economically dependent on Whole Foods for access to consumers) might thus alter their choices on one of more of these fronts to try and get a higher rating.

4. Herbert A. Simon, "Organizations and Markets," *The Journal of Economic Perspectives 5* (1991): 25–44.

5. Alfred D. Chandler Jr., *The Visible Hand: The Managerial Revolution in American Business* (Cambridge, MA: Harvard University Press, 1993; original published 1977).

6. I realize that a lot of Malone, Yates, and Benjamin's work, and Vijay Gurbaxani and Seungjin Whang's work, draws from seminal earlier work by Friedrich Hayek (1937), Ronald Coase (1945), and Oliver E. Williamson's work, perhaps even later work by Sanford Grossman, Oliver Hart, and John Moore, and a host of other excellent economists and social scientists. I am not

attempting a systematic analysis of the literature here, but a brief discussion of some intellectual foundations.

7. Malone, Yates, and Benjamin, "Electronic Markets," 487.

8. Oliver E. Williamson, *Markets and Hierarchies: Analysis and Antitrust Implications* (New York: Free Press, 1975).

9. Vijay Gurbaxani and Seungjin Whang, "The Impact of Information Systems on Organizations and Markets," *Communications of the ACM* 34, 1 (1991), 59–73.

10. Ibid., 71.

11. Ibid., 71–72.

12. See, for example, Erik Brynjolfsson and Lorin Hitt, "Beyond Computation: Information Technology, Organizational Transformation and Business Performance," *Journal of Economic Perspectives* 14, 4 (2000): 23–48, or Timothy F. Bresnahan, Erik Brynjolfsson, and Lorin M. Hitt, "Information Technology, Workplace Organization, and the Demand for Skilled Labor: Firm-Level Evidence," *Quarterly Journal of Economics* 117 (2002): 339–376, or Prasanna Tambe, Lorin Hitt and Erik Brynjolfsson, "The Extroverted Firm: How External Information Practices Affect Innovation and Productivity," *Management Science* 58(2012): 678-697.

13. James Quinn, "Strategic Outsourcing: Leveraging Knowledge Capabilities," *MIT Sloan Management Review*, July 15, 1999. http://sloanreview.mit.edu/article/strategic-outsourcing-leveraging-knowledge-capabilities.

14. Henry Chesbrough, *Open Innovation: The New Imperative for Creating and Profiting from Technology* (Cambridge, MA: Harvard Business School Press, 2003), and Eric von Hippel, *Democratizing Innovation* (Cambridge, MA: The MIT Press).

15. Hila Lifshitz-Assaf, "From Problem Solvers to Solution Seekers: The Permeation of Knowledge Boundaries at NASA," http://ssrn.com/abstract=2431717.

16. See, for example, the Harvard Business School Case OpenIDEO, 2012. http://www.hbs.edu/faculty/Pages/item.aspx?num=41519

17. Linus Dahlander and David M. Gann, "How Open Is Innovation?" *Research Policy* 39 (2010): 700

18. Rachel Botsman, "The Sharing Economy Lacks a Shared Definition," http://www.fastcoexist.com/3022028/the-sharing-economy-lacks-a-shared-definition.

19. See http://www.web-strategist.com/blog/2014/12/07/collaborative-economy-honeycomb-2-watch-it-grow.

Chapter 4

1. See the link to OB1 at https://www.usv.com/portfolio#2015.

2. The video is posted on YouTube and available at https://youtu.be/nuRgHbTU9pk.

3. Benjamin Weiser, "Ross Ulbricht, Creator of Silk Road Website, Is Sentenced to Life in Prison," *New York Times*, May 29, 2015. http://www.nytimes.com/2015/05/30/nyregion/ross-ulbricht-creator-of-silk-road-website-is-sentenced-to-life-in-prison.html.

4. Andy Greenberg, "Inside the 'DarkMarket' Prototype, a Silk Road the FRI Can Never Seize," *Wired*, April 24, 2014. http://www.wired.com/2014/04/darkmarket.

5. Brad Burnham, "Introducing OB1," *USV Blog*, June 11, 2015. https://www.usv.com/blog/introducing-ob1.

6. Ibid.

7. For example, let's consider what happens when you swipe your credit or debit card. Data about the transaction is communicated via networks built by companies like VISA and MasterCard. Your account is then debited and the merchant's account is in turn credited. The bank that issued the credit or debit card is the trusted third party that verifies and clears the transaction.

8. The details of the problem are not important for what follows here. Briefly, Clay has to generate a number (called the *nonce*) that, when appended to the identifier number associated with the list of transactions (the "block"), and then "hashed" using the SHA-256 hash function, yields an output that satisfies a particular mathematical property (e.g., has a value less than some minimum, or has a bunch of zeroes at the beginning). It is very computationally intensive to actually find this nonce-identifier combination, but once the combination has been found, it is very easy to verify that the combination satisfies the mathematical property.

9. Albert Wenger, "Bitcoin as Protocol," *USV Blog*, October 31, 2013. https://www.usv.com/blog/bitcoin-as-protocol.

10. Dionysis Zindros, "A Pseudonymous Trust System for a Decentralized Anonymous Marketplace," *GitHub Gist*, 2015, https://gist.github.com/dionyziz/e3b296861175e0ebea4b.

11. Melanie Swan, *Blockchain: Blueprint for a New Economy* (Sebastopol, CA: O'Reilly Media, Inc., 2015).

12. Primavera De Fillipi, "Ethereum: Freenet or Skynet?," Talk presented at the Berkman Center for Internet & Society, Harvard University, Cambridge, MA, April 15, 2014.

13. Lawrence Lessig, *Code and Other Laws of Cyberspace* (New York: Basic Books, 1999).

14. Vitalik Buterin, "Decentralized Protocol Monetization and Forks," *Ethereum Blog*, April 30, 2014. https://blog.ethereum.org/2014/04/30/decentralized-protocol-monetization-and-forks.

15. It is likely that architecting it "optimally" is impossible, based on a set of results from a branch of economics called *mechanism design*.

16. Chris Dixon, "Some Ideas for Native Bitcoin Apps." *CDixon Blog*, October 4, 2014. http://cdixon.org/2014/10/04/some-ideas-for-native-bitcoin-apps.

17. Jemima Kelley, "Nine of the World's Biggest Bank Join to Form Blockchain Partnership," *Reuters*, September 15, 2015, http://www.reuters.com/article/2015/09/15/banks-blockchain-idUSL1N11L1K720150915#k5rPvtF0 AteX3fFK.97; Jemima Kelly, "Three Banks Join #3 Blockchain Consortium Taking Total to 25," *Reuters*, October 28, 2015, http://www.reuters.com/article/2015/10/28/us-global-banks-blockchain-idUSKCN0SM1U120151028#2r AUwQDFjkKbPeS1.97.

18. Bitcoin has this feature, although, as of 2015, this was just a couple of percent of the total miner revenue.

19. Buterin, "Decentralized Protocol Monetization and Forks."

Chapter 5

1. See Steven Johnson, *Future Perfect: The Case for Progress in a Networked Age* (New York: Riverhead Books, 2012), a study of what Johnson calls the new world view of "peer collectivism."

2. Alex Williams, "That Hobby Looks Like a Lot of Work," *New York Times*, December 16, 2009. http://www.nytimes.com/2009/12/17/fashion/17etsy.html.

3. Julie Schneider, "Quit Your Day Job: Yokoo," *Etsy Seller Handbook*, 2012. https://blog.etsy.com/en/tags/quit-your-day-job.

4. Althea Erickson, quoted in Anne Rice, "Q&A Part Two: Etsy's Public Policy Director on Trade laws and Regulations," *Roll Call*, September 9, 2014. http://blogs.rollcall.com/technocrat/etsys-althea-erickson-on-trade-laws-regulations-and-etsys-sellers/.

5. Carey Dunne, "How One Woman Makes Almost a Million a Year on Etsy," *Fast Company*, February 15, 2015. http://www.fastcodesign.com/3042352/how-one-knitter-makes-almost-1-million-a-year-on-etsy.

6. Etsy announced Shaffer's exit from its marketplace on PRWeb (see http://www.prweb.com/releases/2015/ThreeBirdNestLeavesEtsy/prweb1292 4751.htm).

7. David's story appears at http://blog.relayrides.com/2014/03/pro-tip-make-thousands-renting-out-your-own-vehicle-fleet.

8. Royal Society of Arts, "Microbusinesses Outgunning Large Firms in the UK's Fastest Growing Industries," *RSA*. https://www.thersa.org/about-us/media/2015/microbusinesses-outgunning-large-firms-in-UK-fastest-growing-industries.

9. Dane Stangler Robert E. Litan, "Where Will the Jobs Come From?" *Kauffman Foundation Research Series: Firm Foundation and Economic Growth*, November 2009. http://www.kauffman.org/~/media/kauffman_org/research%20reports%20and%20covers/2009/11/where_will_the_jobs_come_from.pdf.

10. Sam Hodges, quoted in Midori Yoshimura, "Interview: Funding Circle Co-Founder Sam Hodges Talks Regulations, Factors Driving P2P Lending in the US." http://www.crowdfundinsider.com/2015/05/68361-interview-funding

-circle-co-founder-sam-hodges-talks-crowdfunding-regulations-factors-driving
-p2p-lending-in-the-us/.

11. In the long run, Airbnb is likely to alter the business prospects of traditional bed-and-breakfasts as these establishments begin to see a decline in demand, especially in markets where they were the "only game in town." As of 2014, in Manhattan, it appears that Airbnb is having a significant impact on the bed-and-breakfast industry, but not through direct competition. Rather, these businesses appear to be "collateral damage" in the ongoing regulatory tussle between Airbnb and New York City. See, for example, http://observer .com/2014/12/manhattan-bed-breakfasts-face-extinction and http://www .crainsnewyork.com/article/20140921/HOSPITALITY_TOURISM/140919814/ bb-be-gone.

12. There are at least three ways of computing GDP. The production approach sums the money spent on goods and services while subtracting intermediate forms of consumption (e.g., the cost of materials). The income approach adds up all incomes paid to households for factors such as production, labor, capital, and rent. The expenditure approach adds up the monetary value of all purchases made, under the assumption that all goods and services are produced for sale. Different countries use different combinations in their eventual reported GDP. For example, Britain combines all three into a single measure. The United States reports the first measure as GDP, and the second measure as GDI (gross domestic income.).

13. There are other problems with GDP, but I have chosen to focus on those that have specific consequences for capturing the economic impacts of the sharing economy. The best general reference to these issues I have come across is from the Stiglitz-Sen Commission, available at https://www.vorarlberg.at/pdf/ berichtderstiglitz-kommis.pdf.

14. For an excellent survey of different approaches to automated recommendations, see http://ieeexplore.ieee.org/xpls/abs_all. jsp?arnumber=1423975&tag=1.

15. Eric Brynjolfsson, Yu Hu, and Michael D. Smith, "Consumer Surplus in the Digital Economy: Estimating the Value of Increased Product Variety at Online Booksellers," *Management Science* 49, 11 (2003): 1580–1596, 1581.

16. Anindya Ghose, Rahul Telang and Michael D. Smith, "Internet Exchanges for Used Books: An Empirical Analysis of Product Cannibalization and Welfare Impact," *Information Systems Research* 17, 1 (2006): 3–9. http://pubsonline. informs.org/doi/abs/10.1287/isre.1050.0072.

17. Alexander Tuzhilin and Gedas Adomavicius, "Toward the next Generation of Recommender Systems: A Survey of the State-of-the-Art and Possible Extensions," *IEEE Transactions on Knowledge and Data Engineering* 17, 6 (2006): 734–739. http://ieeexplore.ieee.org/xpls/abs_all. jsp?arnumber=1423975&tag=1.

18. Prasanna Tambe and Lorin M. Hitt, "Job Hopping, Information Technology Spillovers, and Productivity Growth," *Management Science* 60, 2 (2013): 338–355.

19. One might instead consider using the term "efficiency" of capital or "productivity" of capital. However, these words have specific (and somewhat distinct) meanings in economics that don't fully capture what I'm trying to communicate.

20. Clay Shirky, from a talk at the Collaborative-Peer-Sharing Economy Summit, New York University, May 30, 2014.

21. Robert Gordon, "US Economic Growth Is Over: The Short Run Meets the Long Run," in *Think Tank 20: Growth, Convergence and Income Distribution: The Road from the Brisbane G-2- Summit* (Washington DC: Brookings Institute, 2015), 188. http://www.brookings.edu/~/media/Research/Files/Interactives/2014/thinktank20/chapters/tt20-united-states-economic-growth-gordon.pdf?la=en.

22. Hal R. Varian and Carl Shapiro call this the "demand-side economies of scale" in their book *Information Rules: A Strategic Guide to the Network Economy* (Cambridge: Harvard Business Books, 1999).

23. See http://oz.stern.nyu.edu/io/network.html for more discussion of network effects.

24. Thomas R. Eisenmann, Geoffrey Parker, and Marshall W. Van Alstyne, "Strategies for Two-Sided Markets," *Harvard Business Review* 96, 4 (2006): 581–595. https://hbr.org/2006/10/strategies-for-two-sided-markets.

25. Of course, there may be other traditional economies of scale that could lead to the eventual dominance of one or two firms because of several circumstances—by getting drivers to sign on and retaining them; or learning by doing in launching in a new market; or learning by doing in dealing with local regulators.

26. A transcript (from panel 4) of the workshop, titled "The 'Sharing' Economy: Issues Facing Platforms, Participants, and Regulators," is available at https://www.ftc.gov/system/files/documents/videos/sharing-economy-workshop-part-4/ftc_sharing_economy_workshop_-_transcript_segment_4.pdf. A copy of the full workshop agenda, and an invitation for public comment prior to it, is available at https://www.ftc.gov/system/files/documents/public_events/636241/sharing_economy_workshop_announcement.pdf.

27. See the video at http://video.pbs.org/widget/partnerplayer/2365538931.

28. Georgios Zervas, Davide Proserpio, and John Byers, " The Rise of the Sharing Economy: Estimating the Impact of Airbnb on the Hotel Industry," Boston University School of Management Research Paper No. 2013–16, May 7, 2015). http://dx.doi.org/10.2139/ssrn.2366898.

29. Alison Griswold, "Airbnb Is Thriving. Hotels Are Thriving. How Is that Possible?" *Slate*, July 6, 2015. http://www.slate.com/articles/business/moneybox/2015/07/airbnb_disrupting_hotels_it_hasn_t_happened_yet_and_both_are_thriving_what.html.

30. Jennifer Surane, "New York's Taxi Medallion Business Is Hurting. Thanks to Uber and Lyft." *Skift*, July 15, 2015. http://skift.com/2015/07/15/new-yorks-taxi-medallion-business-is-hurting-thanks-to-uber-and-lyft.

31. Josh Barro, "Taxi Mogul, Filing Bankruptcy, Sees Uber-Citibank Plot," *New York Times*, July 22, 2015. http://www.nytimes.com/2015/07/23/upshot/taxi-mogul-filing-bankruptcy-sees-a-uber-citibank-plot.html?abt=0002&abg=1.

32. Andrey Fradkin, "Search Frictions and the Design of Online Marketplaces," September 30, 2015. http://andreyfradkin.com/assets/SearchFrictions.pdf.

33. Thomas Piketty, *Capital in the 21st Century* (Cambridge, MA: Harvard University Press, 2014), 571.

34. Ibid., 471.

35. Samuel P. Fraiberger and Arun Sundararajan, "Peer-to-Peer Rental Markets in the Sharing Economy," NYU Stern School of Business Research Paper, March 6, 2015. http://dx.doi.org/10.2139/ssrn.2574337.

36. We also detected a fourth effect—the idea that people who used to buy low-end cars will now "buy up to rent out"—but as of 2015, its magnitude was fairly small in our analysis.

Chapter 6

1. David Hantman, "Fighting for You in New York," *Airbnb*, October 6, 2013. http://publicpolicy.airbnb.com/fighting-for-you.

2. In the summer of 2014, Peers.org ceased its collective action model, and repurposed the organization as a for-profit, Peers.com, which I discuss in greater detail in chapter 8. Mishelle's statement appears at http://action.peers.org/page/s/legalize-sharing-ny.

3. It remains unclear whether Airbnb activity significantly alters the supply of affordable rental housing. In San Francisco, city officials contend the impact is high, while Airbnb's own economic analysis suggests otherwise. See http://www.scribd.com/doc/265376839/City-Budget-and-Legislative-Analysis-Report-on-Short-term-Rentals and https://timedotcom.files.wordpress.com/2015/06/the-airbnb-community-in-sf-june-8-2015.pdf. Regardless, the magnitude of any impact is dwarfed by other larger effects like those of population growth or rent control. See http://www.nytimes.com/roomfordebate/2015/06/16/san-francisco-and-new-york-weigh-airbnbs-effect-on-rent/airbnb-is-an-ally-to-cities-not-an-adversary.

4. Share Better, "About the Campaign," 2014. http://www.sharebetter.org.

5. New York State Office of the Attorney General, "Airbnb in the City," October 2014. http://www.ag.ny.gov/pdfs/Airbnb%20report.pdf.

6. "The 'Sharing' Economy: Issues Facing Platforms, Participants, and Regulators," Federal Trade Commission workshop transcript, June 9, 2015. https://www.ftc.gov/system/files/documents/public_events/636241/sharing_economy_workshop_transcript.pdf.

7. Ibid.

8. Jeremy Heimans and Henry Timms, "Understanding 'New Power,'" *Harvard Business Review*, December 2014. https://hbr.org/2014/12/understanding-new-power.

9. For a great introduction to alternative theories of regulation, see Bronwen Morgan and Karen Yeung, *Introduction to Law and Regulation: Text and Materials* (Cambridge, UK: Cambridge University Press, 2007).

10. Molly Cohen and Arun Sundararajan, "Self-Regulation and Innovation in the Peer-to-Peer Sharing Economy," *University of Chicago Law Review Dialogue* 116 (2015): 82–116. https://lawreview.uchicago.edu/page/self-regulation-and-innovation-peer-peer-sharing-economy.

11. Avner Greif, "Reputation and Coalitions in Medieval Trade: Evidence on the Maghribi Traders," *The Journal of Economic History* 49, 4 (1989): 857–882.

12. Ibid., 865–866.

13. Ibid., 867.

14. Douglass C. North, 1994. "Economic Performance Through Time," *The American Economic Review* 84, 4 (1994): 359–368.

15. Daron Acemoglu and James Robinson, *Why Nations Fail* (New York: Crown Business, 2012); Peter Blair Henry, *Turnaround: Third World Lessons for First World Growth* (New York: Basic Books, 2013).

16. Douglass C. North and Barry R. Weingast, "Constitutions and Commitment: The Evolution of Institutional Governing Public Choice in Seventeenth-Century England," *Journal of Economic History* 49, 4 (1989): 303–332, 303.

17. See Peter Barton Hutt and Peter Barton Hutt II, "A History of Government Regulation of Adulteration and Misbranding of Food," *Food, Drug, and Cosmetic Law Journal* 39 (1984): 2–73, 12. Hutt and Hutt discuss the role of government in preventing the adulteration of food in the past, tracing guidelines that existed in ancient times, as well as specific rules and penalties that were in the Theodosian Code of 438 AD.

18. North, "Economic Performance," 366.

19. Adam Thierer, *Permissionless Innovation: The Continuing Case for Comprehensive Technological Freedom* (Fairfax, VA: Mercatus Center, George Mason University), vii. http://mercatus.org/sites/default/files/Permissionless. Innovation.web_.v2_0.pdf.

20. Sofia Ranchordàs, "Innovation Experimentation in the Age of the Sharing Economy," *Lewis and Clark Law Review* 19 (forthcoming). http://ssrn.com/abstract=2638406.

21. April Rinne, "Lessons from Microfinance for the Sharing Economy," *Sharable*, November 27, 2012. http://www.shareable.net/blog/lessons-from-microfinance-for-the-sharing-economy.

22. See, for example, Anindya Ghose and Panagiotas G. Ipeirotis. "Estimating the Helpfulness and Economic Impact of Product Reviews: Mining Text and Reviewer Characteristics," *IEEE Transactions on Knowledge and Data Engineering* 23, 10 (2011), 1498–1512.

23. The nongovernmental source of information need not necessarily be part of a digital user-generated system. In spring 2015, a feature article on the nail salon

industry appeared in the *New York Times*, http://www.nytimes.com/2015/05/10/nyregion/at-nail-salons-in-nyc-manicurists-are-underpaid-and-unprotected.html. The article revealed that many of the women in the industry were being grossly underpaid and working under dangerous conditions. The article also exposed the fact that the salons, while apparently subject to regulations, were not in fact being regulated at all. None of the workers interviewed had ever seen an inspector in their workplace, and most of the workers were entirely unaware of their rights and of the industry's apparent safety standards.

Within days of the publication of the *New York Times* article, New York's governor, Andrew Cuomo, had announced that he would use "emergency rule changes" in order to give regulators greater authority to punish nail salons that mistreat workers while also making it easier for employees to gain licenses to legally work in the profession.

Why did the governor suddenly wake up to this regulation crisis? What we know for certain is that a popular campaign, initiated by a newspaper article and subsequently driven by the outrage of salon workers and customers, was the catalyst for change rather than any existing regulatory mechanism.

24. http://techcrunch.com/2012/12/09/balancing-innovation-and-regulation-in-the-sharing-economy.

25. There are a number of excellent overviews of self-regulatory organizations and self-regulation in general. The best I've read is by Julia Black, "Decentering Regulation: Understanding the Role of Regulation and Self-Regulation in a 'Post-Regulatory' World," Current Legal Problems 54, 103 (2001). I've also benefited from reading Saule T. Omarova, "Wall Street as Community of Fate: Toward Financial Industry Self-Regulation," *University of Pennsylvania Law Review* 159, 411, (2011); from discussions with Sofia Ranchordàs and Molly Cohen on self-regulation, and from conversations with Sara Horowitz about "new mutualism." Other good readings include Orly Lobel, "The Renew Deal: The Fall of Regulation and the Rise of Governance in Contemporary Legal Thought," *Minnesota Law Review* 89, 342 (2004), which argues for alternative to the government as a regulatory actor, and Ian Bartle and Peter Vass, "Self-Regulation and the Regulatory State," http://www.bath.ac.uk/management/cri/pubpdf/Research_Reports/17_Bartle_Vass.pdf. Cohen and Sundararajan, "Self-Regulation and Innovation," provides a brief history of SROs and suggests a number of other SRO references.

26. Many of these factors implicitly point to a potential weakness of relying on SROs: namely, they may not emerge as a credible representative of all stakeholders, that they may lack enforcement capabilities, that they may not be perceived as independent. Regarding the final point, a frequent concern about self-regulation, dating back to medieval guilds, is that an SRO will somehow be "captured" by large industry participants. See Sheilagh Ogilvie, "The Economics of Guilds," *Journal of Economic Perspectives* 28 (2014): 169–192 (arguing on 169 and 170 that the behavior of guilds can best be understood as being aimed at securing rents for guild members and legal privileges for the guild). However, as the Nobel Prize–winning economist George J. Stigler has famously posited in his "capture theory" of regulation, over time, governmental regulation may also

be supplied to serve the interests of the regulated industries. See id at 335–336. See also George J. Stigler, "The Theory of Economic Regulation," *Bell Journal of Economics* 2 (1971): 3–21 (outlining theories of regulation and arguing that regulation functions primarily for the benefit of the regulated industry).

27. "The 'Sharing' Economy: Issues Facing Platforms, Participants, and Regulators," Federal Trade Commission workshop transcript, June 9, 2015. https://www.ftc.gov/system/files/documents/public_events/636241/sharing_economy_workshop_transcript.pdf.

28. Bill ALUR was predated by a similar law passed by the Amsterdam city council in January 2014, which allowed short-term rentals for up to 60 days a year, imposing a 5.5% tourist tax on the ensuing revenue.

29. Benjamin Edelman and Michael Luca, "Airbnb A," Harvard Business School Case 912–019, December 2011 (revised March 2012).

30. See http://techonomy.com/conf/14-detroit/techonomic-tools/economics-sharing.

Chapter 7

1. See the website concerning the lawsuit, which is addressed to Uber Drivers (with pull-down menu options to translate it into more than 75 languages and dozens of links to other pertinent sites), at http://uberlawsuit.com/.

2. Jianming Zhou and Ryder Pearce, "Do On-Demand Workers View Themselves as Independent Contractors or Employees?" *SherpaShare*, June 15, 2015. https://sherpashare.com/static/resources/SherpaShare-IndependentContractorEmployeeSurveyResults.pdf.

3. See the full docket report for the case, *O'Connor et al v. Uber Technologies, Inc. et al* https://dockets.justia.com/docket/california/candce/4:2013cv03826/269290. Judge Chen's decision (filing #251) is available at https://docs.justia.com/cases/federal/district-courts/california/candce/3:2013cv03826/269290/251.

4. Quoted in Dan Levine and Edward Chan, "Uber and Lyft Fail to Convince Judges," *Business Insider*, March 2015. http://www.businessinsider.com/uber-and-lyft-fail-to-convince-judges-their-employees-are-independent-contractors-2015-3#ixzz3UIFTYbVy.

5. I have heard Teran discuss this at two separate events in the second half of 2015: the TAP Conference in New York on October 1, and the White House Summit on Worker Voice, October 7. See an op-ed by Sapone at http://qz.com/448846/the-on-demand-economy-doesnt-have-to-imitate-uber-to-win/.

6. Mark Warner, "Asking Tough Questions about the Gig Economy," *Washington Post*, June 18, 2015. https://www.washingtonpost.com/opinions/asking-tough-questions-about-the-gig-economy/2015/06/18/b43f2d0a-1461-11e5-9ddc-e3353542100c_story.html.

7. Quoted in Christina Reynolds, "Reality Check: Hillary Clinton and the Sharing Economy," *The Briefing*, July 16, 2015. https://www.hillaryclinton.com/p/briefing/updates/2015/07/16/reality-check-sharing-economy/.

8. Robert Reich, "The Share-the-Scraps Economy," *Robert Reich*, February 2, 2015. http://robertreich.org/post/109894095095.

9. An audio transcript of the New Champions annual meeting for 2015 is available at http://www.weforum.org/sessions/summary/rise-demand-economy.

10. The abstract for the study, "Can Sharing be Taxed," forthcoming in the *Washington Law Review*, is available at http://ssrn.com/abstract=2570584.

11. Alan S. Blinder, *How Many U.S. Jobs Might Be Offshorable?*, CEPS Working Paper No. 142, Princeton, NJ, March 2007, 2. https://www.princeton.edu/ceps/workingpapers/142blinder.pdf.

12. Alan S. Blinder and Alan B. Krueger, *Alternative Measures of Offshorability: A Survey Approach*, National Bureau of Economic Research Working Paper No. w15287, 2006, http://www.nber.org/papers/w15287.

13. Blinder, *How Many U.S. Jobs*, 35.

14. The McKinsey study is at http://www.mckinsey.com/insights/business_technology/four_fundamentals_of_workplace_automation.

15. Frank Levy and Richard J. Murnane, *The New Division of Labor: How Computers Are Creating the Next Job Market* (Princeton, NJ: Princeton University Press, 2004).

16. Erik Brynjolfsson and Andrew McAfee, *The Second Machine Age: Work, Progress, and Prosperity in a Time of Brilliant Technologies* (New York: W.W. Norton, 2014), 9.

17. Ibid., 9–10.

18. Ibid., 10.

19. Ibid., 180.

20. David Card and John E. DiNardo, "Skill-Biased Technological Change and Rising Wage Inequality: Some Problems and Puzzles," *Journal of Labor Economics* 20, 4 (2002): 733–783.

21. A different example of this point comes from the National Hockey League in the United States. In 1989, the NHL made public its annual salaries for players. Over the next five years, average salaries spiked; in 1989, the average salary for a player was $200,000 and by 1994, average salaries were three times that amount.

22. Michael Hammer, "Reengineering Work: Don't Automate, Obliterate," *Harvard Business Review* 68 4 (1990): 104–112. https://hbr.org/1990/07/reengineering-work-dont-automate-obliterate.

23. Ibid.

24. Devon Fidler, "Here's How Managers Can Be Replaced by Software." *Harvard Business Review*, April 21, 2015. https://hbr.org/2015/04/heres-how-managers-can-be-replaced-by-software.

25. Ibid.

26. Quoted in Susan Page, "Sen. Mark Warner: Rethinking the Social Contract in the Age of Uber," *USA Today*, June 3, 2015. http://www.usatoday.com/story/news/politics/2015/06/03/capital-download-mark-warner-gig-economy/28414187.

27. Emily Badger, "The Rise of Invisible Work," *CityLab*, October 31, 2013. http://www.citylab.com/work/2013/10/rise-invisible-work/7412.

Chapter 8

1. Justin Fox, "Uber and the Not-Quite-Independent Contractor," *Bloomberg View*, June 23. 2015. http://www.bloombergview.com/articles/2015-06-23/uber-drivers-are-neither-employees-nor-contractors.

2. The SS-8 form is available at http://www.irs.gov/pub/irs-pdf/fss8.pdf; detailed supplementary guidelines are available at http://www.irs.gov/Businesses/Small-Businesses-&-Self-Employed/Independent-Contractor-Self-Employed-or-Employee.

3. Fox, "Uber and the Not-Quite-Independent Contractor."

4. Often called the "congressional watchdog," GAO investigates how the federal government spends taxpayer dollars. The report is available at http://www.gao.gov/assets/670/669766.pdf.

5. Liz Gannes, "It Takes a New Kind of Worker to Make 'Instant' Happen," *Re/code*, 2014. http://recode.net/2014/08/05/it-takes-a-new-kind-of-worker-to-make-instant-happen/.

6. Elizabeth Kennedy, "Freedom from Independence: Collective Bargaining Rights for Independent Contractors," *Berkeley Journal of Employment and Labor Law* 26, 1 (March 2005): 155–157. http://scholarship.law.berkeley.edu/cgi/viewcontent.cgi?article=1348&context=bjell.

7. Ai-Jen Poo is Director of the National Domestic Workers Alliance. See the website at http://www.domesticworkers.org.

8. Marcella Sapone, "The On-Demand Economy Doesn't Have to Imitate Uber to Win." *Quartz*, June 15, 2015. http://qz.com/448846/the-on-demand-economy-doesnt-have-to-imitate-uber-to-win.

9. For a helpful, early discussion of the topic see Gannes, "It Takes a New Kind of Worker." A useful discussion of the issues and momentum by Caroline O'Donovan in 2015 is available at http://www.buzzfeed.com/carolineodonovan/meet-the-new-worker-same-as-the-old-worker#.umQGJQbGY.

10. Seth D. Harris and Alan B. Krueger, "A Proposal for Modernizing Labor Laws for Twenty-First-Century Workers: The 'Independent Worker,'" *The Hamilton Project* (Washington, DC: Brookings Institute, December 2015). http://www.hamiltonproject.org/assets/files/modernizing_labor_laws_for _twenty_first_century_work_krueger_harris.pdf.

11. H. W. Arthurs, "The Dependent Contractor: A Study of the Legal Problems of Countervailing Power," *The University of Toronto Law Journal* 16, 1 (1965): 89–117.

12. See Lauren Weber, "What If There Were a New Type of Worker: Dependent Contractor?" *Wall Street Journal*, January 28, 2015. http://www.wsj.com/articles/what-if-there-were-a-new-type-of-worker-dependent -contractor-1422405831.

13. http://nextamericaneconomy.squarespace.com/thought-briefs/2015/7/7/ barriers-to-growth-in-the-sharing-economy.

14. Harris and Krueger, "A Proposal for Modernizing Labor Laws."

15. John J Horton, "Should Online Labor Markets Set a Minimum Wage?," Blog posted October 29, 2011. http://john-joseph-horton.com/should-online -labor-markets-set-a-minimum-wage/.

16. Decisions and Orders of the National Labor Relations Board, v. 344, December 16, 2004, through August 17, 2005. Washington, DC: US Government Printing Office.

17. Mark R. Warner, "Asking Tough Questions about the Gig Economy." *Washington Post*, June 18, 2015. https://www.washingtonpost.com/opinions/ asking-tough-questions-about-the-gig-economy/2015/06/18/b43f2d0a-1461 -11e5-9ddc-e3353542100c_story.html.

18. "Common Ground for Independent Workers," *WTF*, November 10, 2015, https://medium.com/the-wtf-economy/common-ground-for-independent- workers-83f3fbcf548f#.nxpr7mck5.

19. https://fu-web-storage-prod.s3.amazonaws.com/content/filer_public/c2/06/ c2065a8a-7f00-46db-915a-2122965df7d9/fu_freelancinginamericareport _v3-rgb.pdf.

20. Arun Sundararajan, "The New 'New Deal'? Sharing Responsibility in the Sharing Economy," *Policy Network*, October 30, 2014. http://www.policy -network.net/pno_detail.aspx?ID=4762.

21. Peter Barnes, *With Liberty and Dividends for All: How to Save Our Middle Class When Jobs Don't Pay Enough* (San Francisco: Berrett-Koehler Publishers, 2014).

22. See Evelyn Forget, "The Town with No Poverty," February 2011, at http:// public.econ.duke.edu/~erw/197/forget-cea%20%282%29.pdf and Derek Hum and Wayne Simpson, "A Guaranteed Annual Income? From Mincome to the Millennium," *Policy Options* (January/February 2001): 78–82, at http://archive. irpp.org/po/archive/jan01/hum.pdf.

23. Warner, "Asking Tough Questions."

24. Shelby Clark, "'Uber' Benefits: The New Safety new for the On-Demand Economy," *Forbes*, July 22, 2015. http://www.forbes.com/sites/valleyvoices/2015/07/22/uber-benefits-the-new-safety-net-for-the-on-demand-economy.

25. Nathan Schneider, "The New Guilded Age," *New Yorker*, October 12, 2015. http://www.newyorker.com/business/currency/the-new-guilded-age.

26. Steven Deller, Ann Hoyt, Brent Heuth, and Reka Sundaram-Stukel, "Research on the Economic Impact of Cooperatives," June 19, 2009 (update from 2007). Madison: University of Wisconsin Center for Cooperatives. http://reic.uwcc.wisc.edu/sites/all/REIC_FINAL.pdf.

27. See the SELC website at http://www.theselc.org/.

28. See an introduction to Rustrum's Digital-Cooperative 101 at http://rustrum.com/digital-cooperative-101/.

29. See, for example, Nathan Schneider and Trebor Scholz, "The Internet Needs a New Economy," November 8, 2015. http://www.thenextsystem.org/the-internet-needs-a-new-economy/. Their concurrent thinking from late 2014 is also interesting, for example, by Scholz, "Platform Cooperativism vs. the Sharing Economy," *Medium*, December 5, 2014 (https://medium.com/@trebors/platform-cooperativism-vs-the-sharing-economy-2ea737f1b5ad#.v78qh7ewj) and by Schneider, "Owning Is the New Sharing," *Shareable*, December 21, 2014 (http://www.shareable.net/blog/owning-is-the-new-sharing).

30. See Elinor Ostrom, *Governing the Commons: The Evolution of Institutions for Collective Action* (Cambridge, UK: Cambridge University Press, 1990).

31. http://www.fastcompany.com/3057014/fed-up-with-uber-and-lyft-drivers-plan-to-launch-competing-app.

32. Lisa Gansky, "Collaborative Economy Companies Need to Start Sharing More Value with the People Who Make Them Valuable," *Fast Company*, December 4, 2014. http://www.fastcoexist.com/3038476/collaborative-economy-companies-need-to-start-sharing-more-value-with-the-people-who-make-th.

33. Adam Werbach, from remarks at the Social Capitalist (SOCAP) Markets Conference, September 2–5, 2014, Fort Mason Center, San Francisco, California.

34. Quoted in Schneider, "Owning Is the New Sharing."

35. See https://www.inkshares.com/projects/the-fairshare-model.

36. Om Malik, "Uber, Data Darwinism and the Future of Work," *Gigaom*, March 17, 2013. https://gigaom.com/2013/03/17/uber-data-darwinism-and-the-future-of-work.

37. Josh Dzieza, "The Rating Game," *The Verge*, October 28, 2015. http://www.theverge.com/2015/10/28/9625968/rating-system-on-demand-economy-uber-olive-garden.

38. Daniel Fleder and Kartik Hosanagar, "Blockbuster Culture's Next Rise or Fall: The Impact of Recommender Systems on Sales Diversity," *Management Science* 55, 5 (2009): 697–712.

39. Mike Dudas, "Employment Data Portability in the Marketplace Economy." *Just Dudas*, December 28, 2013. http://mikedudas.com/2013/12/29/employee-data-portability-in-the-marketplace-economy.

40. Ibid.

Chapter 9

1. Michael Spence, "The Inexorable Logic of the Sharing Economy," *Project Syndicate*, September 28, 2015. https://www.project-syndicate.org/commentary/inexorable-logic-sharing-economy-by-michael-spence-2015-09.

2. Klaus Schwab, *The Fourth Industrial Revolution* (Geneva: The World Economic Forum, 2016).

Index